MW00483396

JAGUAR
THE SPORTING HERITAGE

IN ASSOCIATION WITH THE JAGUAR DAIMLER HERITAGE TRUST

First published in Great Britain in 2000 by
Virgin Publishing Ltd
Thames Wharf Studios
Rainville Road
London
W6 9HA

Text copyright © Paul Skilleter, 2000

The right of Paul Skilleter to be identified as the Author of this Work has been asserted by him in accordance with the Copyright, Designs and Patents Act, 1988.

This book is sold subject to the condition that it shall not, by way of trade or otherwise, be lent, resold, hired out or otherwise circulated without the publisher's prior written consent in any form of binding or cover other than that in which it is published and without a similar condition including this condition being imposed on the subsequent purchaser.

A catalogue record for this book is available from the British Library.

ISBN 1 85227 889 7

Art direction and design by Derek Slatter and Katherine Spokes at Slatter-Anderson.
Printed and bound in Italy by Lego

JAGUAR
THE SPORTING HERITAGE

PAUL SKILLETER

Virgin

Contents

INTRODUCTION

By Paul Skilleter

"THE RACE TRACK IS THE SPIRITUAL HOME OF JAGUAR."

That emphatic statement came from Dr Wolfgang Reitzle, Jaguar's chairman, during the historic unveiling of the first ever Jaguar Formula One car on 25th January 2000. This momentous occasion took place 77 years after a young motorcycling enthusiast founded, with a partner, the company which would become Jaguar Cars.

The young man was, of course, William Lyons, and without him there would have been no Jaguar car and no Jaguar competition story to tell. Sir William (he was knighted in 1956) was absolute master of Jaguar right up until his retirement in 1972. Sir William was not, however, simply an industrialist. He knew what the customer wanted and sold it at the right price, but he was also an artist. His talent for styling motor cars was unique and he produced some of the most beautiful automotive designs ever seen, from the SS Jaguar 100 to the XJ6.

It was William Lyons who, from the earliest days, appreciated that motorsport could bring his company far more publicity than it could ever afford to buy. In fact, over the years, Jaguar has enjoyed an abundance of media coverage wonderfully disproportionate to its size! The fact is that the marque caught the imagination of the press and public early on, and today this interest in and affection for Jaguar is greater than it has ever been. But Lyons never allowed his personal enthusiasm for motorsport to overrule his natural caution; he knew that overspending on motor racing had been the ruin of some companies and he always ensured that Jaguar's ventures into competition were judicious and cost-effective.

One of his governing principles was that Jaguar would never enter a branch of the sport in which it did not stand a very good chance of winning. This brought about the very focused Le Mans programmes of the 1950s: by concentrating on just one type of race, Jaguar could produce "the perfect car", and the result was five victories in the space of seven years. These wins elevated Jaguar from being just a small manufacturer of specialist cars to a world force in the luxury car business. Yet the Le Mans winning C- and D-types were designed, built and maintained by the same remarkable team of people who were also developing Jaguar's road cars. They evolved into the world's most versatile and integrated automobile design team.

The competition initiative in the 1950s was certainly a team effort but, at the risk of leaving out those whose contributions were also vital, some individuals besides Sir William Lyons do deserve special attention.

Right: **William Lyons, aged about 20, photographed in Blackpool on his Harley-Davidson. One of his favourite motorcycles, it came from America – 30 years later the U.S. would be clamouring for Lyons' own products!**

Bill Heynes CBE directed the entire road and race engineering programmes at that time and, with Walter Hassan and Claude Baily, designed the XK engine which lay at the heart of Jaguar's successes during that period. Malcolm Sayer's technical input to the C-, D- and E-types was considerable, although he is best remembered for the brilliant shapes he created for these cars. R. J. Knight MBE was the man who, assisted by the likes of Tom Jones, engineered these vehicles; Bob Knight was probably the most gifted engineer in the luxury car field during the 1950s and 1960s - quite apart from his prowess at race car engineering! Norman Dewis, chief development driver, drove the cars for tens of thousands of miles in testing, a good proportion of the time at over 100 mph, making a vital contribution to the legendary reliability of the Le Mans Jaguars.

Above: **William Lyons appreciated his drivers; here Tazio Nuvolari enjoys a conversation with him at Silverstone in 1950 but the 58-year-old Italian ace was too unwell to drive this XK 120, which had been painted in Italian racing red especially for him.**

Organising Jaguar's assault on the Le Mans races of the 1950s was the quite unique figure of Frank Raymond Wilton England - inseparable from Jaguar's racing story. A Daimler apprentice, Lofty (he was 6ft 4ins tall) first worked for "Brooklands Boys" Sir Henry Birkin and Whitney Straight in the early 1930s. Then came several seasons with ERA before he moved to Alvis where (apart from distinguished service during the war in the RAF) he stayed until coming to Jaguar in September 1946. As Jaguar's race team manager from 1951 to 1956 he oversaw five Le Mans victories, yet his main job was still managing the service department! Works mechanic Joe Sutton paints this pit counter portrait of the man: "Lofty England was a one-off. You'll never find a bloke anything like him, anywhere in this world. I'll tell you for why. While the job was there, Lofty was there. He didn't leave it to somebody else to see that it was done, he stayed and saw it done. If we'd got to be up early in the morning, no matter what time, four, five or six, who was the first bloke there? Lofty. But one of the things that really endeared him to me was his pit counter manner - there were cars bashing by at 150 mph, but Lofty didn't have a loud hailer like some of 'em, he used to lean over and say, 'Joe, have you checked so and so?', and he wouldn't speak any louder than that but you could hear every word he said. With any job anywhere - so far as I was concerned, Lofty was at the top of the tree."

When Sir William Lyons retired in 1972, Lofty England became Jaguar's chairman and chief executive, though in 1974 he retired early, elements of the new BL regime not being to his liking.

In common with a number of manufacturers, Jaguar eventually found it more effective to place their competition programmes in the hands of outside teams; here, too, were some strong personalities. Bob Tullius was co-founder of and driver for the immensely successful North American racing team Group 44 (his former partner, Brian Fuerstenau, was sadly killed in a plane accident in 1993). With the backing of Graham Whitehead and Mike Dale of Jaguar in North America, Group 44 took the V12 E-type and XJ-S to victory in important US championships, and later returned the Jaguar name to Le Mans with the Group 44-built XJR-5.

Above: Team manager extraordinaire: Lofty England, hand raised in typical headmaster style, directing operations in the Jaguar pits during the 1950 TT.

Sir John Egan, Jaguar's chairman from 1980 to 1990, and Roger Putnam (director of sales and marketing) had the vision to see that it was time for Jaguar to return to motor sport in Europe. It was Tom Walkinshaw who took the XJ-S to victory in the European Touring Car Championship in 1984, a little over 20 years after the great German enthusiast and Jaguar distributor, Peter Lindner, made it possible for Peter Nöcker to win the first such championship with his Mk 2. Tom Walkinshaw and the TWR team went on to produce two Le Mans wins, of course, and three World Sportscar Championships with the XJR Group C cars, not to mention the Daytona 24 Hour race, too.

In 1989 the Ford Motor Company purchased Jaguar and the injection of capital has allowed Jaguar to embark on a huge expansion programme which will see a return to a full model range once more. With the coming of new, smaller and more affordable saloons and sports cars, Jaguar needs to reach a new and younger generation of potential customers - one major reason why the company entered Formula One in the year 2000.

Above: **William Lyons with Lofty England and a C-type in the United States, the market which took Jaguar to its heart. Centre is Max Hoffman, then Jaguar's East Coast distributor.**

The road to success in Formula One is a long and hard one but both Jaguar (now with Jonathan Browning as MD) and Ford are determined to succeed. Given the considerable skills and commitment within the Jaguar Racing team and at Cosworth Racing, success is sure to come.

I am sure that Sir William Lyons, if he were still with us, would be delighted with Jaguar's involvement in Formula One. He occasionally contemplated Jaguar entering Grand Prix racing - though way back as a teenager riding a stripped Harley-Davidson in seaside sprints, he could hardly have envisaged that one day, a company he was to found would compete against the greatest marques in the world at the very pinnacle of motorsport.

Swallow and S.S.1

"Making a success of a business venture - that was my original aim in life," so claimed Jaguar founder Sir William Lyons. His passion for motorsport helped fuel his drive for success and in fulfilling his ambition he was to create a sporting legend. . .

"THIS MACHINE, INTRODUCED ONLY A YEAR AGO AT THE REQUEST OF MANY FAMOUS SPEED MEN IN THE COUNTRY, HAS PROVED ITSELF THE IDEAL SIDECAR FOR ALL SPEED EVENTS." *1926 Swallow catalogue*

As he grew up in his home town of Blackpool, young Bill Lyons developed the sort of fascination for motor-cycles that only a schoolboy can sustain. By the time he left school in 1918 at the age of 17, he had formed, along with a few like-minded enthusiasts, the Blackpool, Fylde and District Motor Club.

At 18 he owned a Sunbeam before graduating to a Harley-Davidson 'Daytona', which he used to win a speed hill climb at Waddington Fells in the Forest of Bowland.

But while the young Lyons' hobby was flourishing, his early career was less buoyant. After school he nearly headed into the ship-building industry but instead spent a brief spell at Crossley, the Manchester-based car-maker. However, this proved not to his liking and by 1919 he was working for Brown and Mallalieu, a newly established motor sales business in Blackpool. Resourceful and energetic, Lyons was hungry for success and keen to put his talents to work in a business venture of his own.

Then in the summer of 1921 a new family arrived in King Edward Avenue where William lived with his parents. This event was to change the whole course of his life and, ultimately, result in the Jaguar car. The Walmsleys had come from Stockport and their son, also called William, had brought with him the hobby-cum-business he had started there.

He now commenced making his 'Swallow' sidecar in the double garage at the back of 23 King Edward Avenue. Panelled in shiny, unpainted aluminium and built at the rate of about one a week if everything went well, these stylish 'chairs' immediately attracted the young bike enthusiast down the road. The two met and Lyons, who saw a great business opportunity if production levels

Above: **The very beginning: William Walmsley on his Brough Superior S.S. 80 and William Lyons in a Swallow sidecar, photographed in King Edward Avenue, Blackpool around 1922.**

Below: **Lyons' own Harley-Davidson attached to a Model 4 Swallow sidecar – the most popular of the range and which provided the financial spring-board for the partners to move into coachbuilding.**

Above: **The Blackpool works about 1924; early employees Harry Teather and Cyril Marshall read *The Amateur Photographer* with Model 4s providing the backdrop. Note the 'Scrapper' competition chair on the floor.**

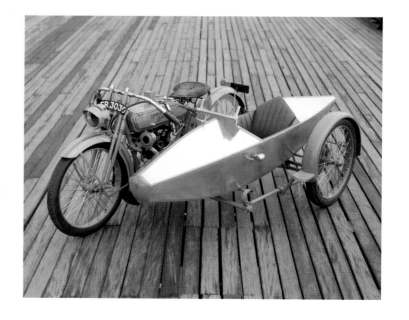

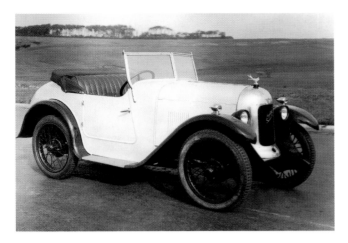

could be raised, persuaded Walmlsey - who was almost ten years his senior - to form a partnership with him.

The result was the Swallow Sidecar Company, established early in 1922 and financed by a £1,000 overdraft guaranteed jointly by the two fathers. Lyons' instincts, however, were soon proved right: the business expanded rapidly and a range of 'chairs' came on stream - including competition models. Lyons, the sporting enthusiast, even persuaded two entrants in the 1924 Sidecar TT on the Isle of Man to use a Swallow, and Harry Reed (founder of the DOT motor cycle company) achieved second place. Another user was Jack Emerson, years later to become part of the XK engine development team.

During the 1920s Swallow gained the custom of several well-known motor-cycle racers, including the Sunbeam works rider George Dance and also Bert Le Vack, who was twice world speed record holder with a Brough Superior. A Swallow 'Scrapper' was even used for record breaking, with Dougal Marchant taking 16 world speed and endurance records in 1926, achieving in the process 86.35 mph for the flying kilometre (an episode that may have lingered in William

Top: **A Blackpool-built Austin Swallow 'open sports' two-seater, photographed circa 1927 when it cost £175 (a novel hardtop was extra).**

Middle: **The Wolsely Hornet Swallow came in January 1931. This is the Hornet Swallow 'Special', the most sporting of these little six-cylinder cars.**

Left: **The Austin Swallow was in no way a sports car, but was a lot more decorative than a standard Austin 7 and was easy to drive, too. This is a later, Coventry-built, car.**

Below: **The rider and passenger survived this brush with a sandbank at Brooklands in the early 1930s!**

Lyons' mind when, 22 years later, he sanctioned the famous XK 120 speed runs in Belgium).

Meanwhile, the company had grown to become the Swallow Sidecar and Coach Building Company, the business having expanded to include a car paint and trim facility as part of Lyons plan to move into the automobile business. In 1927 they launched the first of their own four-wheel products, a Swallow-designed body on an Austin Seven chassis. Backed by a huge order from Henly's, the Austin Seven

Swallow was an immediate success, offering affordable individuality at a time when Britain's depressed economy (the General Strike had occurred the year before) was causing many people to downsize their motoring aspirations.

The success of the Austin Seven-based car forced Lyons to relocate in 1928 to a former ammunition factory in Foleshill, Coventry, in order to find the necessary skilled labour and premises large enough to accommodate the fast-growing automobile business. Soon the Austin was joined by bodies on other chassis including Fiat, Swift, Standard and Wolseley. The most sporting of these was the Wolseley Hornet, with its miniature six-cylinder overhead camshaft engine. But more significant was the Standard, as it brought Lyons into direct contact with R. W. Maudslay and John Black at Standard. This liaison was to result in Lyons being able to produce a car of his own.

"LAST YEAR I DESCRIBED THE S.S.1 AS THE CAR WITH THE £1,000 LOOK. THIS YEAR IT MIGHT BE CALLED THE CAR WITH THE £1,500 LOOK. AND IT COSTS ONLY £325." *Harold Pemberton,* Daily Express, *1932*

The transition from coachbuilding to the creation of a marque in its own right came in 1931, thanks to Standard agreeing to supply Swallow with a 'special six-cylinder chassis'. The S.S.1 was the result, "a name which was agreed upon after a long argument with Maudslay and Black," recounted Sir William many years later, "which resulted in my determination to establish a

Right: **More room! Swallow moved to this building in Cocker Street, Blackpool, in 1926 after the original Bloomfield Road premises became hopelessly inadequate for the rapidly expanding little company.**

Right: The first-ever RAC Rally was in March 1932 and several S.S.1s entered. The original S.S. had a rather boxy passenger compartment – Lyons had intended a lower roofline and was furious when Walmsley altered it while he was in hospital having his appendix removed!

marque of our own. There was much speculation as to whether S.S. stood for Standard Swallow or Swallow Special – it was never resolved." Due to its specially commissioned frame, the S.S.1 was glamorous indeed, sitting very low – "two short people can shake hands across it," exclaimed the *Daily Express*. This sporting stance was accentuated by the long-bonneted, low-roofline body which Lyons had styled for it. The car, along with a Standard Little Nine-based S.S.2, was first shown at the October 1931 London Motor Show at Earl's Court, and aroused considerable interest, especially when the price was revealed – £310, very little for a car which aped the appearance of cars like the Gurney-Nutting and Mulliner-bodied Bentleys costing over four times this price.

Below: Another of the S.S.1 entries in the 1932 RAC Rally: this is probably the cream and carnation red car of Kathleen, Countess of Drogheda – though a deputy obviously drove in the final tests at Torquay.

With this original 1931 car, William Lyons produced something rather ahead of its time – what would later be called in the States a 'personal car'. It was not to be categorised as simply a sports car or coupé but was intended as a personal statement of individuality by the owner – cars like, many years later, the Ford Thunderbird in the US and the Ford Capri in the UK. Lyons seemed to know instinctively what the customer required, and produced it at the right price. Just on 500 of the original S.S.1 were made, but while the car was nicely equipped in the Swallow fashion, the cycle-winged body was not very durable and the performance from the 45 bhp side-valve engine hardly matched the coupé's extravagant looks. Nevertheless Lyons' first car was involved in a form of 'motor sport' almost from the start, with five of the new S.S.s taking part in the

Above: The S.S.1's Alpine Trial debut brought mixed success with two out of the five not finishing; but Koch and Orssich (tourer and coupe) managed sixth and 11th respectively in their class - the Bugattis (like the one in the background) were quicker.

February 1932 RAC 1,000-mile rally to Torquay. This, the first 'RAC Rally', was little more than a moderately arduous road run around the country. S.S. entrants included Kathleen, the Countess of Drogheda, and E.F. Huckvale: as Edward Huckvale was Swallow's company secretary, this last car can be nominated as Lyons' first 'works' entry, although it is likely that A.G. Douglas-Clease of *The Autocar* actually drove the car.

The rally winner was decided by a test at Torquay which involved driving as slowly as possible! This favoured cars with fluid-flywheel transmissions, and a tall young man by the name of F.R.W. England did well in a Daimler Double-Six. In less than 20 years' time, Lofty England would be master-minding William Lyons' successful assault on the world's most famous motor race, the Le Mans 24-Hours...

Tacitly acknowledging the shortcomings of the S.S.1, Bill Lyons ensured that a completely revised S.S. appeared at the 1932 Earl's Court show, its new, longer frame allowing more room and more balanced styling. Vincent Prideaux-Budge gave the new car its continental debut when he took his 20 hp coupé on the Monte Carlo Rally, which started

Above: Bonnet removed and rally plate covered, Humphrey Simons' S.S.1 retires from the 1933 Alpine with head gasket failure.

in January. A skid in France resulted in front axle damage and much loss of time, but otherwise the car ran well and was classed as a finisher. Then, in March 1933, the coupé was joined by a four-seater open tourer. It was this ostensibly more sporting model which, perhaps prematurely, enticed William Lyons into forming his first 'works team'. The event was the 1933 International Alpine Trial, an infinitely greater challenge than the RAC Rally. Entrants had two major goals: either the Alpine Cup for teams, or the Glacier Cup for an individual car.

"ONLY THOSE WHO HAVE ACTUALLY TAKEN PART IN THE ALPINE TRIAL CAN REALISE WHAT A REALLY GRUELLING TEST OF A CAR IT IS. A MISTAKE ON ONE OF THE INNUMERABLE HAIRPIN BENDS MAY, IN FACT PROBABLY WILL, MEAN A HORRIBLE DEATH FOR THE CREW." *Douglas Clease in* The Autocar

In fact the three tourers which comprised the S.S. team were all privately entered by their drivers, who were lent the cars on the understanding that they paid all their own expenses! Painted respectively red, white and blue, the trio of cars were given a splendid send-off by the staff at Swallow Road (as the road leading to the Foleshill factory had become known) as they departed for the start in the Italian Alps. A fourth tourer was prepared for Georg Hans Koch, the S.S. distributor in Vienna, while a coupé was entered by the Austrian Count Peter Orssich. Lyons had at least managed to pick experienced crews: the lead drivers were Humfrey Symons, a noted journalist and rally driver; Charles Needham, who had won a Glacier Cup in the previous year's Alpine with an Invicta; and finally Miss Margaret Allan. A remarkable lady, Miss Allan had already gained fame racing a massive Bentley at Brooklands, had driven in trials and rallies, and won a *Coupe des Alpes* and the Ladies' Cup with a Wolseley Hornet Special in the 1932 Alpine.

Above: **Miss Margaret Allan's car (right) halts alongside the Symons car at St Moritz for cylinder head work; neither car was classified as a finisher on the 1933 Alpine, however.**

The problems began early. In an effort to counter the sidevalve engine's power deficiency, new high compression aluminium heads had been fitted at the Merano start, and these soon warped. Cylinder gasket failure followed on all the team cars. "We lasted two days," recalled Margaret Allan, "and we stopped with water running out of the exhaust pipe." Needham alone limped on, using most of the spare cylinder heads.

It might be thought that William Lyons' first team entry in a major competition was a

Above: A.G. Douglas Clease takes the S.S.1 tourer, top up, through a gorge during the 1934 Alpine Trial. He wrote graphically about the event afterwards for *The Autocar.*

disaster, but this was not really the case. The individually-entered tourer of Koch made 14th best performance of 121 starters in this particularly tough Alpine, and his fifth place in class was, after all, behind four Bugattis (three of them supercharged) and a Hotchkiss. He was also the highest British finisher in that 2-3 litre class. And despite their problems, the S.S. team had been running well ahead of the Daimler-Benz team during the first day. Much had been learned, and it would all be applied to good effect on the next 'Alpine' - by which time (1934) Swallow would be operating within a newly-formed company, SS Cars Ltd.

At the beginning of 1934 another S.S.1 completed the Monte Carlo Rally; its driver, Sydney Light, became a key member of the company's second assault on the Alpine Trial. Only Charles Needham remained from the 1933 effort, while making up the team of three was A.G. Douglas Clease.

He wrote about the 1934 rally afterwards in *The Autocar*, explaining that the radiator cap was sealed since replenishment was allowed only at the end of each day, but emphasising that none of the cars would have needed water over the entire six days. Obviously the cylinder head problems had been overcome and in fact engine consultant Harry Weslake had obtained a little more power too. Douglas Clease went on to describe "roads which are narrow and loose, and zig-zag their way up the mountain side, with a wall of rock on one side and a sheer drop on the other." The descents, though, were worse than the climbs. "It is a case of accelerating downhill in second, braking before reaching the hairpin - you dare not touch the brakes on the loose surface, and accelerating to the next bend."

None of the team cars lost marks over the first three days but conversely, on the fourth day, none climbed the Stelvio Pass within the time allowed. Other cars in the same class did - Talbot and Opel included - so sheer lack of power was to blame. Then that night Sydney Light ran off the road after a puncture and had to retire, though thanks to the points scoring system, the S.S. team still managed a third in class behind Talbot and Adler. A fourth tourer, that of F.W. and A.L. Morgan, came fourth in the same capacity (2-3 litre) class for individual entrants, but the factory-owned S.S.2 tourer driven by racing driver Norman Black and Reuben Harveyson was excluded for a reason perhaps unusual on an international rally: its crew overslept!

So ended the S.S.1's works-backed career in international rallying. There was no Alpine Trial in 1935, and by 1936 a very much more sporting machine from S.S. would be contesting the event.

Elsewhere, the S.S.s continued to appear, the RAC Rally attracting over the next couple of years all the variants on the chassis - besides the fixed-head coupé and tourer, a fastback saloon (the Airline) joined the range in September 1934 and, finally, a drophead coupé in March 1935. But the best results were still being obtained in *concours d'élégance* events, beauty contests where points were awarded for presentation, rather than power/weight ratios. These *concours* were taken seriously at the time and manufacturers, including S.S., were keen to advertise their successes. The S.S.s were attractive cars and, especially where a price element entered into it, they did consistently well.

The S.S.1 tourer, although it may have been derided by owners of established sporting models like MG and Riley, had definitely shown promise in 'proper' events. The bigger-engined car could achieve virtually 85 mph, its handling was respectable, and it had proved quite tough and reliable. It was worth building on - and the most significant offshoot of the S.S.1 did just that. The S.S.90, William Lyons' first two-seater, had been announced along with the drophead coupé in March 1935.

The '90' heralded something altogether more convincing from S.S and soon the scoffers were going to have to eat their words.

Left: All types of S.S.1 entered some sort of competition - this is an S.S.1 Airline tackling a re-start on the awesome Brooklands test hill in 1938.

Driving an S.S.1

The original S.S. looks something of an oddity to modern eyes, and in many ways it was pretentious. Climb inside and that long bonnet stretches out in front of you, but put your foot down and no surge of power comes in response. Nevertheless, the car bowls along well enough, and new, the 20 hp version could do around 75 mph - at least 10 or 15 mph faster than the average British family saloon of the day. Visibility from inside is not too restricted, though the rear seats are really suitable only for children.

The second-series S.S.1 was a quite dramatic improvement in every direction. The seven inches added to the wheelbase gives a lot more space inside and adult rear passengers are allowed legs... To those used to 1930s cars, the S.S.1 handles reasonably well. The steering, though heavy for parking, is nicely weighted

and surprisingly accurate at speed, and the six-cylinder engine is smooth and flexible (no wonder Lyons remained loyal to the big-capacity 'six').

New, the 1933 model S.S. 1 could reach 85 mph, with 60 mph obtainable in third gear - enough to give quite brisk motoring today. The Bendix self-servo brakes are perfectly adequate and handling is neutral, the rear end easy to control if slid on loose surfaces.

The S.S.1 tourer is, in fact, an unexpectedly sporting car and some of its adherents today prefer it to the later two-seaters from the S.S. stable - principally because, as a genuine four-seater, it is more practical.

Swallow and S.S.1

Technical specifications

SWALLOW SIDECARS

YEARS CURRENT
1920-1939 Models 1 to 15, including competition versions (nb: no Model 13)

The first Swallow sidecars were eight sided and made in a shed at the rear of no. 5, Flowery Field, Stockport by William Walmsley, who sold them at £28 each. This sidecar was catalogued as the 'Model 1' Coupé Sports De Luxe, price £23.10s, when proper manufacture began under the auspices of the Lyons and Walmsley partnership, trading as the Swallow Sidecar Company, Blackpool from 1922.

The first competition sidecar was the Model 6 of 1927 (price £15). The most popular sidecar was the simpler and lighter five-sided Model 4, like the Model 1 also of polished aluminium and of which many hundreds were built. The last new model range was the '15' of 1936 by which time the products, now on well-sprung frames, were being sold under the slogan "Car Comfort at Sidecar Cost".

Although the Swallow sidecar range was discontinued during 1939, SS Cars produced more than 9,000 utility versions for military use during the war.

The Swallow name was sold after the war and is now owned by Watsonian, though has not been used for many years.

SWALLOW MOTOR CARS

YEARS CURRENT

1927 - 1932	Austin Seven Swallow
1929 (only)	Fiat-Swallow
1929 - 1931	Swift Swallow
1929 - 1932	Standard Swallow 9hp
1931 - 1932	Standard Swallow 16hp
1931 - 1933	Wolseley Swallow Hornet
1932 - 1933	Hornet Special

The Austin Swallows (introduced in May 1927) were later joined by coachwork on other chassis initially because William Lyons was upset when he considered he was treated discourteously by Sir Herbert Austin - who failed to keep an appointment with Lyons to discuss the regular supply of Austin Seven chassis. The adoption of Standard chassis proved crucial in making it practical for Lyons to build his own car, however. In November 1928 Swallow completed its relocation to Whitmore Park, an industrial estate in Coventry (postal address: Foleshill) and most of the additional makes bodied by Swallow were made there (there are very few survivors of the original Blackpool built Austin Swallow Sevens).

S.S.1

YEARS CURRENT
1933-1936 (tourer)

SPECIFICATIONS

Engine capacity	2054cc (2,552cc)
Power	48 bhp at 3,600 rpm (62 at 3,600 rpm)
Length	15ft 6ins
Width	5ft 3.5ins
Weight	26 cwt (2,912 lbs)
Wheelbase	9ft 11ins.
Max. speed	84 mph
0-60mph	23 sec
Mpg	18-19

Engine capacity 2,143cc/2,663cc from Oct 1933. The S.S.1 fixedhead coupé and saloon were broadly to the same specification.

Competition results

COMPETITION RESULTS

Sidecar Tourist Trophy Race, Isle of Man, 1924, Harry Reed, 2nd, DOT-JAP/Swallow Model 4; Almond Tinkler, 3rd, Matador-Blackburn/Swallow Model 4; J.W. Taylor, 4th, New Scale/Swallow Model 4

Sidecar World Speed records (class), 1926, Dougal Marchant, 86.35 mph for the flying kilometre and 73.72 mph for the 100 km from a standing start

In addition, Swallow sidecars (either standard or lightweight competition types) were used by a number of riders in a variety of more minor events during the 1920s.

COMPETITION RESULTS

The Swallow-bodied cars were not really suited to any type of competition work except, possibly, the Wolseley Hornet Specials which (occasionally joined by other Swallow products) were entered by some keen owners in trials and other low-key forms of motor sport.

COMPETITION RESULTS

1932
Ulster Rally, August, H. Lantlin, 2nd, 16 hp S.S.1 Coupé

1933
Royal Scottish Automobile Club Rally, A.G. Douglas Clease, 6th overall, 1st in class, coachwork competition, S.S.1 Tourer

1934
Alpine International Trial, A.G. Douglas Clease, Charles Needham, Sydney Light, 3rd in class (team prize, group 2), S.S.1 Tourers

Jaguar - a breed is born

The very first Jaguar motor car was launched at the Mayfair Hotel in London in 1935. The SS Jaguar 100 brought affordable performance motoring, if not to the masses, then to the real enthusiasts, and went a long way towards giving the name Jaguar genuine sporting credentials.

"WITH A DISTINGUISED APPEARANCE, OUTSTANDING PERFORMANCE AND ATTRACTIVE PRICE, THE NEW JAGUAR RANGE REPRESENTS AN ACHIEVEMENT OF WHICH MR LYONS AND HIS TECHNICAL STAFF MAY WELL FEEL PROUD." The Motor, *1935*

In January 1935 SS Cars Ltd was floated as a public company and, after little more than 12 years since he formed the partnership with Lyons, William Walmsley sold out. Big business was not for him and, in any case, Lyons had become increasingly angry with what he perceived as the older man's casual attitude to the business ("Walmsley would take long weekends," one contemporary worker remembers. "From Friday to Friday…"). The originator of Swallow, who undoubtedly possessed a genuine flair for style, then went into caravan manufacture; after suffering ill-health for some years he died in 1961. Sir William send a representative to his funeral.

Walmsley's departure left Lyons, still only in his early thirties, in total control of the company - a control he was to exercise rigidly for the next 30 years or more.

SS Cars' first product was also Lyons' first true sports car. The SS 90 was a beautifully proportioned two-seater derived from a shortened S.S.1 frame (the very first had, uniquely, a

Above: **William Lyons showed the effectiveness of his first two-seater by setting fastest time at the SS Car Club's Blackpool driving tests in 1935.**

round tail); the 75 bhp given by the S.S.1's smooth if somewhat plodding 2,663cc engine was, however, enough to push the car only some of the way towards the speed implied by the model's name.

It wasn't long before the new car was in action, being driven in the fourth RAC Rally by the Hon. Brian Lewis. The car impressed onlookers but Lewis's driving less so; he messed up some of the tests and won no award… This same car was demonstrated by Lyons himself at an early SS Car Club event on Blackpool's sea front. In an impressive display of his own driving skills and the performance of the 90, his slalom run was faster by six seconds than anyone else's.

The 90 was not long to remain the fastest SS: In September 1935 Lyons launched an entirely new range of cars, headed by a 2.7-litre saloon but including a new sports model, the 100. They were called 'Jaguars'. This new model name was chosen by Lyons from a list compiled by his advertising agency. "I immediately pounced on 'Jaguar' for it had an exciting sound to me, and

brought back some memories of the stories told to me, towards the end of the 1914-1918 war, by an old school friend who, being nearly a year older than I, had joined the Royal Flying Corps... He used to tell me of his work on the Armstrong Siddeley 'Jaguar' engine. Since that time, the word Jaguar has always had a particular significance to me."

Crucially, the new Jaguars had a lot more power. This was thanks to Harry Weslake, a forthright West Countryman and a pioneer of 'gas flowing' cylinder heads for extra performance. Harry's opinion of the S.S.1 - which he had helped fettle for the 1934 Alpine - was not high. Perhaps because Weslake, despite all his bluster, was so effective, he and William Lyons got on very well, regardless of the fact that he claimed to have told Lyons exactly what he thought of the S.S.1.

Above: **May 1935 and the Hon Brian Lewis takes the SS 90 prototype (alone of the 90s round tailed) up Shelsley Walsh; he was third in class with a time of 52 seconds in this, the first competitive appearance of a two-seater sports car from SS.**

"YOUR CAR REMINDS ME OF AN OVER DRESSED LADY WITH NO BRAINS - THERE'S NOTHING UNDER THE BONNET!" *Harry Weslake, to William Lyons, on the S.S.1*

Harry designed an overhead valve conversion for the smooth and sturdy 2.7-litre Standard engine and the results exceeded all expectations, boosting power to over 100 bhp; it certainly gave the new SS Jaguar 100 a truly credible performance. Lyons persuaded Standard to make the new head (SS had no machine shop of their own) and he always remembered this whole exercise as one of the biggest break-throughs in the company's fortunes.

Another lifeline was thrown to SS by the arrival in April 1935 of William Heynes as the company's first chief engineer. The 31-year-old Heynes came from prestige car makers Humber, where he had felt stifled, but it still took some five interviews before the cautious Lyons finally entrusted the engineering future of his company to the young man.

Heynes soon discovered Lyons was no ordinary boss; he enjoyed the freedom to pursue new ideas, but there was relentless pressure for progress. "After I'd been there two years, I think, I said to him, 'Mr Lyons, I'd like to take my summer holidays.' He said 'Why? Are you ill?'"

The immediate task facing Heynes was to re-design the S.S.1 chassis for the forthcoming range of Jaguars. "Lyons knew what was wrong, but he didn't know what to do about it, that was the point," remembered Bill Heynes. Steering, brakes and the chassis frame itself were all markedly improved and, together with the new 2.7-litre ohv engine, the Jaguars were pretty formidable motor cars in their class.

This was proved unexpectedly soon by the SS 100. Thomas Henry Wisdom, debonair motoring correspondent and amateur racing driver, persuaded Lyons to lend him one of the new sports cars for the 1936 International Alpine Trial. Perhaps coloured by the mixed record of the S.S.1 in the event, Tommy's expectations of registration number BWK 77 were limited, but "by the end of the first day's run I had a new respect for the car's capabilities".

Crewed by his wife 'Bill', Tommy found that the completely standard 100 was in fact highly competitive; only the 3.3-litre Bugatti of Gaston Descolles was quicker on the timed sections. Then Descolles lost road marks and the Wisdoms were able to claim best performance of the rally. Their success is worth

Above: **Sammy Newsome enjoys a large crowd as he takes his SS 90 through the pylons during an SS Car Club rally; note the upright spare wheel which distinguishes the 90 from the 100 model that replaced it.**

emphasising. Few continental drivers had even heard of the new Jaguar car, but now, from nowhere, the new SS had beaten all-comers in a tough international event, including that 1930s sporting icon, Bugatti.

The 100's excellent power-to-weight ratio made it a good rally car and it was in these events that the car performed best, its competitiveness increased still further when a 3.5-litre engine arrived for the 1938 season. Developed by Heynes and Weslake, it produced a punchy 125 bhp, finally allowing the 100 to live up to its name and, at £445, to become the cheapest of the very few 100 mph cars then available for general sale.

Above: **Tommy Wisdom pauses during the 1936 Alpine Trial.**

It certainly gave the SS an even better chance against its major rival, the BMW 328. The German company's 2-litre sports car, lighter and with independent front suspension, was better-handling than the 100 and tuned versions could often match the SS in a straight line. In typical British road rallies, however, the SS's somewhat crude suspension was compensated for by ample torque and its 'chuckability' in the all-important driving tests which still often decided the winner (Jack Harrop's 3.5-litre won the 1938 RAC Rally and A.F.P. Fane's 328 the 1939 event). If you threw price into the equation, of course, there was no contest: the BMW cost £695 against the Jaguar's £445.

The 100 was less suited to the race track, though. It may have been described by SS Cars as "primarily intended for competition work", but 'competition' in this instance was not intended to embrace circuit racing. William Lyons needed persuasion, therefore, from Heynes - the constant motor racing enthusiast - to allow one car to be developed for the track. This was the 1936 Alpine Trial car which, as the company's first 'racing car', is really the progenitor of the true competition Jaguars which were to arrive in the 1950s.

Wisdom had first run this car, BWK 77, at Brooklands in October 1936, when it must already have been well fettled as it lapped at 105 mph, well over the standard car's top speed. BWK 77 finally left its road-car persona behind when in September 1937, *sans* lights, starter, battery and dynamo and fitted with an early 3.5-litre engine, it was driven by Sammy Newsome (SS Cars' Coventry agent) at Shelsely Walsh. Then Tommy Wisdom took the wheel at Brooklands again and averaged 111.85 mph, surprising the handicappers and winning the first handicap race there in October.

Above: **The 100's unexpected success in the 1936 Alpine Trial rocked the establishment. "If ever the international motoring press found itself drinking the wine of astonishment, like whoever it was in Psalm 60, this was it," wrote Tom Wisdom many years afterwards.**

It was through this car that Walter Hassan came to join SS Cars. Working at the Brooklands-based company of Thompson & Taylor (builders of such famous cars as Malcolm Campbell's *Bluebird* and John Cobb's Napier Railton), Hassan modified an SS 100 for Harold Bradley to use in competition and, doubtless through his friendship with Tommy Wisdom, received a lot of advice and special parts from Bill Heynes at SS. The Bradley car became probably the quickest 100 after the works BWK 77 and, again through Tommy Wisdom, Walter was offered the post of chief experimental engineer at SS Cars. He joined towards the end of 1938, one of his jobs being to continue development of BWK 77.

Previous spread: **Restored SS 90 - a beautiful example of Lyons' first sports car.**

Right: **One of the most remarkable occasions in Jaguar's competition history: William Lyons himself about to win a motor race! Heynes and Newsome appear to be taking the Donington event none too seriously but Lyons (nearest camera) adopts a more thoughtful pose. The year: 1938.**

That year saw the one and only time William Lyons took part in a motor race - possibly setting some sort of record while doing so… At the SS Car Club's May 1938 meeting at Donington Park, Lyons took part in the 'trade' handicap race. Alongside him on the grid, in seemingly identical 100s, were Sammy Newsome and Bill Heynes.

Then, as *The Motor* recounted in its report, "W. Lyons, managing director of the SS Company, simply could not wait on the starting line and was twice hauled back by the starter. When he did get it right, he drove with the most awe-inspiring determination, and despite having tossed up for cars was soon in the lead."

Lyons won, with Newsome close behind and Heynes third. More than that, it transpired that 'the boss' had put up the fastest lap of the day, ahead of all the regular 100 drivers, quicker even than Harold Bradley's Hassan-tuned 3.5-litre 100 in another race. Heynes contended years later that Lyons had insisted on changing cars with him before the race (a claim emphatically denied by Lyons to the author!), but even if DHP 734 had been a little quicker than the others, it is still pretty remarkable that Lyons, with no race experience at all, was able to set fastest time against practised competitors. It seems to indicate that he was as good as any amateur racing driver of his day.

And the unofficial record? Well, has anyone else entered just one motor race, won it, and never ever driven in another?

Meanwhile, some SS 100's had found their way overseas. Australian driver F. J. McEvoy achieved an early success when he won the 2-3 litre class in the Marne Grand Prix at Rheims in 1936, even if the 3.3-litre 'tank' Bugattis dominated the race. The 100's first overseas race victory was secured by Casimiro d'Oliveira who, in a close-fought event, defeated race-prepared Adler and BMW opposition to score a highly popular win in front of his fellow-countrymen at Vila Real, Portugal, in 1937.

In North America, the only 100 with any sort of racing profile was Paul Marx's 3.5-litre. Arriving on the East coast in 1938, Marx joined in with the grandly-titled Automobile Racing Club of America, raced at Thompson, Connecticut and Alexandria Bay, New York State, and also

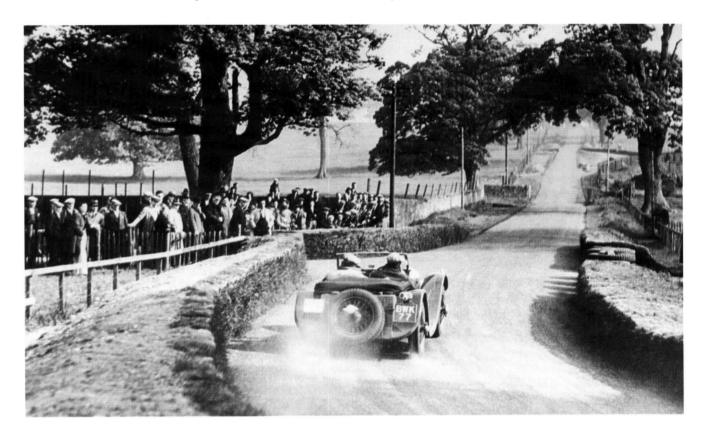

took the 100 up the ARCA's 'home venue', the spectacular Mount Washington hill climb. The car made the ascent in 13 minutes 22.6 seconds, finishing fourth overall (post-war, Jaguars were to do even better there).

Meanwhile, Walter Hassan continued the development of chassis no. 18008, higher compression pistons and the use of an alcohol/methanol fuel mix extracting 169 bhp from the engine. Before war intervened, Sam Newsome made best un-supercharged car time at Shelsely Walsh in June 1939, ahead of Forrest Lycett's 8-litre Bentley. Tommy Wisdom then drove the car at Brooklands again, and reckoned the SS now had a top speed of around 140 mph. On that occasion, he related, "in our final effort, with the car at its peak in practice - an unofficial lap of more than 125 mph - we broke the crank on the way to the start".

Wisdom has left us with some fine descriptions of driving the 100 on the intimidating Outer Circuit. "It was at Brooklands, with its bumpy surface and peculiar configuration, that one paid the penalty for the car's short wheelbase and by no means rigid chassis. There was one point in

Above: **The SS 100 excelled in conditions like these: Newsome tail-slides the hard-worked BWK 77 ready to devour the straight ahead. This is the Bo'ness hill climb, part of the 1937 Scottish Rally.**

particular where, at speeds above about 110 mph any car would take off and fly through the air in traversing the humpbacked river viaduct over the River Wey, and I repeatedly thought my last moment had come. On landing, the SS 100 would veer lurchingly to either right or left, but which way was a matter of pure guesswork. My life was quite likely saved, I think, by some advice which Kaye Don, formerly an habitual breaker of the (outright) Brooklands lap record, gave me: 'Don't grip or fight the wheel on touchdown,' he said, 'just let it go loose in your hands.' Screwing up what courage I could muster, I obeyed, and this did the trick."

Above: The vast open spaces of Brooklands, with its various circuits, saw many appearances by the 100; here Tommy Wisdom in the stripped and modified works 100 (18008) is braving the famous banking as a Talbot overtakes higher up.

Generally speaking, however, the best BMW 328s and Delahayes were quicker than the best 100s, and Lyons never allowed any works-backed cars to run against such opposition in major races. In fact, when a 2.5-litre 100 was entered in the 1938 Tourist Trophy race at Donington (a circuit which, if any, suited the car), he even persuaded the drivers to withdraw and refunded them their entry money. "We knew its limitations in spite of its outstanding performance," he confessed many years afterwards. It was probably a

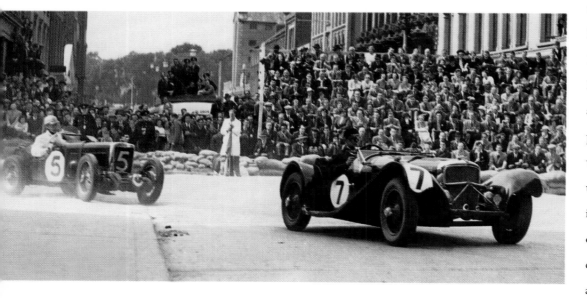

Above: Harold Bradley in his Hassan-tuned SS 100 leads Ernie Robb's J4 MG through the streets of Limerick during the 150 mile race in 1939. Robb later led, then retired - but Bradley didn't realise it and blew up his engine trying to catch the non-existent leader!

wise move - the car would have been left very much in the wake of Delage and BMW. But the 100's known drawbacks also acted as a spur: "It was in fact this limitation which led to the determination to design and produce a new engine," said Lyons.

But the twin overhead camshaft XK unit - despite being dreamed of by Bill Heynes in the 1930s - did not arrive until 1948, and it was the SS 100 which remained Jaguar's flagship sports car, even after 1945, though it was well and truly obsolete by then.

From 1940 SS Cars turned over to war work of all sorts, from airborne trailers to aircraft parts, and it took a great effort for the company to resume car making after 1945. For obvious reasons the name 'S.S.' was dropped and the company became Jaguar Cars Ltd.

"THE 100 TOOK A LOT OF NERVE TO DRIVE REALLY QUICKLY AT GOODWOOD, ESPECIALLY THROUGH FORDWATER, AND I FRIGHTENED MYSELF MORE THAN ONCE. . ." *F. Michael Wilcock, SS 100 racer*

Jaguar's pre-war range re-entered production, minus the 100, but the two-seater remained effective and did well in the UK's very first post-war event, a hill climb at Naish House near Bristol in 1945. Walter Hassan revived the old works racer, chassis no. 18008, and although Brooklands was no more, 'Bill' Wisdom won the Ladies' Prize with the car at the Bouley Bay hill climb in Jersey in 1947. Shortly afterwards this car, which had pointed the way ahead to the XK 120, was sold to pre-war SS 100 campaigner George Matthews.

A range of other de-mothballed 100s were active in the late 1940s, many proving effective amongst the mishmash of cars which emerged from barns and garages to resume various sporting activities. The 100 achieved at least one outright post-war race win in Britain, although it was also the car's last major 'scratch' victory in the UK against current competition. This was on 18th September 1948, in the very first race held at the Duke of Richmond's new motor racing circuit at Goodwood, when Paul Pycroft in his streamlined-bodied 2.5-litre SS 100 took the chequered flag.

Other Goodwood regulars around this period were F. Michael Wilcock and John Craig (later to be a Rolls-Royce director). Recalls Michael Wilcock, "My car was the ex-Cyril Mann 3.5, and although this was at least as fast as Craig's, I was never able to emulate his driving skill. My limit was about 90 mph through Fordwater but John would go through at least 5-8 mph faster...

Below: Paul Pycroft winning the first ever race at Goodwood; his rebodied 2.5-litre 100 had one-piece nose and tail sections which hinged up to disclose the mechanics. The shape even hinted at the XK 120 to come.

"We would certainly hold off the early XK 120s at Goodwood until they came up with the high lift cams and beefed-up suspension, and we had a lot of fun doing it. The ex-Cyril Mann car would walk away from the XKs from 0-100 mph, but of course they pulled away at the top end. My maximum speed was about 120 mph." In fact, at the June

Above: Fortunately, this was
just after the 1947 Alpine!
On the way home, Appleyard
ran the 100 in a Swiss
Automobile Club hill climb
at Les Rangiers - but 'lost it',
ending up against a post.
He was unscathed.

1950 Goodwood meeting, John Craig lapped at 1 min 49 secs (79.30 mph) - a good Formula 500

time and quicker than the 100's old pre-war rivals like Guy Gale's Darracque T150.

Other 100 drivers of the late 1940s included the Canadian 'Spike' Rhiando (with the very

quick ex-Truett 2.5-litre), Les Leston (with another special-bodied car) and Tom Cole. Cole took

his car to the US and finished second to George Huntoon's Alfa Romeo in the feature 100-mile

sports car race at Bridgehampton, Long Island in June 1949. Several SS 100s were by now

competing in the US, including those of 'Johnny' Von Neumann (who would later drive

Porsches for Max Hoffman) and, later, entertainment star Dave Garroway in his well-known

XK-engined car.

Back in Europe, a young man by the name of Ian Appleyard, the son of a Leeds Jaguar dealer,

was to produce one of the SS 100's most extraordinary feats. In April 1947 he acquired a

20,000 miles from new, one-owner SS 100 3.5-litre; after just one prior event locally,

Appleyard and the nine-year-old car entered the 1947 International Alpine Trial. The SS and crew

proved surprisingly competitive and only tyre problems prevented them from finishing higher

than a respectable third in class. The following year was to be much better...

The 1948 Alpine began on 13th July, again at Marseille. A very full entry list contained most

of the leading makes of the day, Allard, Delahaye, Healey, Hotchkiss and Lancia included. The

1,200-mile route went into Switzerland and the final day's run was almost 400 miles, including

five passes. A mere one-minute tolerance was given for being late or early at a control.

Appleyard, crewed by Dick Weatherhead, later wrote up the adventure in Jaguar's house journal and painted a vivid picture of the event.

After the SS had left the 'famous N7', it became much tougher to maintain the 37.5 mph rally average as the car climbed Mont Ventoux, "the French equivalent of Shelsely Walsh, although about thirty times the length". Refuelling was done in motion to save time, Dick Weatherhead "spending about ten minutes perched precariously on the tail as the car bounced and slithered round the hairpins of the Col de Rousset".

Next came the tortuous Grenoble to Aix section, tackled in pouring rain: "the muddy road was like a skating rink and patches of drifting mist and cloud turned what should have been a highly pleasurable dice into a suicidal series of terrifying slides at each corner of the unfenced road."

Several cars did not make it, an Opel ending up on top of a Healey saloon which had gone off earlier. Two timed hill climbs were also involved - the fastest ascent of the Col d'Izoard by any car was made by the good old Jaguar in 7 min 7 secs.

It was somebody else's accident that made Appleyard's 1948 Alpine truly extraordinary. On the descent from the Col d'Allos, a local standing by the roadside made gruesome 'turning over'

Below: Spoils of victory: trophies (including an Alpine Cup) adorn the bonnet of Ian Appleyard's SS 100 following his clean sheet in the 1948 Alpine Rally.

signs, and they stopped to see Donald Healey and Nick Haines dragging someone up to the road. Norman Hiskins' Sunbeam Talbot tourer had left the road and rolled over, its driver saved only because the car ended up across a stream; his co-driver Bill Marsden had been thrown out and was unconscious. Dick Weatherhead was a doctor and did what he could. Help arrived and the SS 100 could go on its way again but its crew were disconsolate: they were a total of 35 minutes late and had only two hours to regain the time.

At first the twisting roads gave them little chance to catch up. Then at Grasse it straightened out "but it was almost too late. We had exactly half an hour left for the 32 miles to the finish - that meant averaging 64 mph all the way towards Nice on roads which were seething with holiday-makers. It was a terrifying ride. "Clocking between 70 and 80 mph most of the way, and with the horn blowing incessantly, we passed obstructive vehicles on whichever side looked the more promising, whilst cyclists scattered before us like chaff in a hurricane. But as we emerged onto the promenade at Nice there was still a minute to go and with the speedo needle creeping up towards the century mark, the Jaguar hurtled towards the final control. Dick was ticking off the seconds now. We'd just do it if nobody got in the way. Those final few yards seemed to take ages as we screeched to a standstill and handed over our route card, it was stamped. We were on time."

After the official examination to see that engine, transmission, horns and lights all still functioned, the *Coupe des Alpes* was assured. Then a final test decided class placings. The SS finished three-tenths of a second ahead of Potter's Allard so that was in the bag too. Dick Weatherhead even won the draw for best navigator!

All was not yet over for the SS 100's rally career, as in May 1949 Ian Appleyard and LNW 100 won their class in the Tulip Rally, finishing second overall. This last international success was a remarkable final tribute to a car which, although completely orthodox, was carefully designed and highly effective.

Above: Later owner of BWK 77 was H.A. Mecran who attempted, unsuccessfully, to beat the car's winning pre-war times at Shelsley Walsh. Here the twin rear wheeled 100 competes in the June 1953 meeting.

Far Left: Tommy Wisdom reunited with his old Brooklands SS 100 in the early 1970s. For many years the motoring editor of the *Daily Herald*, he also persuaded the *Sporting Life* (the UK's horse racing bible) to let him write a motoring column too - "the best informed in the business," according to fellow journalist John Dugdale!

Driving the SS 100

Today, when even driving an XK 120 is a culture-shock to those not used to old cars, getting behind the big wheel of an SS Jaguar 100 is a very different experience again. You sit only two or three inches from the floor in a neat bucket seat with your legs almost straight out in front of you, and look down that immensely long, multi-louvred bonnet ahead.

Starting the engine is easy because there's an automatic choke (actually an auxiliary starting carburettor) so you just switch on and press the starter button. The engine will spring into life with a soft burble from the exhaust and a hissing from the twin SU carburettors. Depressing the clutch to engage a gear can cause the first problem - there isn't much space between steering column and clutch pedal and large-welted shoes are definitely out. But the clutch action itself is smooth and anyone used to XK or early E-type transmissions will be quite at home with the gearbox: the stubby lever snicks through the nicely-stacked ratios very satisfactorily.

The synchromesh is not that strong on second (and absent on first) but, especially with the bigger-

engined car, it is mainly third and top you'll be using.

Both the 2.5 and 3.5 engines are flexible and will pull away from almost tickover speeds in third or top. The 2.5-litre car is not quick by modern standards, and the engine needs revving to its modest limits for brisk motoring, but the 3.5 car is respectably quick off the mark with a still-good performance in top gear, so you can go from, say, 50 mph to 70 mph faster than the average traffic flow.

The car will lope along all day at 70-80 mph. The Girling rod brakes will probably surprise the newcomer with their effectiveness and with large drums and air able to circulate freely through those wire wheels, plus the air-brake effect of the uncompromising radiator and big headlights, fade is not a problem - as long as the rods and compensators are adjusted properly; otherwise the car will slew sideways under hard braking. The 100's worst aspect is probably the hard ride combined with a flexible chassis frame and rather too much weight up high in the scuttle - this has to carry the battery and the heavy brass windscreen. This results in scuttle shake over poor surfaces, while the over-stiff springs can cause the rear end to skitter sideways on corners. On smooth surfaces, grip from the 18-inch tyres is actually quite good and the 100 can be hustled along country roads surprisingly quickly.

Become acclimatised and you will probably end up admiring how dynamically successful the first Jaguar sports car was. Compared with the average British car of the 1930s, the 100 was simply in a different world, while it was also able to challenge the best from the continent in the right event.

S.S.90 and SS Jaguar 100

Technical specifications

YEARS CURRENT
1935	(S.S.90)
1935 - 1940	(SS 100 2.5 litre)
1937 - 1940	(SS 100 3.5 litre)

SPECIFICATION (S.S.90)
Engine capacity	2,663cc
Power	70 bhp @ 4,200 rpm
Length	12ft 6ins
Width	4ft 3ins
Weight	2,520 lbs/(22.5 cwt)
Wheelbase	8ft 8ins
Max. speed	88 mph
0-60 mph	20.5 secs
Mpg	19

SPECIFICATION (SS Jaguar 100 2.5 litre/3.5 litre)
Engine capacity	2,663cc/3,485cc
Power	102 bhp @ 4,600 rpm /125 bhp @ 4,250 rpm
Length	12ft 6ins
Width	4ft 3ins
Weight	2,576 lbs (23cwt)/2,604 lbs (23.25 cwt)
Wheelbase	8ft 8 ins
Max. speed	94 mph/101 mph
0-60 mph	12.8secs/10.9secs
Mpg	20/21

The '100' model replaced the '90' within a year and while the new two-seater looked similar to the old, it came with many improvements including more efficient (Girling rod) brakes instead of cable-operated ones, revised steering and better damping. All these were brought in by Bill Heynes, appointed as chief engineer of SS Cars Ltd in 1935. Above all the '100' had the new overhead valve conversion.

This engine, together with its 1.7 litre and 3.5 litre sister units, powered all Jaguars built from 1937 to 1948, when the 2.5 and 3.5 litre units continued in the Mk V.

The Mk V, for all its old-fashioned looks, had a surprisingly good competition record: the lusty 3.5 litre engine had good low-speed torque and together with fine handling from its very modern, independent front suspension chassis (actually developed for the XK-powered Mk VII), this made the Mk V and excellent rally car. A good many of the cars were rallied internationally, but Cecil Vard from Dublin was the car's greatest exponent and he achieved a remarkable fifth place in 1953 with the type - beating many more modern cars (including Mk VIIs) in the process. This was a good finale for the old 'pushrod' engined Jaguars - though Frank Hann's 3.5 litre was still mixing-it in with modern saloons right into the 1960s in Australia!

Competition results

COMPETITION RESULTS

1935
Shelsley Walsh hill climb, May, Hon. Brian Lewis, 3rd in class (sports cars up to 3,000cc), S.S.90

1936
Marne Sports Car Grand Prix, July, F. J. McEvoy, 1st (2,000cc - 3,000cc class), SS Jaguar 100 2.5 litre
International Alpine Trial, August, T.H. Wisdom/E.M. Wisdom, best individual performance, best performance 2,000cc - 3,000cc class, Glacier Cup, SS Jaguar 100 2.5 litre
Shelsley Walsh hill climb, September, S.H. Newsome, 1st (3,000cc unsupercharged class), SS Jaguar 100 2.5 litre

1937
RAC Rally, March, J. Harrop, 1st general classification, 1st open cars over 15hp, SS Jaguar 100 2.5 litre. T.H. Wisdom, 2nd general classification, 2nd open cars over 15hp, SS Jaguar 100 2.5 litre. Team prize - Harrop/Wisdom/E.H. Jacob (SS Jaguar 100 2.5 litre)
Scottish Rally, J. Sleigh, 2nd open cars over 15hp, SS Jaguar 100 3.5 litre
Vila Real road race, Portugal, Casimiro d'Oliviera, 1st, SS Jaguar 100 2.5 litre
Welsh Rally, July, E.H. Jacob, Best overall performance, 1st open cars over 15hp. Team prize - Jacob/Rankin/Matthews (SS Jaguar 100 2.5 litre)
Shelsely Walsh hill climb, September, S.H. Newsome, 2nd, 5-litre class, fastest unsupercharged car, SS Jaguar 100 3.5 litre
BARC meeting, Brooklands, First October Handicap race, T.H. Wisdom, 1st (111.83 mph average), SS Jaguar 100 3.5 litre

1938
SS Car Club meeting, Donington, May, W. Lyons, 1st, 'trade' handicap race, SS Jaguar 100 3.5 litre
RAC Rally, May, J. Harrop, 1st, open cars over 15hp, SS Jaguar 100 3.5 litre
Welsh Rally, July, Mrs V.E.M. Hetherington, 1st, open cars over 15hp, SS Jaguar 100 3.5 litre
Paris-Nice Trial, T.H. Wisdom, 1st, 3-litre class SS Jaguar 100 2.5 litre
ARCA New London TT, Connecticut, Paul Marx, 3rd, SS Jaguar 100 3.5 litre
Mount Washington hill climb, New Hampshire, Paul Marx, 4th, SS Jaguar 100 3.5 litre

1939
Monte Carlo Rally, January, J. Harrop, 10th equal, SS Jaguar 3.5 litre saloon
RAC Rally, May, S.H. Newsome, 2nd, open cars over 15hp; Gordon/Gibson/Mann, 2nd, club team prize
Shelsley Walsh, June, S.H. Newsome, 1st, 3,001cc-5,000cc unsupercharged cars (42.95sec), SS Jaguar 100 3.5 litre
Welsh Rally, July, W.G. N. Norton, 1st, open cars over 15hp; Miss V. Watson, Ladies' prize (open cars), SS Jaguar 100 3.5 litre
Phoenix Park, Dublin, handicap race, H.E. Bradley, unsupercharged lap record (93 mph), SS Jaguar 100 3.5 litre

1946
Bo'ness Speed Trials, May, N.A. Bean, FTD (40 sec), SS Jaguar 100 3.5 litre
Shelsley Walsh hill climb, June, S.H. Newsome, 2nd, 5,000cc class (46.95secs), SS Jaguar 100 3.5 litre
Prescott hill climb, August, R.M. Dryden, 1st, 3,001-5,000cc class (46.95sec), SS Jaguar 100 3.5 litre
Craigantlet hill climb, August, J.W. Patterson, 1st, unlimited sports car class (99sec) SS Jaguar 100 3.5 litre

1947
Bo'ness hill climb, May, N.A. Bean, 1st, unlimited sports car class (43.4sec), SS Jaguar 100 3.5 litre
Prescott hill climb, June, R.M. Dryden, 1st, unsupercharged cars over 3,000cc, SS Jaguar 100 3.5 litre
Queensland Road Racing Championship race, Lowood, Queensland, Australia, Keith Thallon, 1st, SS Jaguar 100 3.5 litre
Bouley Bay hill climb, Jersey, July, Mrs E.M. Wisdom, best performance by a lady (72secs), SS Jaguar 100 3.5 litre
JCC Eastbourne Rally, June, H.E. Matthews, E.I. Appleyard, L. Parker, 1st class awards, SS Jaguar 100 3.5 litre

1948
International Alpine Rally, July, E.I. Appleyard, 1st, over 3,000cc; Coupe des Alpes, SS Jaguar 100 3.5 litre

1949
Tulip Rally, Holland, April, E.I. Appleyard, 2nd general classification, SS Jaguar 100 3.5 litre

1951
Monte Carlo Rally, January, C. Vard, 3rd, Mk V 3.5 litre saloon, W.H. Waring, 9th, Mk V 3.5 litre saloon

1953
Monte Carlo Rally, January, C. Vard, 5th, Mk V 3.5 litre saloon

The XK era

Tyre squeal was the dominant noise echoing across Silverstone's open spaces one day in August 1949, the skylarks' song high in the blue sky above drowned out by 30 cars roaring around the airfield circuit. Britain's first post-war event for production cars was underway.

"WHAT IMPRESSED ME MOST WAS ITS SHEER BEAUTY. I THINK ALL THE WILLIAM LYONS JAGUARS HAVE BEEN REALLY BEAUTIFUL, AND THE XK 120 MADE SUCH AN IMPACT THAT EVERYBODY WANTED ONE, BUT THEY WERE NEARLY ALL FOR EXPORT SO YOU COULDN'T BUY ONE FOR LOVE NOR MONEY." *Stirling Moss*

In an austere post-war Britain nothing remotely like this had been seen since the Brooklands days of the 1930s. The Silverstone meeting had been proclaimed as "an unrivalled opportunity of watching the car of your choice matched in open competition with its rival in engine size, or in price, to compare its acceleration, road holding, and 'flat out' speed in this race of one hour's duration round the 3-mile Silverstone circuit. A sort of Mobile Motor Show…"

When announced, the event had placed Jaguar in something of a dilemma. Their new XK 120 sports car had made a huge impact at the British Motor Show at Earl's Court in the Autumn of 1948, and aroused even more interest in May 1949 when it rushed almost silently down the

Below: Notice of intent: 30th May 1949, and the new Jaguar XK 120 records over 132 mph in Belgium. Jaguar's test driver then was 'Soapy' Sutton, a remarkable chain-smoking, hang-dog looking character so called because he would often arrive at work having not bothered to remove all his shaving cream!

Above: Leslie Johnson on the way to victory at Silverstone 1949, after fending off the Frazer-Nash challenge (the 'Nash, at £2,724 in the UK, was over double the XK 120's price. Bob Gerard's lost a wheel at Abbey and while this was found, the brake drum was not. Commented *Motor Sport* waspishly afterwards, "It should be worth searching for, in view of the price of F.N. spares").

Jabbeke-Aaltere autoroute in Belgium at 132 mph, an astonishing speed for what was claimed to be a series-built production car.

Yet this most elegant of sports cars was an afterthought which conceivably might never have appeared at all. The XK 120 had been a last-minute inspiration to highlight the newly announced twin-cam XK engine by creating an attention-grabbing roadster for the 1948 London Motor Show. The exercise was, Sir William told the writer in the 1970s, the most rapid he had ever undertaken, the XK's flowing body - Jaguar's first streamlined shape - having evolved from start to finish in some three weeks. Intended for low volume production (a run of 200 or 250 cars was anticipated), the car used, in essence, a shortened version of the still-secret Mk VII saloon's chassis. In the event, demand at the show resulted in a drastic re-think. No one had appreciated the strength of the North American market and Jaguar's West coast distributor, Charles Hornburg, offered to buy the entire first year's production!

But the car had never been designed for racing. A straight-line speed trial of a few minutes' duration was one thing, but a full one-hour race that would test its engine, braking, handling and reliability in front of tens of thousands of spectators was quite another. The doubters said there must be a flaw, it was simply impossible to make and sell a competent 130 mph car for just £1,263, with UK taxes, half the price of anything else as quick.

The publicity rewards from victory would be great, but failure might do lasting damage to Jaguar's marginal credibility. So, in what became a founding principle in Jaguar's competition strategy, William Lyons agreed to enter the XK 120 - but only if he could be shown it would almost certainly win.

Accordingly, Lofty England, Walter Hassan and Jaguar PR man Bill Rankin took a car to Silverstone "and flogged it round for three hours," as Lofty put it, to see if it was indeed fast enough and was likely to last the distance. During the session Lyons himself turned up. More than that, he wanted to try the XK for himself - the first time he had driven on a race track since that frenetic 'trade race' at Donington in 1938.

Below: Bira's XK 120 had been specially finished in blue, with yellow wheels. The XKs' engines were all meticulously assembled and bench-tested but not modified; the most powerful was fitted to Bira's car and gave 158 bhp at 5,200 rpm, actually 2 bhp less than catalogued.

The incident went down in Jaguar lore. Rankin was sitting in the XK's passenger seat at the time; Lyons jumped in beside him, slapped the startled PR manager on the back, and said "Hey, Rankin, I've left my specs behind - tell me where the corners and braking points are!" Then he let in the clutch and roared off. It was an ashen-faced Rankin who staggered from the XK a few laps later...

As the company founder's last drive on a race track ended, so began a competition career for the XK engine that was to produce five Le Mans wins and countless racing and rallying successes the world over.

But when the three XK 120s (probably the only three in existence at that time) lined up for the Le Mans-style start at Silverstone a few weeks later, the result was by no means a foregone conclusion. Some elements of the car, particularly the brakes and cooling, were going to be tested to their limits, with the opposition - especially the very light, race-developed Frazer-Nashes, and perhaps the 4.4-litre V8-engined Allards - likely to be fierce.

Service chief Lofty England, with his former racing experience, had been delegated by Lyons to find good drivers for the XK 120s. Lofty chose people he already knew. The lead driver was

Above: **Leslie Johnson in traffic, Silverstone 1949. It was an altercation with one of the slower cars, a Jowett Javelin, that resulted in HKV 500's damaged bodywork.**

the ERA and Maserati ace Prince Bira of Siam, aged 35 and still at the top of his form. Peter Walker was another rapid ERA driver, while Leslie Johnson had previously raced against Lofty England (he'd also lent Bill Heynes his BMW 328 to examine pre-war). This trio did not disappoint, even if it was a big Allard that led into the first corner after the flag dropped. But, watched by a large crowd which included three coachloads of Jaguar employees, Bira soon took the lead and though Johnson and Walker were in turn harried by Norman Culpan's rapid Frazer-Nash, a Jaguar one-two-three seemed to be on the cards.

Then, with 17 laps completed and going quicker than ever, "Bira swirled into Woodcote Corner fast, bang went a rear tyre and the Jaguar shot backwards into the straw bales," as *The Motor* described it. Bira tried to change the wheel but the jack sank into the soft earth. He was out. Leslie Johnson in HKV 500 (the 'Jabbeke' car) saved the day, however, and led Peter Walker to the chequered flag 44.6 seconds after the hour was up, and after covering 28 laps at an

average speed of 82.8 mph. Walker also had the satisfaction of setting fastest lap at 84.90 mph, though with Bira's demise the team prize was taken by the Healey Silverstones.

So the XK 120, and the XK engine, won their very first race - but should this herald a full works competition programme? Walter Hassan knew, because he had helped design it, that the XK 120 was primarily a refined, high-speed road car, and all the power advantages of the XK engine were being used to overcome the deficiencies inherent in this, principally excess weight. He also knew that motor racing could be an enormous consumer of money, something Jaguar had little of at the time.

Accordingly, on 30th December 1948, Hassan penned a sensibly cautious memo to William Lyons, copied to Bill Heynes and Lofty England: "At the risk of being accused of 'sour grapes' and/or being unduly pessimistic," it said, "I would suggest that unless you are willing to produce a special competition model on the lines of the Healey Silverstone and the special Frazer-Nash, our production models will always carry a tremendous handicap when in competition with such cars." He proposed that the company should allow "one or two" private entrants to race in 1950, and then "have a go in the following year if it is considered desirable". And that is pretty much what happened.

Meanwhile Leslie Johnson travelled to the US and on 3rd January 1950 drove the XK 120 in its first race in America. He failed to win at Palm Springs, Florida (George Huntoon's ex-Indianapolis Duesenberg Special did), but the ex-Walker 1949 Silverstone car gained trophies for best production car and best all-British finisher. It was the privilege of the Cuban Alfonso Gomez Mena to post the first XK 120 race win outside Britain, when he won a road race near Havana.

Above: Cuba saw the XK 120 win its first race outside the UK, driven by Alfonso Gomez Mena. This was in February 1950 when a trickle of XKs were finally leaving Jaguar – all, apart from the six 'works' cars, strictly for export.

The XK engine

The XK engine was perhaps Jaguar's greatest asset for over 35 years. First seen in the XK 120, it powered a succession of brilliant designs throughout the 1950s, including five Le Mans winners, and in the 1960s provided the motive force for yet another epochal two-seater, the E- type of 1961. It was still good enough in 1968 for the XJ6, surely the supreme luxury car of its day. That this same engine also powered an 18 ft 6 ins long limousine, off-shore power boats and a range of tracked and wheeled fighting vehicles merely underlines the versatility, toughness and utter rightness of its design.

The engine was born during Second World War fire-watching discussions at SS Cars' Coventry factory. William Lyons needed a suitable engine to power the new 100 mph luxury post-war saloon he was planning. Chief engineer William Heynes favoured a racing-type twin overhead camshaft design from the start, a configuration which allowed higher engine speeds and thus more power.

But once this then radical engine had been accepted in principle, other crucial influences came to bear - from Walter Hassan, with his solid background of race and practical engineering with Bentleys; from Harry Weslake, the bumptious but gifted cylinder head consultant; and finally, from Claude Baily, designer-draughtsman, quiet but meticulous.

Twin ohc engines had previously been used only in low-volume and expensive motor cars, yet Lyons authorised this exotic format in a large, soft, refined touring car which would be produced in relatively large numbers and be driven everyday by mechanically inexpert owners who would expect to have their cars serviced by the local town garage. To outsiders at the time, this seemed like a huge commercial risk. What about the warranty claims?

But this is an instance of how the normally cautious William Lyons could, when he felt the occasion demanded it, depart markedly from the conventional. He had faith in Heynes, and that faith was amply justified. After a series of prototypes, the final 3,442cc straight-six 'XK' design arrived. With a rigid iron crankcase and lightweight aluminium head, it was powerful, quiet in operation and reliable.

The engine was revealed in the autumn of 1948, and because the new saloon (the MkVII) was not yet ready, made its public entrance in the hastily-designed XK 120 sports car. For two decades, it purred at the heart of every Jaguar built and was the foundation of all Jaguar's competition successes up until the advent of the V12 engine in 1971.

Left: Le Mans 1950, and the Peter Whitehead/John Marshall car (actually owned by Peter Walker) heads for 15th place. Oil on the clutch delayed it but seven-minute stops to laboriously unbolt all four wheels for brake adjustments didn't help either!

Below: Just after the 1950 Le Mans start; all three Jaguars can be seen, with the Haines/Clark car chasing the Morel/Chambas Talbot-Lago coupé.

In Coventry, Jaguar's competition plans had crystallised. In the spring of 1950 six XK 120s were supplied to carefully selected customers who would enter under their own names, although the cars would receive works preparation. One customer, Tommy Wisdom, suggested that a car be loaned to that master of Italian road-races, Clemente Biondetti, who had won the *Targa Florio* in 1948 and 1949, and the *Mille Miglia* twice each for Alfa Romeo and Ferrari: he now became the first person to compete in a works-prepared XK 120, in the 1950 'Targa'.

Only the brilliant Alberto Ascari, in a Ferrari, could pull away from the 52-year-old Biondetti, who kept the Jaguar ahead of stars like Bracco, Marzotto and Villoresi, also driving Ferraris. He was halted only when a connecting rod broke - a failure which was led to all rods being crack-tested, the first instance at Jaguar of a racing experience improving the rest of the breed.

The *Mille Miglia* was next. Again, Biondetti delivered an astonishing drive, this time backed up by three other works-prepared XK 120s. These, making their competition debuts, were driven by their owners: Leslie Johnson (JWK 651), Tommy Wisdom (JWK 988) and Nick Haines (his car later to be registered MGJ 79). Although a broken rear spring slowed the veteran Italian, he still managed to claw back an incredible 53

minutes from the eventual winner. Johnson came fifth, the other two XKs having retired with

relatively minor problems.

While Tommy Wisdom subsequently drove 1,200 miles across Europe to compete in the

Circuit of Oporto, back in Coventry all efforts were being concentrated on preparing the cars of

Johnson, Haines and Walker for Le Mans. For the first time, Jaguar had a car worthy of at least

an experimental sortie in the 24-hour classic, then - as perhaps now - the world's most famous

motor race. The three cars were entered in

the names of their drivers.

By then, Walter Hassan had moved on

to Coventry Climax as, with Bill Heynes

firmly entrenched as chief engineer, he

could not see his career at Jaguar

progressing; Lofty England was now

managing both the service operation and

competition activities. Car preparation

was overseen by Philip Weaver ('borrowed'

from his job as Jaguar's London-based

service representative but never returned!), while Jack Emerson was the engine specialist.

Mechanics were also borrowed as necessary.

Above: **Bert Hadley was invited by Leslie Johnson to share his car, despite Hadley not having driven competitively since well before the war. "I was quite astonished to find that I made fastest (practice) lap times of the three XK 120s," recalled Bert, who played a fine supporting role to Johnson until the XK's clutch failed.**

Although carefully prepared, the XK 120s for Le Mans 1950 were, as Bill Heynes was to

write later, "probably the most standard cars ever to run in this race". The principal departure

from standard was a disc with turbine-like fins sandwiched between brake drum and backplate,

the idea being to cool the brakes which were the car's major weakness, especially since - with

24 gallons of petrol, tools and spares - the cars weighed in at over 30 cwt (3,360 lbs).

Three mechanics were allocated to the cars and they took, as Lofty England recalled, "three

single lift garage jacks I bought for £3 10s each for use at pit stops, which jacks the works team

used throughout the racing days!"

The opposition was tough. In 1949 Luigi Chinetti had provided Ferrari with its first Le

Mans win and he was entered again, the Ferrari co-driven by Raymond Sommer. Other 1950

favourites were the big Talbots, essentially Grand Prix cars controversially equipped with lights

and cycle-type wings. Aston Martin had a team of DB2s managed by John Wyer and there was a

Nash-engined Healey driven by Tony Rolt and Duncan Hamilton. Apart from Jaguar, seven

makes were making their Le Mans debut, including Allard, Cadillac, Jowett and Skoda.

Come 4.00pm on Saturday 24th June and the 60 drivers (three of them women) rushed

across the track to their cars. The veteran Bert Hadley was amongst the first away in Leslie

Johnson's JWK 651 and, gaining the Mulsanne Straight first, thought he had jumped the start.

But it was Rosier in a 4.5-litre Talbot who was to lead the field on the first lap. The Johnson/Hadley car acted as the 'hare' Jaguar and by half distance was a surprising third overall, behind two of the Talbots - and when the Rosier Talbot had to pit for repairs, the white XK actually moved up to second place. Alas, while heading for what seemed a certain third, the white Jaguar coasted to a halt just short of the pits. Weakened by many hours of using the gearbox to slow the car in an attempt to save the brakes, the clutch centre had pulled out.

The Haines/Clark XK came 12th after brake wear problems. Peter Clark recalls, "Our car came in two or three times for attempted brake improvement and, on the last occasion, our works mechanic Joe Thrall said, 'Take it away, Mr Clark, sir, and you needn't bring it back because there's no more bleeding adjustment!'" The Whitehead/Marshall XK 120 soldiered on to 15th.

England and Heynes returned home having learned that no one had a really modern, properly developed car, and that the main ingredients of the XK 120 - engine, drive train and suspension - easily matched the opposition's. According to Lofty, they were "convinced that using the standard mechanical units in a tubular frame with aerodynamically-shaped body and thus lighter in weight, we had a good chance to win the 1951 race." The result was, of course, the XK 120 'C' (for 'competition'), soon known as the C-type Jaguar.

Williams Lyons had not been at Le Mans; instead he attended - as he almost always did - the motor cycle TT on the Isle of Man, though this was also a way of distancing Jaguar officially from the slightly dangerous (in PR terms) Le Mans experiment.

Back home, the XK 120 asserted its dominance once more in the *Daily Express* production car race at Silverstone. More significant, though, was another Jaguar victory. The Dundrod road circuit near Belfast in Northern Ireland hosted the RAC's Tourist Trophy race on 16th September 1950 and the race was attended by the major British works sports car teams.

Previous spread: **Not just the famous raced XK 120s: the car gave hundreds of complete amateurs great fun. Here J.A. Keeling and K.T. Nightingale take Woodcote corner at Goodwood in 1953. By then, XKs were becoming quite modified - note how the bodywork has been cut away to allow more cool air to those sorely taxed drum brakes.**

Below: **Moss heads the works Aston Martins at the start of the 1950 TT at Dundrod in Tommy Wisdom's XK 120. Tommy was a close friend of the Moss family and had driven the Marandez Special of Stirling's father Alfred in the French GP for sports cars in 1936.**

Above: **Stirling Moss, soaked but happy at Dundrod after winning in the XK 120 – which today he remembers as "a particularly special car for me".**

The event also attracted an aspiring young driver by the name of Stirling Moss. He had just graduated from Formula 500 racing to Formula 2 with HWM, but wanted to borrow a works XK 120 for this high-profile event. Jaguar turned him down as too much of a risk; but Tommy Wisdom, who had greater faith in the 20-year-old, offered him the use of JWK 988.

Moss was sensational from the beginning, lapping in practice at 81.39 mph, less than 6 mph down on the Formula 1 lap record set by Peter Whitehead's Ferrari and easily quicker than anybody else. He was if anything more devastating in the three-hour race itself. The weather had turned atrociously wet, making life most unpleasant for drivers and pit crew alike; "the only cheering thing was when the ladies' lavatory blew away opposite the pits!" Lofty England recorded later. Moss - 21 the following day - won and Lyons signed him up as Jaguar's lead works driver on the spot.

By this convincing victory the budding star had reinforced the credibility of the XK 120, which otherwise might have suffered post-Le Mans. Moss related in an interview years later just how important the 1950 TT had been for him, too: "I remember this race terribly well because it was really raining like hell and because the Jaguar was to me fairly difficult to drive; it was a very fast and large car. I think it was the big, big turning point in my career, because I went from driving, professionally, yes, but for HWM which was a small team, to heading up what was then the world's leading sports car team."

Moss's first engagement as a Jaguar team member was at the banked Montlhéry circuit in France, where in October Leslie Johnson had taken JWK 651 with the objective of running for 24 hours at over 100 mph average. Sharing the driving with Moss, he recorded an average of 107.46 mph with a fastest lap of 126 mph: at a time when around 105 mph was a respectable maximum for a performance car, this was an impressive achievement indeed. Johnson also ran JWK 651 in the 1951 *Mille Miglia*, together with Stirling Moss in HKV 500: both cars left the road at almost the same spot and, though driveable, both were forced to retire.

Meanwhile, more XK 120s were reaching customers and large numbers of the cars were being entered in rallies and races. Not that success came automatically; skilled driving and good preparation were essential to achieve good results. At the May 1951 Silverstone meeting, Moss led the now-traditional Jaguar domination: this time the first five places were taken by XK 120s.

In August 1952 Johnson made another ambitious sortie to Montlhéry. This time an XK 120 fixedhead (the hardtop version launched in March 1951) had been prepared for an endurance run. The objective: to average 100 mph for seven days and seven nights, including all stops.

After a false start when a tyre shredded at speed and cut the main battery lead, the wire-wheeled, bronze coupé in fact averaged 100.32 mph, covering 16,851 miles in 168 hours. Nine international or world records fell in the process.

Above: **The Jaguar Driver's Club 1964 meeting at London's Crystal Palace saw a great dice between the much-modified XK 120s of Robin Beck (MXJ 954) and a young Jackie Stewart in Eric Brown's faired-headlamp drophead. Stewart won - and the occasion made such an impression on him that when he helped launch the Jaguar Formula One team in 1999, he mentioned it as one of his career highlights!**

Possibly even more remarkable was another officially observed speed run, this one in a straight line on Jaguar's old hunting ground near Jabbeke in Belgium. Stung into action by a supercharged Pegaso, which in September 1953 had exceeded 150 mph on the autoroute, Jaguar prepared an XK 120 roadster in response. On the cool, still morning of 20th October, Jaguar's chief test driver Norman Dewis hurtled down the highway at an average of 172.412 mph, a velocity which astonished even the Jaguar party!

By this time however, C-types had begun to find their way into private hands and the XK 120 was relegated mainly to club racing. There, in many parts of the world, the car could still give a good account of itself and as late as 1959, Dick Protheroe won his class in the UK's Autosport Championship. And Jackie Stewart, later to be Formula 1 World Champion and founder of what became the Jaguar Racing F1 team in 2000, won at Crystal Palace in an XK 120 as late as 1964.

The XK 120 had proved to be one of Sir William's most beautiful creations; despite its relative cheapness, it was the fastest production car of its day, and also demonstrated that with speed could come docility and comfort. It established Jaguar as a serious sporting marque in the US, and while never designed as a competition car, its performance on the track proved to Jaguar that a Le Mans win was within the company's grasp.

"IN 1954 THE JAGUAR XK 120 AND THE MK VII SALOON REMAINED THE MOST DESIRABLE SPECIALIST CARS IN AMERICA, IF NOT THE WHOLE WORLD." *John Dugdale, Jaguar's first sales executive in the United States*

Left: **Clark Gable was one of the first movie-stars to take delivery of an XK 120; California dealer Chuck Hornburg encouraged many of the Hollywood set to buy Jaguars, making the cars even more fashionable. Jaguar's exports to the U.S. more than trebled between 1950 and 1952.**

Most XK 120s built went to the United States, initially because a war-weary Britain desperately needed to earn dollars, and the UK government reserved precious steel resources for major exporters only.

Perhaps a quarter of XK 120 owners in the U.S. indulged in speed events, although until the Sports Car Club of America gradually helped bring things under control, sports car racing in the US during the late 1940s and early 1950s could be hair-raising. Almost any type of venue was commandeered as a circuit, from town centres to U.S.A.F. bases, with enthusiasm often rather ahead of crowd control.

The XK 120 could compete in either production or modified classes and tended to perform better in the first, where opposition came mostly from Allard, Ferrari, Frazer-Nash and Healey. In the 'modified' class an array of home-brewed specials were powered, in the main, by large-capacity V8 engines.

West coast importer Charles Hornburg's premises on Sunset Boulevard, on the Hollywood/Beverly Hills border, had become a honey-pot to car-loving film stars, and in 1950-51 the XK 120 was 'the' automobile to have. Clark Gable acquired one of the first to enter the US and owned three in succession. Jaguar's XK 120 and Mk VII had little competition. There were no equivalent domestics, nor could there be, since fashion dictated an import. Ferraris were only available in tiny quantities for huge amounts of bucks, and neither BMW or Mercedes-Benz would offer a production sports model for several years.

Chuck Hornburg was keener than the East coast Jaguar distributor Hoffman to promote the marque through racing but his success with the XK 120, thousands of miles from specialist factory support, was limited. On a visit to Jaguar, Hornburg spotted the three lightweight, tubular-framed magnesium-alloy XK 120 bodies which William Lyons had insisted be prepared just in case the XK 120C was not ready for the 1951 Le Mans (it was, of course). He persuaded Jaguar to let him have two of them. This pair of bodies - number LT1 in green, LT3 in white - were mounted on quite standard XK 120 chassis and shipped to the US.

Jaguar-trained technician and America's first World Champion driver-to-be, Phil Hill, took LT3 to third place at Elkhart Lake, Wisconsin in August 1951. But Hill's best results in an XK had come earlier, when from mid-1950 he raced his own alloy-bodied XK 120. His win in this car at

Right: **Palm Beach in Florida was a typical early-1950's American road circuit - and here a mixed field of XK 120, Allard and 'specials' are following the XK 120 course car.**

the first Pebble Beach, California, meeting in November parallels, in US terms, Moss's TT win since the opposition was credible. "I drove with a thrusting kind of fever," related Hill in 1958. "Winning was essential and I just more or less drove over anyone who got in my way..."

Despite help from former Jaguar mechanic Joe Thrall, now freelancing, the two special-bodied cars (termed 'Silverstones' by Chuck Hornburg) were plagued by overheating and brake problems and never really brought home the bacon (later, it was Bob Berry in the UK who showed the potential of these genuine 'lightweight' XK 120s, when in 1954 he built up a highly successful car using the third body).

Other competitors 'added lightness' by constructing their own special-bodied XKs; Coby Whitmore, Phil Hill's brother-in-law Don Parkinson and Sherwood Johnston were three of the most successful.

Above: **Sherwood Johnston leads another XK 120 at Elkhart Lake, Wisconsin in September 1952. That year the Texas-born Johnston was voted 'No. 1 Sports Car Driver' by the SCCA, having won his class in 11 out of 15 events entered.**

Not that the production XK 120 was ineffective. The very standard-looking car of John Fitch and Coby Whitmore won its class in the first long-distance race held in the US, the six-hour event at Sebring on New Year's Eve 1950. Then in 1952, Charles Schott's roadster, co-driven by Moe Carroll, took second place in the first 12-hour race at Sebring; they had been sensible enough to contact Browns Lane for advice on preparation, and it had paid off. The same year - the XK's most successful in the US - Sherwood Johnston from the East coast was the SCCA's champion driver, with 11 class wins in the 13 national qualifying events; most of these were achieved with his re-bodied XK 120.

After 1952, as in Europe, professionals and serious amateurs moved on to the C-type and, later, the D-type. However, some diehards continued with the XK, like Charles Wallace who won his SCCA class in 1954 and 1955, as did Hap Richardson in 1960.

The XK 120 played an active and entertaining role in early American sports car racing, and contributed usefully to Jaguar's reputation. But it took carefully modified cars and the best drivers to achieve the relatively few important outright victories in North America.

The XK 120 also went international rallying - those long-distance road events which were

becoming increasingly tough as the 1950s drew on. Major events like the Alpine and Monte Carlo rallies almost, but not quite, matched Le Mans for press and public interest in Europe.

Easily the most outstanding British rally crew of the early 1950s were Ian and Pat Appleyard.

Above: **Evoking all the atmosphere of an early 1950s event, this XK 120 fixedhead is taking part in a modern rally for historic cars.**

Ian Appleyard was engaged to the eldest daughter of William and Greta Lyons, Pat, when in April 1950 he received one of the works-prepared XK 120s to replace the SS 100 he'd rallied so successfully. The pair's wedding day was carefully planned around the 1950 Alpine Rally! Alone of the six 'works' XK 120s, NUB 120 (as it was registered) did duty exclusively as a rally car.

The XK received much detailed preparation by its driver. "I spent hours thinking out the possible problems we could encounter and making necessary preparations and improvements," said Appleyard of this period. "We used to practice changing wheels, adjusting the brakes, etc." In fact Pat (now Mrs Quinn) remarked that Ian's favourite saying was "Good luck is good preparation meeting opportunity".

It was a policy that worked supremely well, as NUB 120 became probably the most successful (and famous) rally car of its time in Europe. It gave the Appleyards three *Coupes des Alpes*, this hat-trick of penalty-free runs gaining them the first Alpine Gold Cup ever awarded.

A further *Coupe des Alpes* - the fifth for Ian - was won in 1953 with NUB's replacement, a steel-bodied XK 120, registration RUB 120. That same year the Appleyards very nearly won the first international rally championship, but it also marked their last full season. They had proved, though, that the XK was still highly competitive despite the rise of nimbler cars like the 356 Porsche and Triumph TR.

Ian Appleyard was far from the only successful XK rally driver. Maurice Gatsonides (who later invented the speed camera widely used in Europe!) and Ruef Habisreutinger from Switzerland also achieved outstanding results with the car, while Johnny Claes and Jacques Ickx put up one of the most amazing XK rally performances ever. That was in the punishing Liège-Rome-Liège rally of 1951, where the average speeds made it more akin to the *Mille Miglia*, but at 3,000 miles, three times the length! Using the well-worn but obviously still highly effective HKV 500, the original 'Jabbeke' car, musician Claes and journalist Ickx became the first and only pair ever to complete the event with a clean sheet.

Above: **The Appleyards on their way to their fourth (and Ian's fifth) Alpine Cup during their last Alpine Rally; that year, 1953, they used a new (steel-bodied) XK 120 roadster; for 1954 this was fitted with a 2-plus-2 drophead body, then sold the same year.**

Next spread: **Belgians Johnny Claes and Jacques Ickx (father of Jackie Ickx, the Grand Prix driver) took HKV 500 to victory in the 1951 Liège-Rome-Liège. Only 56 out of 126 starters finished the event.**

The Mk VII

Someone once remarked that if the XK 120 had never existed, the Mk VII saloon might today have achieved cult status in motoring terms as the car that launched the magnificent XK engine. As it was, of course, the XK 120 stole its thunder and Jaguar's big saloon of the early 1950s lies firmly in second place behind its glamorous two-seater sibling.

Yet the Mk VII was a car of towering abilities, at least as good in its own class as the XK 120 was in its

own. The Heynes/Hassan/Knight wishbone front suspension, and the long, low-stressed rear leaf springs, plus good weight distribution, produced handling qualities that were amongst the best in the world and quite astonishing for a car whose weight approached 4,000 lbs. Augmenting this was the power and torque of the 3.4-litre XK engine which was designed for it, and which could push the large saloon to over 100 mph.

This combination of qualities made for an unexpectedly competitive circuit racer and a front-runner in international rallying. In both spheres the car enjoyed factory support, and attracted the best drivers.

On the race track, the Mk VII dominated the major annual production car race at Silverstone from 1952 until 1956: the winners in those years being Stirling Moss ('52 and '53), Ian Appleyard ('54), Mike Hawthorn ('55) and Ivor Bueb ('56). Only in 1957 was the car retired, allowing the 3.4 Jaguar to take over its racing laurels.

The Mk VII's record on the European rally scene was even more impressive, in that the competition was tougher and the conditions - often snow and ice, plus winding mountain passes - ostensibly much less suited to a big four-door car. But here the Mk VII's handling qualities came into their own, while the torque of the XK 'six' hauled the big car up the mountains with great effect.

The Mk VII, and the later, more powerful Mk VIIM, was consistently successful in Europe's premier motor rally, the Monte Carlo. This culminated in the win by Ronald Adams, Frank Bigger and Derek Johnston in 1956 - Ulsterman Adams being the outstanding Jaguar saloon rallyist of the 1950s, notwithstanding Ian Appleyard's highly successful drives. Adams' 1956 success gave Jaguar a unique sporting 'double': victory in the 'Monte' and at Le Mans in the same year by the same marque.

"IN THE FINAL BRAKING, ACCELERATING AND MANOEUVERING TEST AT CANNES, APPLEYARD'S TWO RUNS WERE IN PRECISELY THE SAME TIME, 3 SEC. FASTER THAN ANY OF THE 23 SURVIVORS." The Motor, *on the 1952 Alpine Rally*

Although Ian and Pat Appleyard had substantially wound down their rallying, they would have continued their works-backed Alpine assault into the second half of the 1950s with the new XK 140 roadster but for the 1955 Le Mans. As a result of the terrible accident there, the Alpine was amongst several motor sport events cancelled. The three XK 140s, which had been earmarked for Ian Appleyard, Ronald Adams and Eric Haddon, never ran as a team.

Ian Appleyard had in fact tried the updated XK, announced in October 1954, and considered it "much improved" over the XK 120, and offering greater potential even with no extra power. But there was never to be a works-supported XK 140 rally team and although the Appleyards did

run an XK 140 fixedhead (registered VUB 140), it was driven competitively only rarely. However, a fine second overall in the 1956 RAC Rally's General Classification showed that car and crew still had the potential to perform well.

As it was, it was left to others to further the XK 140's cause in rallying. G.H. 'Bobby' Parkes became the type's leading exponent in the UK, entering some 25 British rallies (and three international ones) over a three-year period from March 1955.

Others tried their hand too but ever stronger works teams from BMC, Ford and Triumph, plus the 300SL Mercedes-Benz, relegated these amateur efforts to, at best, the occasional class

Right top and bottom: 'Before and after'... Italian driver Guyot's XK 140 roadster was not so pristine by the end of the 1956 Mille Miglia, but he did finish - and averaged over 70 mph to win his class (open cars under £1,100), ahead of Tommy Wisdom's Austin Healey.

win. Jaguar's official interest was now in the saloons, where up until 1956 the Mk VII remained competitive and the new 2.4 and 3.4-litre 'compacts' showed great promise.

Few XK 140s were raced but one of the most memorable episodes in the car's sporting history concerned Le Mans. Garage proprietor and amateur rally driver Robbie Walshaw had entered his XK 140 fixed in the 1956 24-Hour event, enlisting another amateur, Peter Bolton, to co-drive. The car's preparation by Jaguar included the loan of a D-type head but no radical modifications were carried out. Yet after 12 hours the XK 140 was running 14th overall, and by early afternoon on the Sunday was up in 12th place amidst the sports racing cars. Then disaster struck: the car was black-flagged for allegedly having refuelled a lap too early. The accusation was disputed but the officials' decision was final and at 1.10pm the car came in and drove slowly back to the paddock. It had covered 212 laps, some 1,749 miles, averaging 83 mph.

"This was the worst of luck," said *Autosport*. "Here was a hack car with 25,000 miles on the clock, keeping its end up with the very latest sports racing cars, brought to a standstill by a slight miscalculation - but that is motor racing." It has to be said, though, that Walshaw and Bolton went to Le Mans with no plans whatsoever for pit organisation, and but for help from the *Ecurie Ecosse* team next door their effort might have collapsed much earlier...

Above: **Gallant failure: the Bolton/Walshaw XK 140 streaked ahead of all the other genuine road cars at Le Mans 1956, only to be disqualified in the early hours of the Sunday morning. This is the start.**

The final development of the XK range was the more sophisticated but bulkier XK 150, announced in May 1957; much needed disc brakes were now standard! The car never received proper works support and although private owners manfully entered various international rallies, good results were few. It might just have been different as the well-proven Hadden/Vivian partnership proved when they won the GT class in the 1960 Tulip Rally with their roadster, but instead, Jaguar chose to concentrate on the 3.4 and, later, the Mk 2 saloons.

On the track, several XK 150s competed in the UK but none were quicker than the XK 120s still active, and were soon out-gunned by the new E-type. In the United States Walt Hansgen took third place at Bridgehampton in June 1960 with a stock XK 150S roadster, but again, it was something of a one-off result.

Rather than a race or rally car, the XK 150 is best remembered as a superbly rapid, long-distance touring car (the 3.8-litre XK 150S could top 135 mph and reach 100 mph in 19 seconds). The Jaguar competition torch was rightly handed over to the E-type in 1961.

Below: **The XK 150 was too heavy and old-fashioned to duplicate the successes of the XK 120, but private owners persevered. This fixedhead is competing in the tough 1960 Liège-Rome-Liège long-distance rally.**

Right: **As they will always be remembered: the brilliantly successful team of Ian and Pat Appleyard and their faithful XK 120, against an Alpine backdrop. This is 1952, a year which brought the combination their third successive Alpine Cup.**

Driving the XK 120

The XK 120 was remarkable for a variety of reasons - performance, wonderful styling and price all amongst them. But on the road there was another factor which was as important as any of these: refinement.

In short, Jaguar re-wrote the sports car book with the XK 120. Never before had an ultra-fast two-seater been so comfortable and easy to drive. Previously, high performance had usually come with penalties - a harsh ride, tricky handling and a noisy, brutish engine perhaps amongst them. But the XK 120 swallowed poor surfaces better than most luxury saloons and had a silky-smooth power unit that could take you from 10 mph to 115 mph in top gear alone.

These characteristics still shine through today as you nose that long bonnet out onto the highway, grasping that huge steering wheel which lies so close to your chest. Accelerate and that 'soft' early XK engine is still sewing-machine smooth, with a wonderful flexibility that, if you are content to merely cruise, makes gear changing almost unnecessary - which is convenient as even in the 1950s the Jaguar gearbox was considered somewhat crude, with no synchromesh on first gear and precious little on the others.

The cockpit is rather cramped by modern standards and an 'elbows out' driving style is usually adopted. The handling doesn't have the crispness of something like a contemporary Aston Martin but is utterly progressive. Ignore the roll and on original-type cross-ply tyres it doesn't take much skill to neatly slide and drift the XK 120 through 60-70 mph bends. Those notorious drum brakes? For leisure driving they're no problem. But use all the acceleration between bends and within a few miles the pedal will go hard and retardation will begin to diminish.

Above all, you are aware of the car's beauty. It is like driving mobile sculpture.

XK120, XK140, XK150 & MkVII

Technical specifications

YEARS CURRENT

XK 120	1949 - 1954
XK 140	1954 - 1957
XK 150	1957 - 1961
Mk VII	1950 - 1957

SPECIFICATION (XK 120 open two seater)

Engine capacity	3,442cc.
Power	160 at 5,000 rpm (later versions up to 210 bhp)
Length	14ft 6ins
Width	5ft 1.5ins
Weight	2,912 lbs (26cwt) (fixedhead and drophead versions.were slightly heavier)
Max. speed	120 mph
0 - 60mph	10secs (with catalogued performance equipment 8.6secs)
Mpg	16-18

SPECIFICATION (Mk VII and VIIM saloon)

Engine capacity	3,442cc
Power	160 bhp @ 5,000 rpm (Mk VIIM 190 bhp @ 5.500 rpm)
Length	16ft 4.5ins
Width	6ft 1ins
Weight	3,875 lbs (35.6cwt)
Wheelbase	10ft
Max. speed	102 mph (Mk VIIM 104 mph)
0-60mph	13.7 secs
Mpg	15-18

All XKs were offered in three different body styles: open two seater, fixedhead coupe and drophead coupe. The open two seater ('roadster') was the most popular for racing and rallying. All power outputs are as quoted by Jaguar. Installed bhp was usually a little lower. Specification is given for the definitive sporting XK, the XK 120 open two seater; the XK 140 and XK 150 were heavier and no faster, except that the optional 'S' version of the XK 150 (in either 3.4 or the new 3.8 litre capacity) from 1959 gave an extra 40 bhp approx. which took maximum speed to around 130mph.

The Mk VII saloon was upgraded to the Mk VIIM in October 1954, the enhancements included a more powerful (190 bhp) engine.

COMPETITION RESULTS
(all XK 120 except where stated; the XK 120 achieved many successes the world over and the following represents a selection of the most important)

1948
Jabbeke, Belgium, September, Major A.T.G. Gardner, International class E (2-litre) records (1km f.s. 176.72 mph, 1m f.s. 173.66mph, 5km f.s. 170.52 mph), MG Special/Jaguar four cyl. XJ 2-litre engine

1949
Jabbeke, Belgium, May, National speed records, R. Sutton (1m f.s. 132.596 mph)
One Hour Production Car Race, Silverstone, August, L.G. Johnson, 1st, P.D.C. Walker, 2nd

1950
Palm Beach Production Car Race, January, L.G. Johnson, 4th
Mille Miglia, April, L.G. Johnson, 5th
International Alpine Rally, July, E.I. & P. Appleyard, 1st over 3,000cc, best individual performance, Coupes des Alpes
One Hour Production car Race, Silverstone, August, P.D.C Walker 1st, A.P.R Rolt, 2nd
Shelsley Walsh hill clmb, September, PDC Walker, 1st, production cars over 3,000cc (44.61sec)
Tourist Trophy race, Dundrod, September, S. Moss, 1st, P.N. Whitehead, 2nd; Moss/Whitehead/Johnson, team prize
Pebble Beach, California, November, P. Hill, 1st, D. Parkinson, 2nd

Competition results

1951
Rallye Soleil, France, April, H. Peignaux, 1st, D.O.M. Taylor 2nd
Tulip Rally, April, E.I. & P. Appleyard, 1st general classification
International Trophy Meeting, Silverstone, May, S. Moss, 1st, C. Dodson, 2nd, J. D Hamilton, 3rd
Production Car Race, Spa, J. Claes, 1st (81.22 mph)
RAC Rally, June, E.I. Appleyard, 1st, open cars over 3,000cc, Miss M. Newton, Best Open-car performance by a lady
International Alpine Rally, July, E.I. & P. Appleyard, Best individual performance, Coupes des Alpes, R. Habisreutinger, 2nd, over 3,000cc class, Coupes des Alpes
Liege-Rome-Liege Rally, August, J. Claes/J.Ickx, 1st general classification, J. Herzet/Baudin, 2nd
Johore Grand Prix, Malaya, September, B.R. Hawes, 2nd
Tour de France, September, M. Hache/Crespin, 1st, over 3,000cc class
Watkins Glen GP, NY, S. Johnston, 1st, 3,001-4,000cc class

1952
Monte Carlo Rally, January, R. Cotton, 4th, Mk VII
Daytona Speed Trials, February, fastest stock saloon, T, McCahill, Mk VII (100.9 mph), fastest stock sports car, XK 120 (119.8 mph)
Sebring 12-hour race, Florida, March, C. Schott/M. Carroll, 2nd
RAC International Rally, April, J.C. Broadhead, 2nd, Open car class, Miss M. Newton, Best performance by a lady
Tulip Rally, April, E.I. Appleyard, 2nd, general classification, 1st touring cars over 3,000cc, Mk VII
International Trophy Meeting, Silverstone, May, S. Moss, 1st, production car race, Mk VII (73.32 mph)
International Alpine Rally, July, M. Gatsonides, 2nd general classification, 1st over 3,000cc class, Coupes des Alpes, E.I. & P. Appleyard, Coupe des Alpes and Alpine Gold Cup
Montlhery, France, August, World's and C Class international records inc. 10,000 miles at 100.65 mph average

1953
Monte Carlo Rally, January, E.I. & P. Appleyard, 2nd, Mk VII
Tulip Rally, April, E.I. & P. Appleyard, 1st touring cars 2.4 - 3.5 litre, Mk VII
International Trophy Meeting, Silverstone, May, S. Moss, 1st production touring cars, Mk VII
International Alpine Rally, July, E.I. & P. Appleyard, 1st over 2,600cc class, Coupes des Alpes
Liege-Rome-Liege Rally, August, M. Fraikin/O. Gendebien, 2nd, XK 120

1954
Monte Carlo Rally, January, 5th, R. Adams, Mk VII
Mount Druitt 24-Hour Race, Australia, January/February, Mrs Geordie Anderson, 1st
International Trophy Meeting, Silverstone, May, production touring car race, E.I. Appelyard, 1st, A.P.R. Rolt, 2nd, S. Moss 3rd, Mk VII
International Alpine Rally, July, E. Haddon/C. Vivian, 1st over 2,600cc class

1955
Monte Carlo Rally, January, R. Adams/C. Vard/E.I. Appleyard, Team Trophy, Mk VII
International Trophy Meeting Silverstone, April, production touring car race, J.M. Hawthorn, 1st, Mk VII

1956
Monte Carlo Rally, January, R. Adams. F. Bigger, 1st, Mk VII
RAC Rally, E.I. & P. Appleyard, 2nd general classification, XK 140

1959
Vanwall Trophy meeting, Snetterton, August, saloon and GT race, 1st equal, Sir G. Baillie (3.4 litre) and E. Protheroe (XK 120)
Oulton Park International Gold Cup meeting, closed car race, September, E. Protheroe, 2nd, (XK 140)
Tulip Rally, April, E. Haddon/G. Vivian, 1st GT cars 3,000-4,000cc, XK 150S roadster

C for Competition

If ever there was a single car built for a single purpose, it was the C-type Jaguar. Designed purely to win just one race, the 1951 Le Mans 24-Hours, it did exactly that - and set new lap record in the process.

"IMMEDIATELY AFTER THE WAR, JAGUAR AS A CAR OUTSIDE THIS COUNTRY WASN'T WELL KNOWN. BUT BY WINNING LE MANS IN 1951, WE ESTABLISHED A REPUTATION WORTH HAVING."

Lofty England

The C-type was the car which brought Jaguar international recognition. Yet this beautiful car was the first ever competition model from a company which was almost entirely new to international motor racing. Its originators had never previously designed a race car, nor had the C-type even turned a wheel in anger before it competed at Le Mans. And it had been built in an extraordinarily short time. "We had about seven months," related Bill Heynes, "to design, make and prove a new car from a clean sheet of paper and to complete three cars for the race."

That was because, despite the promising showing of the XK 120s in the 1950 event, Bill Heynes and Lofty England failed to persuade the ever-cautious William Lyons to give them final authorisation to build the new Le Mans competition Jaguar until the all-important Mk VII saloon had been safely launched in October 1950. After that, the pressure from Lyons was inexorable. As it was, the last car was finished just six days before it was due to depart for France.

Given all of this, the successful outcome in June 1951 was certainly remarkable, but it was very nearly a complete disaster.

Jaguar's engineering resources in 1950 were still tiny. There were some 12 people in the design engineering office at Foleshill, including Claude Baily, Bob Knight, Tom Jones and Malcolm Sayer. About the same number were in the experimental shop run by Phil Weaver. No competition department had been set up: all of those involved just had to fit the new competition car into their everyday work.

Above: **The XK120C frame; note areas of stressed steel panelling; this is a production car frame - the tubes on the original 1951 cars were all cut and filed by hand.**

"Three or four of the staff and a little band of stalwarts in the shops worked assiduously on drawings, models and schemes," Heynes later wrote. "We built up frames and bodies in wood, and models in paper and even broomsticks were in demand for mock-up tubular frames. Time went on and our schemes crystallised. It was then that the heat was really turned on; everyone in the little band was working every spare moment that he could find, weekends merged into the normal week and to leave the factory at 8 o'clock was halving a half-day."

Left: 1951 engine bay, showing the small (1.75 inch) carburettors and XK-type wishbone front suspension with drum brakes.

A lot of time was saved by Jaguar's good relationship with its suppliers, who rapidly produced new or modified parts from drawings. And it had always been clear what was needed: installing the XK 120's engine, drivetrain and suspension in a lighter frame, and enclosing it with a more aerodynamically efficient body.

The well-triangulated, multi-tubular frame which emerged seemed fairly typical racing practice at the time but in fact it contained a number of clever features, including a stressed-skin element - an advanced concept for 1950. The suspension was evolved by Bob Knight using XK 120-type wishbones at the front and a live rear axle.

Brakes had been the XK 120's weakest point. The C-type used the latest self-adjusting Lockheed type on the front, the brake drums better cooled thanks to the centre-lock wire wheels now used for quicker wheel changing.

The one crucial item which made a Jaguar Le Mans car feasible was the XK engine. Essentially a production 3,442cc unit, none of the modifications made to it needed to be extreme and many of them would find their way onto road Jaguars in due course. Enclosing this blend of ingenuity, good design and solid, production-car engineering was an aluminium body of considerable beauty. The design was the work of Malcolm Sayer, formerly of Bristol Aircraft. His influence at Jaguar was to become profound.

After the war Sayer had left Bristol and in 1948 travelled by cattle-boat to Baghdad to establish a faculty of engineering at Baghdad University - only to find that "the university existed only on paper!"

He ended up managing an agricultural machinery business instead, though while in Iraq he learnt from a German professor an unusual mathematical technique for expressing curvatures as figures. "I think a lot of hard work and argument can be saved by the use of mathematics," he

Above: The C-type's aluminium bodyshell was beautifully made by Abbey Panels; this is the bonnet assembly.

wrote later, "to give a series of co-ordinates for any three-dimensional shape. It is quicker, more precise and free from guesswork, and can be applied to almost any curve with a little experience."

In denominating complex body shapes mathematically, Sayer pre-empted the computer which would become an integral part of vehicle body design 40 years later (sadly, he was not destined to see this happen; he died in April 1970 from a coronary thrombosis).

Sayer - who at one point was engineering stress consultant for the 1951 Festival of Britain! - came to Jaguar on the recommendation of another Bristol man, Phil Weaver. Bill Heynes immediately took to this slightly unusual person. "He'd no sense of money," Heynes recalled. "We gave him a reasonable wage but he was always short of money; he used to rent houses and not pay the rent and get turned out... In the end I fixed it so we bought him a house and stopped the money from his wages to pay for it. He was a charming bloke."

Malcolm Sayer's arrival completed the key elements of the tightly-knit team which produced not only five Le Mans wins but also an astonishing array of road cars. As a stress engineer his input to the design of the C-type's frame was crucial, and he created for the XK 120 "C" - as it was officially known - a body shape that was efficient, practical and attractive.

Finally, the first of three cars, XKC 001, was ready for testing at Silverstone and the MIRA test track. All the drivers except the Italian Biondetti managed to get track time on the new car prior to the team's departure for France.

As was to be an (almost) invariable rule, the competition cars were driven, not trailered, to

Below: **Successfully completed on time, the three C-types are ready to be driven to their first race - Le Mans 1951. Just one mechanic was assigned to each car.**

the circuit. "The reason for that," Lofty England would explain, "was 1) it didn't cost much, 2) we thought people should see that our motor cars were capable of being driven on the road, and 3), if anything was going to fall off, then by the time you've driven across France on their bumpy roads, it would fall off. Much better to know before you start!"

Similar economics applied to the pit crew: Lofty, Phil Weaver and Jack Emerson drove the C-types, with just two mechanics, John Lea and Joe Sutton, following in a Bedford 13cwt van.

That was it. Bill Heynes drove down in his Mk VII in time for the Wednesday practice session and William Lyons was to arrive later in the Dunlop aeroplane. The team was based at the *Hotel de Paris* in Le Mans town, taking over the hotel's garage too.

Surprisingly, the new Jaguars had remained entirely secret and so the gleaming, ultra-modern cars made a big impact when they arrived at Le Mans. Nevertheless, they were not necessarily viewed as certain race winners, especially by the local press. Of the 60 entrants, the smart money seemed to be on the six 4.5-litre Talbots, similar to the previous year's winner but faster, the 4.1 and

Above: Over 50 years on and the C-type Jaguar is one of the most revered of the classic sports racing cars. These three are pictured at the 1998 Goodwood Revival meeting.

2.6-litre Ferraris (though none of the six were works entered), or even perhaps the big 5.4-litre, 250 bhp V8 Chrysler engined Cunninghams from the United States. Nor could Aston Martin, with five entries including three 140 bhp DB2 team cars, be discounted despite their smaller engine size.

As with the XK 120s the previous year, the C-types were ostensibly entered by their drivers, all but one of them having driven the works-prepared XK 120s the previous year. The pairings were Clemente Biondetti/Leslie Johnson, Stirling Moss/Jack Fairman, and Peter Walker/Peter Whitehead. Only the 38-year-old John Eric George Fairman, who had won his class at Le Mans in 1949 with an HRG, was new to Jaguar: he was chosen by Moss as a reliable co-driver, and on the recommendation, claimed Fairman, of *The Autocar*'s sports editor, John Cooper.

The Jaguar team posted its serious intentions at the mid-week practice session when Walker in XKC 003 circulated at well under Rosier's 1950 lap record, averaging over 104 mph - in the dark! Not all was plain sailing though: Johnson and Biondetti in XKC 001 had engine trouble which necessitated a rebuild by John Lea at the local Peugeot garage. Then the somewhat inadequate Marchal headlamps turned out to be an obsolete type - and although the latest variety

Above: A good view of the 1951 C-type with many of those responsible for its design and operation (left to right): Tom Jones, George Price, Jack Lea, Frank Rainbow, Gordon Gardner, Phil Weaver and Cyril Harris. The full-windscreened car is ready for the 1952 *Mille Miglia*.

arrived after 'words' by Lofty England to M. Marchal Jnr, they still required new shells. Recalled Lofty, "Phil Weaver and I had already reverted to our role as mechanics but Bill Heynes then joined in and made the new backshells." And when Moss collided with the rear of Morris-Goodall's Aston Martin during the Thursday night's practice, "I then showed my ability as a sheet metal worker!"

The race began on Saturday 23rd June in the same wet, overcast weather that had characterised practice. Moss, Walker and Biondetti were the starting drivers who ran across the track to their waiting C-types at 4 o'clock that afternoon. As start positions were determined not by practice times but by engine capacity, almost a quarter of the field streamed under the Dunlop bridge ahead of the Jaguars. To the excitement of the British contingent, however, Moss was second to the Argentine Froilán González in his Talbot at the end of the second lap, and after three more *tours* was ahead of the 'Pampas Bull', with Biondetti moving to third.

After four hours and the first Jaguar refuelling stops, Moss remained in the lead, reeling off the laps with a smoothness which belied his speed. On the 20th lap he broke the old lap record,

Below: The unmistakable figure of F.R.W. 'Lofty' England in the Jaguar pits at Le Mans 1953. Alongside him are (from right) William Lyons, Bob Berry, Bob Knight and Bill Heynes, while just behind are Norman Dewis and Alfred Moss, Stirling's father.

and was to shatter it twice more to leave it at 4 min 46.8 secs, or 105.2 mph average. The Walker/Whitehead and Biondetti/Johnson C-types lay second and third.

But then, drama. Biondetti, driving a consecutive stint in Jaguar no. 23, had completed 50 laps when he noticed a sudden loss of oil pressure. He toured round to the pits where John Lea found there was plenty of oil in the sump, but none circulating in the engine. "However, nothing could be done using only the parts and tools carried on the car which at the time was the rule," recounted Lofty, so the car was retired.

William Lyons, his plane delayed by the bad weather, missed the start but when he finally arrived at 10pm he found his cars still running in first and second positions. Midnight came and went, then on lap 94 Moss in the lead car failed to come past the pits. The same oil failure had occurred and the Jaguar had clattered to a halt on the grass after Arnage corner.

Above: **Success! The winning C-type of Whitehead and Walker is besieged by photographers after its historic 1951 Le Mans win.**

Catastrophe now faced the Coventry team: what initially had seemed to be an unmitigated triumph looked like becoming a total disaster. By this time the cause of the failure had been discovered. A weld on the main oil feed pipe had simply broken due to engine vibration. The third C-type seemed certain to suffer the same fate.

Nothing could be done except instruct Peter Walker and Peter Whitehead, who had inherited first place, to keep the revs down and drive as smoothly as possible.

They did. In fact, the near-standard XK 120 of Lawrie and Waller lapped faster in the last two hours than the C-type.

Fortunately the opposition had wilted and XKC 003 was under no pressure for the remaining, nail-biting, hours. Peter Whitehead drove the final stint, taking the Jaguar to an historic victory some 45 minutes ahead of the Talbot of Meyrat and Mairesse. The C-type had covered 2,243.886 miles at an average speed of 93.495 mph.

Back in 1950 Heynes had qualified his conclusions that Jaguar could win Le Mans with the phrase "given reasonable luck". Certainly, that reasonable luck only just held in 1951!

It is hard to appreciate today exactly how important that 1951 Le Mans victory was for Jaguar. Today the company is a world-recognised brand, 'Jaguar' ranking 18th in a worldwide recognition survey which included commercial icons like Coca Cola, IBM and Disney. Back then,

Above: To end his 1951 season, Moss won two five-lappers at the September 1951 Goodwood meeting - ahead of Hugh Howarth, one of the quicker XK 120 drivers of the period.

however, it was a minor specialist car maker turning out a few thousand quite pretty cars a year, without a racing pedigree and far from being part of the establishment.

The result was also important for Britain. Today the world centre for race car engineering, in 1951 it was all very different. No British car had won anything worthwhile since the war and BRM's V16 Formula 1 car was fast becoming simply an embarrassment. Lagonda had been the last British car to win Le Mans, way back in 1935. Jaguar's success raised the profile of the entire British motor industry.

For Jaguar itself, the commercial benefits from that first Le Mans win exceeded all expectations, thanks to front-page headlines and hundreds of column inches in the world's press. Lofty England put it like this:

"I know this from personal experience. When I first started going to the States in 1948 when we were just starting to get into the market, people didn't even know what a Jaguar was. If you were in a Jaguar car people would pull up beside you and say, 'What is it?' But as soon as we won Le Mans, people who were interested in motor cars immediately knew what a Jaguar was and the name went forward very, very quickly."

The team went home to headlines from a near-ecstatic British press, and to a rapturous reception at Coventry. Jaguar was now firmly on the map.

Jaguar entered the C-types in only two other events that year. The narrow, hedgerow-lined Dundrod road circuit in Northern Ireland could not have been more different from the long straights of Le Mans but in the RAC Tourist Trophy race, the young Stirling Moss took the lead from the start and was never headed. Peter Walker came second, while fourth was taken by newcomer Major Tony Rolt. A reserve driver, he took over from an unwell Leslie Johnson at just over half distance and proceeded to bring the C-type up from seventh and, somewhat unusually for a reserve driver, broke the lap record in the process! It secured him a place in the Jaguar team for 1952.

Moss was victorious in the C-type's final 1951 appearance, winning two races at Goodwood at the end of September - the first time the car had been seen in action on the British mainland.

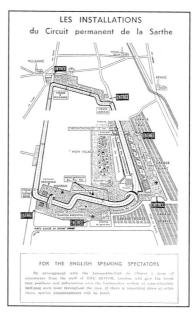

LES INSTALLATIONS
du Circuit permanent de la Sarthe

FOR THE ENGLISH SPEAKING SPECTATORS

Left: Schematic diagram of the 8.38 mile Le Mans course as it was in the early 1950s, comprised of public roads closed for the event. The first 24-Hour race there took place in 1923.

"TODAY ALL PRODUCTION CARS USE THEM AND THEY CAUSE HARDLY ANY PROBLEMS. BUT THAT'S BECAUSE WE HAD ALL THE PROBLEMS IN 1952!"

Stirling Moss on disc brake development

Right: A wonderful snapshot by mechanic John Lea of the Jaguar pits at Dundrod 1951, with Lofty (centre) flanked by Stirling Moss and Tony Rolt. Considering the conditions, everyone is looking remarkably cheerful!

Right: Stirling Moss brings the disc-braked C-type - still with its trade plates on after the drive from England - to the start area for the May 1952 *Mille Miglia.*

Stirling Moss was Jaguar's 1952 season-opener when he drove XKC 003 to fourth place at Goodwood in the Easter meeting, reeling in handicap leader Geoff Duke's new DB3 Aston Martin at the rate of six seconds a lap. Few spotted that the C-type was using a new type of brake which was to have such a profound effect on both race and road cars...

The Dunlop Wheel & Rim Co. had recently evolved a disc brake for aircraft use and when one of their engineers suggested applying it to cars, Jaguar was its obvious development partner - the two concerns had long worked together on tyres and other components. At the suggestion of Norman Dewis, who had become Jaguar's chief tester earlier in 1952, this major new brake testing programme was centred around the C-type and not just the XK 120.

All sorts of problems were encountered though. Among the most serious was boiling brake fluid caused by the very high temperatures generated. When this happened, the brake pedal would go almost to the floor, a phenomenon which the imperturbable Norman Dewis came to accept as routine but which deterred some team drivers to the extent that later, if there was a choice, they chose a drum-braked C-type!

The first endurance event entered by a disc-braked C-type was the 1952 *Mille Miglia*, the Italian classic considered to be a suitably gruelling test. Norman Dewis agreed to be Moss's co-driver and on 26th April he left Coventry in the C-type. It was convoyed by Bob Berry and mechanic Frank Rainbow in a somewhat overburdened Mk VII.

The event was made all the more interesting by the works entry of the brand new Mercedes-Benz 300SL coupés - which very nearly failed to start as the Italian scrutineers objected to the cars' unorthodox 'gull wing' doors! The C-type started the hair-raising 1,000 mile race - run over public roads, some of which were still open to normal traffic - at 6.19am. Dewis wrote an account of the race afterwards, describing how they started "with a series of professionally corrected back end slides which brought forth loud cheers from the rain-soaked spectators."

Before the route climbed out of populated areas for the 440 miles of mountain driving, the competitors had to contend with enthusiastic but apparently fearless crowds. "As seen through the windscreen this took the form of a forest of faces turned in our direction with the narrowest of paths down the centre barely wide enough for safety. Everyone swayed to and fro like a cornfield in a strong breeze as we roared past them at speeds of 100-plus."

After two hours the pair closed up on and overtook Taruffi's 4.0-litre Ferrari Spyder. In the town of Pescara, Moss had to pass a baulking Alfa Sprint on the inside on wet cobbles. Recorded Norman: "Looking back I was just in time to see the Alfa disappearing through a shop window!"

Next, the C-type caught up with pre-war ace Rudolph Carracciola in one of the new 300SLs; it seemed faster on the straights (an impression which was to have serious repercussions for Jaguar later that year) but "was no match on the bends, the C-type brakes being much superior."

Alas, the Jaguar was doomed not to finish. On a winding mountain road the C-type swung wide and glanced off a boulder. Moss pressed on "and it was only when the front wheels refused to follow the steering wheel that Stirling stopped for investigation." The steering rack had broken free and it was not safe to continue racing. Bracco's Ferrari won, beating the German challenge in the end; just 274 out of 608 cars finished the event.

Moss did win at the May *Daily Express* meeting with XKC 002, though there were problems with the other two cars and Lofty England complained of poor preparation. After that, the race side was given more resources.

Meanwhile, the first 'customer' C-types were being completed. These were based on a rationalised version of the 1951 works cars. First customer Duncan Hamilton debuted his new car in the British Empire Trophy race on the undulating, 3.8 mile circuit on the Isle of Man. Tommy Wisdom received the new C-type he co-purchased with Bill Cannell and entered it in the Monaco Grand Prix for sports cars. Stirling Moss fielded the well-used XKC 003 but became mixed-up in an accident and was disqualified for receiving outside assistance.

Two of the three original 1951 cars had been prepared for the 1952 Le Mans race, plus a new car, XKC 011. Mechanically they were little changed, but they now looked markedly different. Because of the apparent swiftness of the 300SLs in Italy, within six weeks of the 24-Hour race they were all fitted with entirely new bodyshells - against the advice of Phil Weaver. He distrusted the new cooling arrangements this entailed, and knew there wouldn't be enough time for proper testing.

The longer tails and lower noses were designed to increase maximum speed. The lower bonnet line called for a shorter radiator, achieved by mounting the normally integral header tank on the bulkhead. That was not unsound in itself (it is almost universal today) but the long run of piping connecting the two was too small in diameter and constricted the water. The defect was not discovered in the short time remaining for testing.

Jaguar's 1952 Le Mans was a brief affair. All three cars seriously overheated in practice, to the extent that they had probably ruined their engines even before starting the race. Two cars were hurriedly fitted with standard 'tall' radiators, the bonnets acquiring an unsightly bulge, but it was too late. The third car, driven by Ian Stewart and Peter Whitehead, had to remain on the original system and duly expired first, after 16 laps.

Stirling Moss, paired with Peter Walker, did get up to second place but had dropped to eighth when, during the second hour, he too retired.

Below: A worried-looking Duncan Hamilton brings one of the ill-fated, 'droop snoot' C-types to scrutineering, Le Mans 1952. But the Jaguar team were beaten even before they started due to a disastrous modification to the cooling system - which had been plumbed (though not designed) by an engineer named Roy Kettle!

Newcomers Duncan Hamilton and Tony Rolt - joint sixth at Le Mans in 1951 with the

3.8-litre Nash-Healey - struggled on the longest, Hamilton coasting and slipstreaming other cars.

Replenishment was allowed on the 28th lap (up from 25 from the previous year) but to no avail:

as John Lea poured the water in, so it ran out of the exhaust pipe…

The Mercedes? They won as they pleased, finishing first and second with Herman Lang and

Herman Reiss driving the first closed car ever to win at Le Mans. But most galling of all for

Jaguar, at an average speed which the C-types, even in 1951 specification, could have beaten (the following year this fact was unkindly driven home when the Belgian-entered production C-type, in much the same mechanical trim as the 1952 Jaguars, exceeded the Mercedes' 1952 winning total by 20 miles and was 10 mph faster on top speed).

Above: **The first time a disc-braked car ever won a motor race: Stirling Moss after his 1952 victory at Rheims in Tommy Wisdom's production C-type.**

Spirits were raised when Moss won at the Rheims Grand Prix meeting shortly afterwards, driving Tommy Wisdom's XKC 005. This was the first win ever by a car equipped with disc brakes. Then in July, Ian Stewart won the Jersey Road Race for *Ecurie Ecosse*, driving the Scottish team's new production C-type.

In the aftermath of the 1952 Le Mans debacle, and partly the result of it, came a comprehensive re-organisation of the related departments and for the first time a dedicated competition shop was set up, this under Phil Weaver.

Goodwood saw the year's final appearance of a works Jaguar, on 27th September when Rolt (drum brakes) beat Stirling Moss (disc brakes)! Afterwards he related his tactics, which were to go flat out from the start to take advantage of his opponent's discs, taking a couple of laps to warm up and become fully effective. And as it was just a five-lap sprint, his drums were in no danger of giving out before the chequered flag came out.

As the season closed, Jaguar announced that a competitions manager was to be appointed. Mortimer Morris-Goodall, a veteran of ten Le Mans races himself, would take over many of Lofty England's duties, in theory allowing Lofty to concentrate fully on his 'day job' - still that of running the service operation. In the event, England and Lyons still made all the decisions and 'Mort' was to last only one season.

"LET THERE BE NO MISTAKE. THE JAGUAR 120C JUSTIFIES ABSOLUTELY THE OVERWORKED TERM OF THOROUGHBRED..."

The Motor C-type road test, 1952

1953 was to be a good year for Jaguar, but although no less than five C-types ran in the *Mille Miglia*, only one finished. The works-sponsored cars of Moss/Mortimer-Goodall and Rolt/Len Hayden (the latter had just joined as Jaguar's first full-time race mechanic) went out with, respectively, rear axle trouble and oil starvation. Nor did the *Daily Express* Silverstone meeting bring Jaguar their usual success, although Peter Whitehead's new C-type (co-driven by Tom Cole)

Above: At Jabbeke, *The Motor* recorded 143.7 mph 'mean' when they road tested the production C-type. In fact, Norman Dewis was asked to do the driving, the staff testers not feeling confident enough at these speeds!

won the Hyeres 12-Hour race just one week before Le Mans.

None of this really mattered. What did was Le Mans. Now counting for the new Manufacturers' Championship announced in March, 18 marques were represented and the drivers' list read like a Formula 1 programme. Ferrari looked very strong with four cars, Villoresi partnering world champion Alberto Ascari in a 4.5-litre coupé, with Hawthorn and Farina in a 4.1-litre car. Then Fangio, Marimon and Kling led the highly-fancied Alfa Romeo team; Lancia fielded three supercharged D20 coupés. Cunningham was there in force with three Chrysler-engined cars, while the British contingent included the new DB3S 3.0-litre Aston Martins and two J2 Allards.

It was clearly going to be a classic race. Mercedes-Benz was the only big name missing, claiming to have proved all they needed with the 300SL the previous year.

Unusually, the Jaguars were flown part of the way to Le Mans in 1953, being air-lifted from Lydd airport in Kent to Le Touquet, from where they were then driven to Le Mans. Outwardly, as they lined up opposite the packed grandstands on 13th June, the C-types appeared much the same as the 1951 cars, and this plus only minimal practice laps somewhat lulled the opposition into a false sense of security. Most thought it was going to be Ferrari this year. But there had been

significant changes under the C-type's skin, most aimed at reducing weight.

The result was a car which now weighed around 110 lb (or 5%) less than before. Power was

up as well, to around 220 bhp, but Jaguar's ace card at Le Mans 1953 was the disc brake which,

thanks to exhaustive testing, particularly by Norman Dewis, was now reliable. It gave the C-type

a vital edge.

Compared with the frustration all too evident in the Jaguar pits in 1952, there was almost an

air of relaxation this time round. Lofty, the mechanics and the drivers all knew that testing had

been thorough, the car proven over thousands of miles. All the C-types had lapped during

Thursday's practice at under the previous year's lap record.

"The cars were so good", said Lofty, "we didn't even practise on Friday night. We sat down

and decided what speed we should run the race at."

Their confidence was not misplaced. Soon after the start, there was shock amongst the

Ferrari, Alfa Romeo and Cunningham teams when, after just four laps, Stirling Moss in the British

Racing Green C-type led the field of 60 past the grandstands, a cheer from the crowd just audible

above the sonorous howl of the Jaguar straight-six.

In fact the only major interruption to Lofty's pre-planned schedule came quite early when, on

lap 20, Moss pitted - the engine was misfiring. A plug change didn't cure it and he came in again.

This time a clogged fuel filter was diagnosed; the filter was removed and the engine barked

healthily once more.

Below: **Practice, 1953 Le Mans, and a remarkable photograph as not only did the photographer capture just the eventual winning C-type in focus, but pressed the shutter exactly as it passed another no. 18 in the pits. The latter 'spare' car (XKC 012), used by Norman Dewis to complete some practice laps, had inadvertently been given the same number which nearly resulted in Rolt and Hamilton being disqualified. Lofty England had to sort out the situation with the officials.**

Above: Peter Whitehead in the C-type he shared with Ian Stewart; their role was that of 'sweeper', with instructions to finish at all costs, ready if the leading struck trouble. They finished fourth.

Opposite: Duncan Hamilton takes disc-braked C-type to victory, Le Mans 1953; the cold-air scoop for the Weber carburettors can clearly be seen on the bonnet.

All this had cost ten minutes and given the lead to the Villoresi/Ascari Ferrari. But Tony Rolt in Jaguar no. 18 immediately slashed five seconds off his average lap times and overtook the Ferrari. By the second hour the pecking-order was established: the Rolt/Hamilton car no 18 was controlling the race out in front, pursued by the Ascari/Villoresi 375 '*Mille Miglia*' Ferrari, with one of the two surviving 3.4-litre works Alfas just about in the hunt some way behind.

Until, that is, at about half distance. By then, the 'endurance' aspect of the race was beginning to bite and the quickest Alfa had dropped out. Moss and Walker had climbed from 21st to fourth behind the Peter Whitehead/Ian Stewart C-type. Third was held by the rumbling, fuel-injected 5.4-litre Cunningham C5R. Up front, it was becoming a battle of attrition between the Rolt/Hamilton C-type and the big Ferrari; but pit stops apart, the Jaguar was always in front.

Now the advantages of the Jaguar's disc brakes could be fully realised. After 12, 14, 16 hours of racing they could still be used to the full, whereas the Ferrari drivers were having to contend with a longer, harder pedal and increasing stopping distances as the 375's drum brakes gradually lost efficiency. Duncan Hamilton wrote in his book *Touch Wood*: "First light coincided with the arrival of the usual mist and our disc brakes really paid dividends; I was never in danger of overshooting at Mulsanne whereas poor Ascari was obliged to brake early just to make sure."

But Ascari and Villoresi, the former having shattered the lap record, kept in the fight until after midday Sunday; then, after increasing use of the gearbox to slow the car, the over-taxed clutch began to slip and, shortly after, the red car had no drive.

This left Tony Rolt and Duncan Hamilton to win almost at a canter. All four C-types finished, covering 9,873.6 miles between them at an average speed of 102.85 mph. Just the big Cunningham of Fitch and Walters, finishing 87 miles behind Stirling Moss and Peter Walker, prevented a Jaguar one-two-three. As it was, the Whitehead/Stuart C-type came fourth, ahead of the Marzotto/Marzotto 4.1 Ferrari MM. The very standard Belgian-entered C-type of Laurent and de Tornaco came ninth, ahead of another Cunningham. It was a totally convincing demonstration by the Coventry firm.

And the true role of the disc brakes? They have often been credited for Jaguar's 1953 victory but that somewhat over-states the case. It was the whole package that achieved victory.

"I THINK IT WAS QUITE UNFAIR TO JAGUAR TO SAY THEY WON LE MANS IN 1953 BECAUSE THEY WENT THERE WITH DISC BRAKES. THEY WON BECAUSE THEY HAD A HELL OF A GOOD MOTOR CAR."

John Wyer, Aston Martin team manager

The year's main objective achieved, this race saw the last official full works C-type team in action. The support which the factory provided to private entrants during the remainder of the season was for public relations not World Championship points. Phil Weaver had taken XKC 011 to the Isle of Man, and had missed Le Mans because of it, but in the British Empire Trophy Race there even Moss could not hold the Aston Martin DB3S of Reg Parnell.

The Astons did not enter for Rheims (they were less suited to this 'speed' circuit) and Jaguar released another non-lightweight C-type, 012, for Moss and Peter Whitehead, who won.

Just one works-owned Jaguar appeared at the British GP meeting on 18th July, but Rolt retired when, unusually, a piston broke up. By now, quite a few production C-types were in action and three privately entered C-types entered the Spa 24-Hour race on 25th/26th July. The *Ecurie Ecosse* entry of Sir James Scott-Douglas and Guy Gale secured a good second place, mainly on reliability, with third taken by Laurent's Belgian-entered car.

For the Goodwood 9-Hours in August, however, Jaguar made two of the Le Mans cars available (052 and 053), plus 012. The C-types dominated the race for some eight hours, with the Moss/Walker car leading followed by Rolt and Hamilton. Then within minutes of each other, both were out with ruined bearings due to oil starvation. Goodwood is really a series of inter-

Below: **Jaguar's staff give the victorious 1953 Le Mans C-type an enthusiastic welcome. The effect of Jaguar's motor racing successes on the workforce was an unexpected bonus. Said Bob Berry, "There is no doubt that the overall quality of our workforce and its dedication to Jaguar was improved dramatically as a result of our racing efforts".**

linking corners with few straights, and oil surge was a problem for the Jaguars (Lofty, though, blamed it on Walker and Hamilton having their own private dice...). The surviving works Jaguar, driven more steadily by Peter Whitehead and Ian Stewart but disc brakes still glowing red into the night, came third behind two Aston Martin DB3Ss, with two *Ecurie Ecosse* C-types fourth and fifth.

Right: **Duncan Hamilton and (just obscured) Tony Rolt and their wives savour their moment of victory at Le Mans 1953. A happy Stirling Moss and Peter Walker look on.**

The Jaguars finished behind two Astons again in the Dundrod TT as well, Moss having to push his car across the line to finish fourth on handicap after gearbox problems which affected all three works-prepared cars entered. If Jaguar had been interested in winning the first Manufacturers' World Championship, this was the race that lost it for them. Ferrari ended up

with the most points but nobody at Browns Lane was at all bothered. Again, Le Mans had been the only true goal, and the 1953 event had demonstrated to a huge worldwide audience the marque's dominance in the one race that really counted.

Likewise, Jaguar had decided not to enter the final FIA championship event, the 1,900 mile Carrera Panamericana. A reconnaissance by Lofty England, Stirling Moss and Tom French of

Above: **Jaguar appeared to have the 1953 Goodwood 9-Hours race all sewn up but with an hour to go both Moss (seen here during a 3 min 24 sec stop to repair minor collision damage) and Rolt (partnered respectively by Walker and Hamilton) dropped out with no oil pressure.**

Dunlop revealed what Lofty expected: the huge cost and difficult logistics would not be justified by the relatively limited publicity the event would bring Jaguar outside Mexico. That some American manufacturers took the event seriously is indicated by Lofty's observations that Lincoln probably spent $2,000,000 on publicity alone - a sum that would have more than paid for Jaguar's entire competition activities in the 1950s.

One C-type had been prepared for the event just in case, but XKC 038 was sold to Duncan Hamilton instead. Duncan had crashed his first C-type, MDU 212, most comprehensively at

Below: **Rheims 1953, and Moss grabs some refreshment after winning the first 12-Hour race there by four laps, partnered by Peter Walker. Note the body-belt which Moss always wore. This was the day Mike Hawthorn had his great battle to win the French GP for Ferrari in one of the closest finishes ever seen.**

Oporto just after Le Mans 1953, rebuilt it and put up fastest lap at the final Goodwood meeting of the year. MDU 212 was then sold and Duncan drove XKC 038 (registered OVC 915) in 1954.

Meanwhile, *Ecurie Ecosse* had been fielding no less than four production C-types, with Ninian Sanderson joining the regular drivers. But when they acquired the 1953 works C-types (051, 052 and 053) for the 1954 season, everyone knew that Jaguar must have a new car planned for the forthcoming Le Mans... and it was the D-type which appeared for the 1954 event.

The Scottish team had a good number of successes during 1954 but, like Duncan Hamilton's efforts in OVC 915, these were restricted to non-Championship events. Other C-type private owners were having fun too, Michael Head driving his ex-Wisdom/Cannell C-type through Scandinavia with his wife and tools (no tender car!), often over muddy and poorly surfaced roads, to compete in Finland and Sweden. The C-type covered 1,140 miles over two sorties, completing six practice sessions and winning all four races entered.

The Jaguar, reported Head later, performed "as if it had been leading the most sheltered life… perhaps the last of the sports cars which could be driven all over the continent and… yet be able to give its driver a good chance of success". Likewise, Duncan Hamilton claimed to have taken only "the sort of spares any keen motorist would take with him on a motoring holiday" during his frequent continental excursions.

The final appearance of a C-type at Le Mans was in 1954. Roger Laurent and Jacques Swaters entered a factory-prepared car under the banner of *Ecurie Francorchamps*. Remarkably for an outdated design, it achieved fourth place.

Below: Adaptable: the C-type was sometimes entered in road events by private owners..This is Axel Glans and Luc Descollonges during the one such rally. Ian Appleyard himself was due to rally a C-type in 1953, but changed to another XK 120 (RUB 120) instead.

Above: Two of the finest C-type drivers in the US are shown in this picture - Walt Hansgen (left) and Masten Gregory (in car). With them are Chuck Hornburg, who promoted the C-type in racing, and Jerry Cheeseborough. Year circa 1953.

Previous spread: A gloriously atmospheric shot of noted XK 120 exponents Armand Roboly and Col. John Simone having a go in the Tour de France with the former's C-type (025). No great result was recorded, however.

Of the 53 C-types built, no less than 18 were sold new in the United States. There had been great interest in the car ever since its 1951 Le Mans win (the French 24-Hour race was followed perhaps even more keenly then in the US than it is today), and as the 1952 season got underway, the XK 120 was in danger of being completely outclassed by more specialised opposition in SCCA modified classes.

Finally, production C-types began to trickle in, the first two being dispatched to Hornburg (West coast) and Hoffman (East coast) on 1st August 1952. In the hands of Phil Hill, 007 won at Elkhart Lake before reaching California, where another win for Hill resulted at Torrey Pines in December. Hoffman's 009 won the Seneca Cup race at Watkins Glen, New York state, driven by John Fitch.

While the majority of US-bound C-types were shipped in 1952, most did not go racing until the 1953 season and then not all were particularly successful, although a third place was scored at the Sebring 12 hours early in 1953. Phil Hill was increasingly driving Ferraris now, but the bespectacled, 21-year-old Masten Gregory purchased 015 and won his first race with it, first time out, at Golden Gate Park, San Francisco.

When in August 1953 the C-type was burnt out at Floyd Bennet Field, Long Island, Gregory purchased 022 on the spot and raced it the same day! In his first event abroad, Gregory finished 14th in January 1954 in the Argentine 1000 km race. Masten's brother Ridelle also won in a

C-type (033), a novice event at March Field, Riverside, in November 1953.

By 1954 the C-type was, in Jaguar's terms, obsolete, but Walter Hansgen, to become America's most active Jaguar driver, was victorious at Thompson Raceway in New England and Roy Wyllie won the Seneca Cup at Watkins Glen. He made it three in a row for the C-type by repeating the feat in 1955 too.

In the west, Louis Brero was victorious in the 6-Hour race at Torrey Pines, California, towards the end of the year. Carroll Shelby drove a C-type in 1954 too, winning twice at Fort Worth, Texas, in 020.

The C-type which remained competitive longest in the US was surely 030. Placed fourth in the Sebring 12-Hours in 1953 (Harry Gray/Bob Gegan), it was owned by Gordon MacKenzie of Millbrook, NY, in 1958 and was raced through the 1960s, updated with a 3.8 engine and E-type independent rear suspension. But by 1955, the D-type was winning in North America and the C-type slipped into history.

The C-type was both aesthetically pleasing and thoroughly functional. It re-wrote the Le Mans rule book, ushering in a new era of professionalism in sports car racing. It also changed Jaguar's future, literally overnight. By 4.00pm on 24th June 1951 the world was a different place for the small Coventry manufacturer - because from then on, all the world knew about Jaguar.

Below: **First race for the C-type in America, Elkhart Lake: two cars ran, Phil Hill winning in Hornburg's XKC 007, then in third place behind Walters' Ferrari came George Weaver, giving New York distributor Max Hoffman's 009 its baptism.**

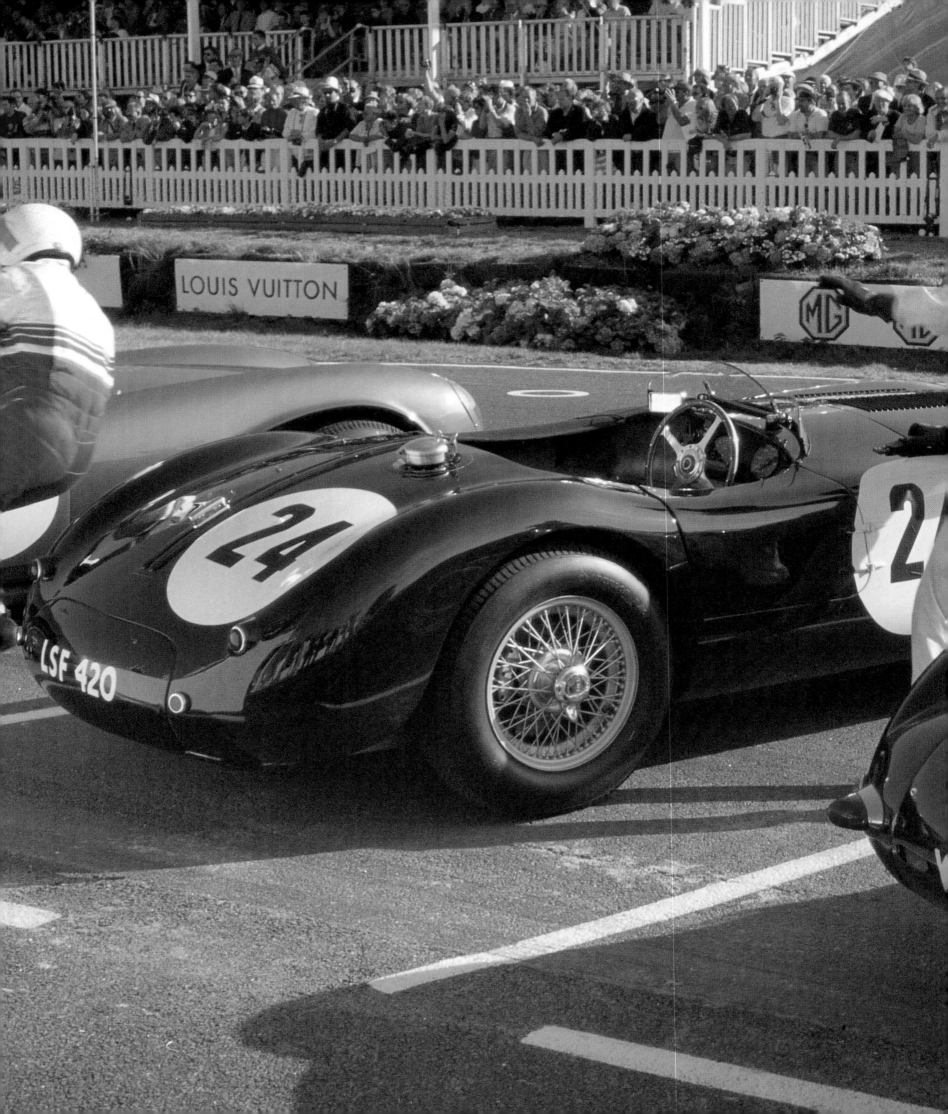

Driving the C-type Jaguar

The C-type has often been described as a great road car, not just a race car. Perhaps this is because of the production-based nature of the car, and from the flexible, easy-going nature of the long-stroke XK engine, still in a relatively 'soft' state of tune. Certainly, a number of owners chose to drive their C-types over long distances to events in the 1950s, while today, this adaptability is prized - it gives more opportunities for

getting enjoyment from an investment which today often represents the better part of half a million pounds! Of course, some examples now go much faster than they did originally, thanks to the continuing

development of the XK engine for 'historic' racing. But a reasonably standard C-type remains a fast car, with acceleration similar to that of a 3.8 E-type unless Le Mans gearing is being used.

Some drivers find the car's handling a little quirky, perhaps because the front and rear suspensions were not designed at the same time. Trying its old road-test car, XKC 015, again many years later, Road & Track described it as cornering "in a series of arcs, no one of which quite matches the radius of the curve". It responded best to confident driving, "entering each turn at maximum velocity and loading both ends of the car to their extremes. Then the car can be steered with power and it all works well."

It certainly worked well at Le Mans, and it is still a wonderful car to drive some 50 years later.

C-type Jaguar

Technical specifications

YEARS CURRENT
1951 - 1953

SPECIFICATION (production C-type)

Engine capacity	3,442cc
Power	200 bhp @ 5,800 rpm
Length	13ft 1ins
Width	5ft 4.5ins
Weight	2,240 lbs (20cwt)
Wheelbase	8ft
Max. speed	145 mph
0-60mph	8.1secs
Mpg	16-18

Competition results

COMPETITION RESULTS

1951
Le Mans 24-hour race, June, P.N. Whitehead/P.D.C. Walker, 1st (93.49 mph)
Tourist Trophy race, Dundrod, September, S. Moss, 1st, P.D.C. Walker, 2nd, L.G. Johnson/APR Rolt, 3rd; Team prize

1952
International Trophy Meeting, Silverstone, May, production sports car race, S. Moss, 1st
Grand Prix de France, Rheims, Sports car race, June, S. Moss, 1st over 2,000cc class (98.2 mph)
Goodwood 9-Hours race, August, S. Moss, 1st, J. D. Hamilton, 2nd
Shelsley Walsh, August, P.D.C. Walker, 1st in class, best production car

1953
Sebring 12-Hours, March, S. Johnston/R. Wilder, 3rd
Le Mans 24-Hour race, June, A.P.R. Rolt/J.D. Hamilton, 1st (105.85 mph), S. Moss/P.D.C. Walker, 2nd
Rheims 12 Hour race, July, 1st, S. Moss/P.N. Whitehead
24-Hour race, Spa, July, Sir J. Scott-Douglas, 2nd
Goodwood 9-Hours race, August, J. Stewart/B. Dickson, 3rd

1954
Le Mans 24 Hour race, June, R. Laurent/J. Swaters, 4th
Rhems 12-Hour race, July, R.Laurent/J. Swaters, 3rd
Leinster Trophy Race, Wicklow, July, J. Kelly, 2nd
Goodwood Trophy Meeting, September, R. Salvadori, 1st unlimited sports car race

The dramatic D-type

This 190 mph technical masterpiece, designed, built and prepared totally within Jaguar, was to achieve a hat-trick of spectacular Le Mans victories in the 1950s.

"WHEN WE GOT THERE FOR SECRET TESTING, EVERY FRENCH NEWSPAPER
HEADLINE WAS 'A NEW JAGUAR WILL BE AT LE MANS SATURDAY'!"

Lofty England on testing the new D-type, 1954

The early 1950s proved a period of explosive growth for Jaguar, unequalled until the full effects
of the company's extensive new-model programmes took effect some 50 years later. During
1953 Jaguar production broke the 10,000-a-year barrier for the first time as the new Browns
Lane factory came fully on stream. The Mk VII and XK 120 were selling in ever greater numbers,
stimulated by new model variants and by competition successes: the XK 120 and Mk VII were still
delivering results in rallying while the C-type had now triumphed twice at Le Mans.

It was while the XK120C was still winning that Bill Heynes and the engineering department
set about designing its successor. They were driven, as Bob Berry remarked, by "the relentless
pressure of the competition, the growing commercial importance of success, the totally human
and understandable desire to ride the crest of the wave for as long as possible". The new car,
naturally, came to be called the D-type and like its predecessor, was created to achieve just one
objective - winning the Le Mans 24-Hour race.

Design goals included better aerodynamics than the C-type, with the driver sitting lower and
with greater protection from the elements - important at Le Mans, especially during cold, wet

Above: **The 'XK 120C Mk II'
at the Le Mans test day on
8th May 1954; this prototype
incorporated all the D-type's
advanced features but never
itself raced. For this test it
used an experimental fuel
injection system.**

nights. On the way to achieving this, and for greater
rigidity and strength, aircraft construction methods
were applied for the first time to a race car; in fact the
D-type employed design and build techniques which,
15 years later, would be universal amongst Grand Prix
cars. A prototype was made to prove these new
features, which included the engine and front
suspension carried in a square-section, tubular
aluminium frame which was welded to a rigid central
'tub' of aircraft-riveted aluminium panels. The XK120C Mk II (or 'C/D prototype') worked so
well that Heynes toyed with the idea of using the car in the 1953 Le Mans, before settling for a
lightened, Weber-carburetted C-type. However, the prototype dramatically cut the time it took
for the D-type proper to be designed, built and tested.

At just 12ft 10ins long and 5ft 5.5ins wide, the D-type was a wonderfully efficient package;
its small frontal area plus Malcolm Sayer's superb, flowing body shape gave the car a remarkably
high top speed for the horsepower available - vitally important at Le Mans with its long straights.

Above: **Lofty England (centre) stands over the new D-type on its first 'secret' test at Le Mans in May. Rolt lapped at 4 min 22.2 secs, five seconds below the existing record (reg. no. should have been 'OVC', a clerical slip-up that wasn't noticed for some time!).**

Promising test sessions followed at Rheims and Le Mans (the roads closed for a rally). The drivers for the latter test were to be Peter Walker and Tony Rolt, but Walker was delayed at Le Havre when he found his passport had expired: he turned up later by taxi; "After he arrived," recalled Lofty England, "I noticed a little man in a cap, smoking a Gauloises cigarette and I asked Peter, 'Who is he?' The reply: 'He is the taxi driver and wants £28!' So I had to produce the money to pay him!"

A storming last-minute lap by Tony Rolt cut five seconds from Alberto Ascari's 1953 lap record and sent out a warning that this new Jaguar meant business. It may even have dissuaded Lancia from entering Le Mans that year; Jaguar were already genuinely disappointed that Mercedes had decided not to run - but they, like Lancia, had a Formula 1 programme underway.

Three D-types lined up under a threatening sky for the start of the 1954 24-Hour race, looking quite futuristic with their distinctive tail fins, added by Sayer for directional stability at speed. Lofty England had secured equally distinctive registrations for the cars: Stirling Moss and Peter Walker were in OKV 2, the 'hare' car; Duncan Hamilton and Tony Rolt had OKV 1; and Peter Whitehead and Ken Wharton drove OKV 3.

As expected, it was the big red 4.9-litre Ferrari of Froilán González and Maurice Trintignant which initially made the running. The D-types were plagued by misfiring, eventually tracked down to a fine grey dust in the fuel which had compacted in the all-too-efficient fuel filters. It was soon cured, but their ill-luck continued, with Moss retiring after brake failure at around 170 mph. "The little serrated drive at the end of the Plessey pump came loose and he went down the escape road at the end of Mulsanne," explains Tom Jones. "He came back to the pits and we put it back on, and he wouldn't get back into the car!"

Meanwhile Wharton and Whitehead were sidelined by, effectively, gearbox problems, which left Hamilton and Rolt battling through what was now atrocious weather in pursuit of the flying

Ferrari. Then, during the early afternoon, when González tried to drive away following a routine pit stop, his V12 failed to fire... Paul Frere watched the drama: "At this moment Rolt, blinded by the rain, tried to stop at his pit, but a hundred arms waved him on to continue his run at whatever cost."

Left: Le Mans 1954, and no. 12 (Moss/Walker) makes a pit stop. Later Stirling lost the brakes' servo assistance at the end of the Mulsanne straight...

The D-type tore off again and the seconds, then the minutes, ticked away as the Ferrari still refused to respond despite the attentions of, perhaps, more mechanics than were strictly allowed. Finally, the engine caught and González slithered away; 97 seconds later Rolt came by and the race was on again - except that the Jaguar driver simply could not see and came in again for a visor, at which point Lofty put Hamilton in the car to chase the 345 bhp Ferrari.

"How I tried," related Duncan in his book, *Touch Wood*. "The gearing of our D-type was such that we could pull 5,600 rpm in top gear on the straight. This corresponded to something just over 170 mph. I saw suddenly that the rev counter was reading 5,900 and realised that I was getting wheelspin at 170 mph in top gear..." But González was "impossibly good" and in one of

Below: Rolt and Hamilton just after the end of the 1954 Le Mans. They had covered 2,521 miles to the winning Ferrari's 2,523.5 miles after 24 hours of racing...

Above: **Historic moment – the D-type's first victory. Peter Whitehead takes the chequered flag at Rheims, 4th July 1954.**

the closest finishes ever seen at Le Mans, was some 2.5 miles ahead of the Jaguar as the 24th hour arrived. So ended the D-type's first race: a defeat, but an honourable one.

Its first win came soon afterwards, at the Rheims 12-Hours in July, where OKV 3 took the chequered flag driven by Wharton and Whitehead. Moss retired with a failed propeller shaft - and he had severe problems in the TT at Dundrod in September. In fact, compared to the "generally lovely old 'C'", the D-type was definitely not Moss's favourite Jaguar: "A precision instrument tailor-made for Le Mans," he told Doug Nye, "and not at all a rough-road nor aerodrome circuit racer." Jaguar's preoccupation with Le Mans also meant too few outings for Stirling and no one was surprised when he left Jaguar for Mercedes.

"NORMAN DID 193 MPH WITH THE D-TYPE ON THE MULSANNE STRAIGHT - MALCOLM SAYER HAD SAID IT WOULD DO 190 PLUS." *Tom Jones, designer, on the 1955 Le Mans D-type*

For Le Mans 1955 a much-revised D-type was evolved. The original car with its integral alloy subframe had proved difficult to repair, so a change to a detachable steel frame was made. This was inspired by motorcycle practice. "Heynes sent me off to the Motorcycle Show to study steel tubing and the joints," recalls Tom Jones. There the Norton and BSA people guided him towards Reynolds 531 high-tensile steel tubing as used for motorcycles. Malcolm Sayer produced a sleeker body, and power was up to some 270 bhp thanks to a new cylinder head with larger inlet valves.

Below: **Peter Whitehead is congratulated by Bill Lyons as the D-type is besieged after its Rheims victory. Its running average speed had been 105 mph for the 12 hours.**

Mike Hawthorn was chosen by Lofty England to replace Moss for 1955. His first race for Jaguar was in XKD 406, the last of the 1954 works cars which was in the States for display at the New York Auto Show. Briggs Cunningham, winding down his own Cunningham sports car project to race Jaguars instead, persuaded William Lyons to let him run it at the Daytona Beach speed trials (driven by Phil Walters it achieved 164.136 mph), and then talked Lyons into allowing him to enter the D-type in the Sebring 12-Hours.

Hawthorn, partnered by Phil Walters, survived an arduous race on Sebring's 5.2 miles of burning concrete, fending off a challenge by the Ferrari of Taruffi and Schell. The D-type was using a lot of oil and water and its disc brakes were wilting, but the Ferrari suffered worse ("I drove the whole of my final spell with no brakes at all, slowing the Ferrari entirely on the gearbox," complained Taruffi afterwards.)

Mike Hawthorn found racing in the US differed somewhat from Europe. "I heard a frightful clanging noise and looked round to see a fire engine racing me. It was a great monster festooned with ladders and things, with characters in long-tailed helmets clinging on all over it, just like a scene from an old-time film comedy. I managed to keep clear of this lot and got on with the motor racing!" He did, to good effect, and secured a significant first-time-out win for the D-type in America's most important sports car race. Highly creditable for a 'show car', though it fuelled demand from local drivers for the D-type which, unfortunately, the factory could not meet.

Above: **Pre-race Le Mans 1954 and the tools and equipment of OKV 1, the Rolt/Hamilton car. Only items carried on the car could be used during the race.**

Although 'customer' versions of the car were planned, the first D-type private entry was an ex-works 1954 car (OKV 1), purchased by Duncan Hamilton. He continued his far-roaming activities by taking it to Agadir in Morocco (where he had to retire from the Circuit of Agadir with brake trouble) and then to Senegal, where he managed third place in the immensely fast Grand Prix of Dakar. "A little light on the helm, but perfect," said Duncan of the D-type at its maximum - the Dunlop representative calculated the D-type's top speed at 183 mph, respectably near to the speed the long-nose works cars were to achieve at Le Mans later that year.

Ecurie Ecosse ran their two brand-new D-types at Silverstone in May 1955; these (XKD 502 and 503) were the first customer or 'production' D-types, essentially short-nose versions of the

1955 works cars, though lacking the big-valve 'wide-angle' cylinder head. The team had a pretty torrid time at the Nürburgring later that month, where the limitations of the D-type's quite primitive rear suspension were well and truly shown up as both Desmond Titterington and Jimmy Stewart crashed. Paul Frere, who drove, and crashed, a works D-type there the following year, described the car as "just like a frightening, ferocious beast on the bumpy, twisting ring".

"AS MOTOR RACING COSTS US SEVERAL HUNDRED THOUSAND POUNDS A YEAR, WE CANNOT AFFORD TO BE SENTIMENTAL ABOUT IT."

Sir William Lyons in a letter to driver Peter Walker

For Le Mans, Hawthorn was partnered by Formula 500 champion Ivor Bueb, brought in to replace Desmond Titterington, who had been injured at the Nürburgring. Three other works D-types were entered, driven by the old firm of Rolt and Hamilton; Norman Dewis (replacing Jimmy Stewart, another Nürburgring casualty) and Don Beauman; and, for Briggs Cunningham, Bill Spear and Phil Walters. Finally, Browns Lane prepared one of the new 'customer' D-types for *Ecurie Francorchamps*. A mighty contest was in prospect as Mercedes had rejoined the fray with the *Mille Miglia*-winning 300SLR plus an awe-inspiring driver line-up which included the pairing of Moss and Fangio.

But for Jaguar the event was clouded with tragedy even before it began. Travelling to the race, John Lyons was killed when his Mk VII skidded on oil and collided with an

Above: Jaguar's competition shop, with the new 1955 'long nose' D-types taking shape. In the centre is Bill Heynes: as engineering director, Heynes was ultimately responsible for all Jaguar's competition programmes - and for their success.

army bus in France. It fell to Lofty England to break the news to William Lyons that his only son had died. The conversation was, Lofty recalled, "the most unpleasant thing I had to do in my life". But there were no thoughts of withdrawing the Jaguar team. Despite this personal tragedy, William Lyons obviously considered that his son would have wanted the team to race.

Three works D-types therefore lined up ready for the start. Externally, the new version was identifiable by its longer nose and 'wrap round' windscreen, part of Malcolm Sayer's new aerodynamic package. Norman Dewis remembers that this new windscreen caused some debate prior to the race. "Rolt and Hamilton wanted two inches cut off the screen - they wanted to look over it if it rained. Beauman wanted it shortened too, but I said there was no need to, the water would not stay, as I'd already tried it in the wet.

"Malcolm said, 'Well, it's up to you, but if you do you'll lose speed down the straight, about 4 mph'. But they wouldn't have it, even though Lofty warned them that there was no spare screen. They put masking tape on and hacked it off. We kept our original screen and we got 192 mph, I think it was, down the Mulsanne Straight, and they got 187 or 188 mph. Malcolm was right, spot on. I believed him - I'd experienced his predictions."

When the flag dropped at 4pm on 11th June, the battle lay between Coventry, Stuttgart and Modena, represented at the start by Hawthorn, Fangio and Castellotti. Hawthorn recorded what happened in his autobiography *Challenge Me The Race*: "A terrific battle developed as the three of us swapped places... I was highly elated when I found that the Jaguar could pass both the Mercedes and the Ferrari on the straight and even if they used my slipstream could not get past again. Duelling with the Mercedes and the Ferrari demanded fantastic concentration and this looked like going on for hours."

Below: The pits area before the start of the 1955 Le Mans. The Claes/Swaters Belgian-entered car is far right next to the Cunningham entry driven by Spear and Walters. No. 8 is the Beauman/Dewis car.

Left: **Mike Hawthorn and Ivor Bueb try and put a cheerful face on their victory, but the toll in spectators' lives made the end of the 1955 Le Mans a solemn occasion in reality.**

Hawthorn found that the 300SLR had a distinct advantage on fast and medium-fast corners thanks to its independent rear suspension. "Fangio took the lead for three laps, but I took him again with a lap of 4 min 6.6 secs for the 8.36 miles at an average of 122.39 mph which remained unbeaten and stood as a new record. At the end of the second hour, there was less than a second separating us after nearly 250 miles of motoring." Soon all but four cars had been lapped.

It was a wonderful duel by two masters of their craft, the cars well-matched even if very different technically - the D-type aerodynamically more slippery and with disc brakes, but a live rear axle, the Mercedes bulkier, with drum brakes assisted by a weird air brake, but with independent rear suspension.

Then, just before 6.30pm, came the terrible accident which blighted the 1955 race. Hawthorn, heading for a scheduled pit stop, overtook Lance Macklin's Austin-Healey 100, pulled over and started to brake. Macklin moved out and was hit by Pierre Levegh's 300SLR. The Mercedes was launched into the air, landed on top of the outside banking and disintegrated, front suspension and engine flying into the crowd opposite the pits.

Only partially aware of what had happened, but knowing that a very major accident had occurred, Hawthorn stopped just past the Jaguar pits (Lofty, fearing that other cars would become involved in the chaos, had prevented the mechanics from jumping into the road as normal so Mike had lost his reference point). As reversing was forbidden, he got out of the car and ran back to the Jaguar pits. His first reaction, on seeing the carnage, was one of horror, especially as he thought it was Fangio who had been flung from the Mercedes and killed.

Mike was consoled by Duncan Hamilton and encouraged by Lofty England: "After we had got through the refuel of all four of our cars, including the Belgian car, I was able to go and talk quietly to Mike and convince him that it was not Fangio, who he greatly respected." Hawthorn did later resume, taking over from Ivor Bueb who had completed his first drive for Jaguar in the most intimidating circumstances, having witnessed the disaster from the pit counter.

The Fangio/Moss 300SLR assumed the lead but the Hawthorn/Bueb Jaguar was still healthy and within striking distance when, early in the morning, the contest was brought to a conclusion by the Mercedes team withdrawing. That left Hawthorn and Bueb to secure a somewhat joyless victory (Claes and Swaters finished third) - and ever since, the debate has continued over who would have won if the battle had run its course.

Following the 1955 Le Mans race, there were widespread repercussions within motor racing, a number of major events being cancelled. Jaguar elected not to publicise its win and instructed its dealers and distributors to do likewise. No works-entered Jaguars appeared in the August Goodwood 9-Hour race, though *Ecurie Ecosse* scored a good second place amongst the works Astons.

Rheims was one of the many post-Le Mans cancellations; perhaps the Tourist Trophy should have been another. The 7.5-mile

Left: **Late night line-up: the Rheims 12 Hours started in darkness. The 1956 D-types are those of (nearest camera) Fairman/Titterington, Hamilton/Bueb, Frere/Hawthorn (with the latter's four-spoke steering wheel) and in the distance, Flockhart/Sanderson. The result was a clean sweep of the first four places by Jaguar.**

Above: **Jack Fairman, looking particularly debonair at Rheims 1956; he came third, partnered by Ulsterman Desmond Titterington.**

Dundrod road circuit did not suit the D-type that well, but "not wishing to disappoint the organisers who we liked", Lofty entered one works car for Hawthorn and local lad Desmond Titterington. Although the field was briefly headed by Bob Berry in the Broadhead D-type, the feature of the race was another Hawthorn/Fangio battle. In an enthralling contest they swapped places, with Hawthorn setting what was to be fastest lap at 96.41 mph.

However, rain handicapped the lone works D-type, the three 300SLRs better at putting the power down in the wet. So although Hawthorn, "driving right on the limit", got ahead of Fangio, Moss finally proved superior despite terrible tyre wear problems. Mike was denied even second place when the Jaguar's crankshaft (most unusually) broke on the penultimate lap. This race too was blemished by accidents, promising C- and D-type driver Bill Smith being killed when his Connaught hit the wreckage of another accident. He was one of three drivers killed that day.

In a rather black season, a little light relief was provided at Snetterton by Duncan Hamilton who spun his D-type backwards across the finishing line when a tyre burst. It was, he said, the only race he could remember winning while pointing the wrong way...

"TRULY, JAGUAR OCCUPIES TODAY THE POSITION HELD IN VINTAGE TIMES BY BENTLEY IN THE AFFECTIONS OF BRITISH ENTHUSIASTS."

Bill Boddy, Motor Sport

1956 was Jaguar's last year in sports car racing. Virtually all the competition work was being done by staff also responsible for road car development, which consequently was suffering. This same manpower shortage meant that there was no D-type replacement for the 1956 season. As Tom Jones says, "The E-type was to be the 1956 competition car. Because of the restricted facilities on the personnel side, the competition car was scrubbed and we continued with the D-type" (in fact a prototype D-type replacement was running by May 1957 but never raced). There was also concern over stringent new regulations at Le Mans, including a limit on fuel consumption aimed at reducing speeds; but in the end, the works involvement continued.

At the Sebring 12-Hour that year, thanks largely to Briggs Cunningham, there was an impressive entry of Jaguars, four D-types running in Cunningham colours. And at Rheims, regarded by Lofty England as a useful fuel consumption test for Le Mans more than anything, a Jaguar 1-2-3 finish certainly made up for failures at Silverstone and the Nürburgring earlier in the year. The Rheims race is best remembered for Duncan Hamilton disobeying the 'maintain position' pit signal; he used the fuel-injected D-type's power to overtake Paul Frere, winning and setting fastest lap, a record. Duncan knew he'd transgressed and said to Lofty at the end of

Previous spread: **Ivor Bueb and the 3.8 litre-engined, fuel-injected XKD 606 on their way to victory at Le Mans, 1957.**

Below: **Le Mans 1956, and the wonderful line up of works long-nose D-types for scrutineering. The spare car is here, too. Note that regulations have demanded full-width windscreens.**

the race, "I suppose I'm in trouble". "Not really", said Lofty, "or you won't be in the future because you will not be driving for us any more." Hamilton was sacked on the spot. (They remained friends though: a little later Lofty received a parcel from Duncan - in it was a mortar board and cane labelled 'To teacher with love'.)

Paul Frere, co-driving with Hawthorn and second to Hamilton, found even the fruits of second place to be fleeting: "A few minutes after the

Above: The start, Le Mans 1956, and the yellow Swaters/Rouselle short-nose D-type (which eventually finished fourth) leads most of the field, ahead of the 300SL which was so comprehensively out-run by the XK 140. Behind the Mercedes is the gaggle of works D-types.

finish, a beautiful girl dressed up in the local costume handed me a magnificent bunch of flowers and an equally magnificent magnum of champagne, and gave me two resounding kisses, which the photographers insisted on repeating for their benefit. This happy interlude was not to last long either, for not only did the pretty Rheims girl disappear suddenly, but so did the flowers and champagne, which had only been brought, apparently, to add tone to the photographs!"

A month later than usual, following numerous alterations to the track, Le Mans 1956 was dominated by fuel consumption: 34 laps had to be covered before refuelling, when a maximum of 120 litres could be taken on, equating to 10.9 mpg. Other new rules aimed at reducing speeds included restricting prototypes to 2.5 litres (which meant that for a year the race was taken out of the Manufacturers' Championship), but crucially for Jaguar, 'series production' cars - ie more than 50 built or scheduled - could run with their usual capacity engines. By this time, thanks to the run of production examples, the D-type qualified for this category.

As Heynes said, the fuel consumption limitation "made it difficult to take full advantage of the power we had available"; but the D-type's efficient shape, extra high gearing and the relative economy of the long-stroke XK engine allowed the car to average 11 mpg with enough speed to give Jaguar an edge. "We were the only people at the track that ran 3.4-litre cars," said Lofty. "Nobody else had a car with a good enough petrol consumption which would allow them to run anything over 3.0 litres."

All this encouraged a strong Jaguar line-up for the race: there were three works-entered long-nose cars (Hawthorn/Bueb, Fairman/Wharton, Frere/Titterington) and a factory-prepared production car for Swaters and Rouselle driving for the Belgian team *Equipe Nationale Belge.* *Ecurie Ecosse* made their Le Mans debut with one of their production D-types driven by Ron Flockhart and Ninian Sanderson.

With no Mercedes-Benz or big-engined Ferraris, a repeat of the Rheims demonstration appeared likely, even though it began to drizzle as the drivers ran across the track to their cars. It was not to be, though, as Paul Frere relates:

"Forewarned by my slide at the start, I entered the big bend after the pits very carefully and, just after the crest of the hill leading to the Esses of *Terte Rouge*, I began applying the brakes at a spot at which I considered would give me ample time to slow down for the corners. Alas! It was already too late. The mere touch of my foot on the brake pedal was sufficient to lock the wheels... I did what I could, entering on the very edge of the road, but it was wasted effort: the car spun round and crashed into the earthworks."

Above: **Disaster for Jaguar! The D-types of Paul Frere and Jack Fairman limp off after spinning on the slippery road just two laps into the 1956 Le Mans race. De Portago's Ferrari also comes to grief and retires.**

Worse was to follow. Fairman had spun too, then de Portago's Ferrari came down the hill "spinning like a top" and crashed into Fairman's D-type. The two Jaguars hobbled away but Frere had to abandon his when a rear tyre rubbed against the bent rear bodywork and burst.

As Paul walked back to face Lofty England he realised not only was Fairman missing, but Hawthorn in the injected car was no longer coming by. "It was then that the full magnitude of the disaster was borne upon me. Through my fault Jaguar were going to be deprived of a victory which would have been theirs for the taking, and on which they depended to sell thousands of cars all over the world."

In fact Lofty "made not the slightest reproach", but that only made Paul feel worse! The Hawthorn/Bueb car was suffering a misfire from a longitudinal crack in the injector tube, but by the time the problem was dealt with they had lost 22 laps, a huge deficit. Lofty: "There was little point in going out again, so I said to them, 'Well, I reckon if we have a real go we'll finish eighth'. 'Right', they said, 'we're on!' They were flogging round while it rained nearly all the time and they came in soaking wet.

"I would say to Mike, 'What's it like?' and he'd say, 'Wet'. And after another three hours soaking, 'Still wet!' They were just enjoying themselves..."

Meanwhile Paul Frere was suffering agonies, though there was a ray of hope as the *Ecosse* car was now attacking. After a close battle through the night, Flockhart and Sanderson pulled out a lap lead on the DB3S of Moss and Collins. "When the car crossed the finishing line," Paul related, "my eyes were full of tears: the *Ecurie Ecosse* had saved the day."

Hawthorn and Bueb? Remarkably, they hauled themselves up to sixth - and received £30 prize money for their trouble...

As far as Jaguar were concerned, by 1956 the D-type was obsolete. There had been no time to produce a successor, so it was decided to pull out of racing for a year, then return with a new car. A press release to this effect was issued on 13th October 1956; it acknowledged that the racing programme had benefited the product but at the same time had imposed "a very heavy burden on the Technical and Research Branch of the Engineering Division". So ended a highly successful, and unusually single-minded, works motor racing programme which not only made the Jaguar name known and respected worldwide, but also elevated the status of the whole British motor industry.

Circumstances conspired to prevent Jaguar ever returning officially to racing as constructor and entrant. Firstly, there was a major fire at the Browns Lane plant on 12th February 1957 and a huge effort was required before production could resume. This pushed competition matters into the background, but above all was the need to apply to road-car projects the remarkable talents of the team which had produced such successful race cars. Despite its rapid growth, Jaguar was still under-resourced compared to larger rivals and, with a clutch of Le Mans wins

Below: **Mike Hawthorn and Ivor Bueb made a great effort to regain some of their lost laps after being delayed by a faulty petrol feed pipe on their injected 3.8 D-type. They finally took sixth place in the 1956 Le Mans.**

now under its collective belt, the company had all the sporting credentials it needed. So although the D-type's successor, known as E2A, was running by May 1957, thoughts of re-entering the sport lessened as the year drew on. Motor racing increasingly seemed a luxury rather than the necessity it perhaps once was. And the longer Jaguar stayed out, the more difficult it became to re-enter the sport.

The competition shop, though, continued to function for a considerable period, supporting selected private entrants - especially Briggs Cunningham, Duncan Hamilton and *Ecurie Ecosse*. Cunningham received what amounted to full works backing for the March 1957 Sebring 12-Hour race: a 1956 works car with the first 3.8-litre engine was flown out and Hawthorn and Bueb were delegated to drive it. Hawthorn finished third behind two works Maseratis - which surprised everybody by lasting the distance. He might have done better but for a brake seal failure due to the intense heat which entailed blanking off the rear brakes altogether.

Below: Sebring, 1957; Walt Hansgen is sitting in one of the Cunningham-entered D-types. Behind in sunglasses is Alfred Momo; his Momo Corporation was at this time in Queens, New York, next to Cunningham's Jaguar distribution centre. The driver standing is Russ Boss who, with Hansgen, was to take the Momo-prepared D-type to fifth. They are in one of the many old wooden sheds on the airport site used by the teams for servicing.

But the D-type still made a deep impression on those who saw it perform, including a young Walter Hill, there to watch the 12-Hours and take part with his XK 140 in an amateur race afterwards. "More than the car's appealing and familiar Cunningham paint scheme of blue stripe on white was its stunning sound and performance - the beautiful, lithe shape, the strong yet crisp exhaust note, its smooth, almost slippery motion, told me I was seeing something truly special... I never got over it." 30 years later, Walter Hill recreated the Sebring car, complete with Lucas fuel injection, in his own workshops out of an XK-SS.

The XK-SS was a new model announced by Jaguar on 21st January 1957, targeted at the North American market. Essentially a road-equipped production D-type, the model had come about at the instigation of Briggs Cunningham. He wanted to race the D-type in Sports Car Club of America events but the club would not accept the D-type as a production sports car. So the idea arose of dressing the car up with windscreen, bumpers and luggage rack and announcing it as a 'new' road car. "We agreed to build 50 examples, the number needed to qualify," recalled Lofty.

In fact there was no chance of that number ever being produced, but it did seem a useful way of utilising the 30-odd production D-types which had been languishing unsold at Browns Lane since 1956 (Jaguar had, for once, over-estimated demand!). List price for the XK-SS was $6,900 - cheaper than the Mercedes-Benz 300SL road car and much faster, with a 0-100 mph time of around 14 seconds.

However, while the XK-SS made a stupendous road burner, the SCCA still categorised it as 'modified', and Cunningham did not pursue a serious racing programme with the XK-SS. Two cars sold to Canada did achieve some success however, and one went to Hong Kong where it won the Macau Grand Prix in both 1959 and 1960, albeit against somewhat motley opposition.

Above: **The 150 mph-plus XK-SS of 1957 was meant to be a dual-purpose road/race car; a few did achieve success on the track though most became collector's items before too long. Note luggage rack, vestigial bumpers which hint at the E-type's to come, and the top which attaches to the full width windscreen.**

Above: A wonderful paddock view of American sports car racing in the late 1950s, the short-nose D-type next to Ferrari.

A total of 16 XK-SS cars were originally made, out of 67 D-types which went down the production line at Browns Lane. Like the £3,878 production D-type, the XK-SS cost Jaguar more than the list price to build *and* failed to sell well. The factory fire in February 1957 became a convenient reason for not continuing with either version of the famous Le Mans car! However, at Le Mans that year, the marque was completely dominant; five Jaguars started and five finished, taking the first four places and sixth too. The 1951 win might have been the company's greatest, but this was a supreme result.

Three of the cars and all the engines were prepared at Browns Lane. Two cars were entered

by *Ecurie Ecosse*, both long-nose types they had just bought from Jaguar. *Ecurie Nationale Belge* ran the yellow short-nose car that had come fourth in 1955, and the French-based *Los Amigos* team ran a similar car. Duncan Hamilton entered his own long-nose car, another recent purchase from Jaguar.

The race was *Ecurie Ecosse*'s finest hour - or 24 of them. Although the 412 Ferraris were spectacularly fast, both Collins and Hawthorn were soon out. The Maseratis of Moss and Behra were also quick but they too retired within four hours. After that, the race belonged to Jaguar - though not all the D-types were trouble free. The Hamilton car's ignition somehow became retarded during the night, producing a very hot exhaust. Masten Gregory pitted with the Vyback canopy over the passenger compartment blistered and burnt. Duncan, due to take over, asked Gregory how the

Far left: Australia has consistently loved Jaguars; here Bib Stillwell and Bill Pitt, two of the greatest Australian D-type drivers, lead a string of single-seaters at Bathurst in 1958.

Right: William Lyons talks to Norman Dewis who is about to take Harold Hastings, Midlands editor of *The Motor*, round the new banked circuit at MIRA in 1954. The car is the original D-type prototype, XKC 401, now owned by the Jaguar Daimler Heritage Trust.

car was. "Goes fine with it on fire," said Gregory laconically. The overheated exhaust had burnt through both the silencer and the floor, and every time the driver lifted his foot from the accelerator, flames shot up. "All we could do was bolt a piece of plate about ³/₁₆ths inch thick onto the floor" said Lofty; but it worked and the drivers set about recovering a two-hour deficit..

At the end of the 24 hours, Flockhart and Bueb in the 3.8-litre fuel-injected D-type were leading, followed by Sanderson and Lawrence in the second *Ecosse* car. Third came the French entry of Jean Lucas and Jean Brussin, and fourth Paul Frere and Freddy Rouselle. After a Ferrari interloper (Lewis-Evans/Severi) Hamilton and Gregory followed in sixth.

The race was effectively the D-type's finale in Europe, a glorious climax to the career of a quite remarkable sports-racing car. *Ecurie Ecosse* were never to attain the same heights again but continued to field their D-types for some years yet, including the extraordinary event dubbed the 'Race of Two Worlds' at Monza, a challenge match supposedly between the best European cars and American 'Indy' cars. At the same circuit in 1957, Captain Ian Baillie of the Life Guards used his 1955 production D-type to set six international speed records, including 140.67 miles in one hour.

In 1958 five D-types ran at Le Mans once again; this time, all five failed. The Sports Car Constructors' Championship - which now included Le Mans again - had decreed a maximum engine capacity of three litres, a ruling which helped to ensure that a D-type would never again finish, let alone win, at Le Mans again.

Ecurie Ecosse devised their own 3.0-litre version of the XK engine, but both their cars failed after an hour. Two other privately entered D-types crashed, though Duncan Hamilton and Ivor Bueb in the former's factory-prepared car showed that the D-type was still surprisingly competitive. Moreover, the works-built 3.0-litre 'wide-angle' head engine it used was also proving durable. Weather conditions turned bad but did not deter two-times Le Mans winner Bueb; Lofty England told this story about 'Ivor the driver':

"It was very wet and misty, and Ivor was the most fantastic bloke at night… He actually got into the lead, in front of all the Ferraris, and Von Tripps (one of the Ferrari drivers) came to me and said 'This bloke Bueb of yours, he's just incredible. I was going as fast as I could possibly go down the straight, there was a fast bend and he just came past me as if I was standing still.'"

In fact Lofty was concerned that Duncan was failing to maintain the same pace and felt he needed

Above: **The production D-type of Frere and Rouselle undergoing a routine pit stop during the 1957 Le Mans race in which they finished fourth. The spare wheel is being changed while this overhead view also gives a good view of the Weber-carburetted 3.4 litre engine.**

Previous spread: **Duncan Hamilton drives his ex-works long-nose D-type in typically determined manner at a BARC meeting in 1958. Hamilton was undoubtedly the greatest of all the D-type private owner/drivers.**

motivating. Duncan, he knew, was sensitive about his age and would always deflect questions about it. "So I thought to myself that the only hope of getting him to go any faster was his age. So I got the pit signal put out - 'age 41'. Next lap it said 'age 40'. And every second he took off I'd put his age down one, and every second he lost I put his age up!"

It seemed to work, but the weather remained wet and, in second place to the Olivier Gendebien/Phil Hill Ferrari during the 19th hour, Hamilton went off the road in a big way. The D-type turned over but landed straddling a stream, saving Duncan from serious injury, although it resulted, as Lofty said, in "a slight session in this very comfortable hospital in Le Mans".

There Lofty visited Hamilton to find he was bemoaning his lost winnings. "Boy, I've been lying here watching thousand franc notes fly out. 7,454 francs", he said. "273 bottles of gin." Duncan always counted his losses and winnings in gin...

Ecurie Ecosse soldiered on in 1959 and 1960 with the D-type but their single entries failed to finish both times - though Flockhart and Halford were in fourth place before retiring in 1960 (victor with Olivier Gendebien was Paul Frere, finally achieving his ambition of winning Le Mans).

Below: **Le Mans 1958 - Jack Fairman looks determined as, foot hard down, he urges the** *Ecurie Ecosse* **3-litre D-type forward. Alas, he and Gregory did not finish.**

Left: The Hamilton/Gregory 3.8 litre D-type sweeps out of the Esses on the way to sixth place at Le Mans in 1957. Other D-types filled the first four places that year! Chasing the Jaguar is the Aston Martin DBR/1 of Salvadori and Leston which later dropped out with transmission problems.

"JAGUAR NEVER HAD A BUDGET FOR COMPETITION. THEY JUST DID IT."

Andrew Whyte, Jaguar historian

Why were Jaguar so successful at Le Mans in the 'classic years' - even in 1957, well after the car was obsolete? The reasons are not too difficult to discern: first, there was the sheer reliability of the car. This came in some measure from the many production-based components used, including engine, front suspension and rear axle; and although some of these parts might not have been directly interchangeable with those of the road cars, Jaguar could still take advantage of reliability proven over hundreds of thousands of road miles in all conditions. And as the old saying goes, to finish first you first have to finish.

Second, the D-type benefited from relatively efficient aerodynamics by the standards of the mid-1950s. For example, the Maserati 450S V8 engine - reckoned to be the equal of the contemporary Ferrari V12 - gave some 420 bhp compared with the Jaguar's 300-odd bhp, but at Le Mans the Italian car was slower than the D-type on the Mulsanne straight, let down by its poor body shape.

134

Finally, Jaguar systematically developed one basic design for one type of race. This meant they were free of having to produce a car suitable for the Constructors' Championship which involved a variety of different races such as the *Mille Miglia* and the Nürburgring. Ferrari and Maserati, by contrast, were handicapped by this requirement, as well as an instinctively mercurial tendency to experiment with an unnecessarily wide variety of chassis and engine combinations.

In contrast, by 1957 the D-type had completed three seasons of racing and - in modern parlance - was thoroughly 'de-bugged'. Chassis and engine were also well proven by 24-hour test cycles. Here, the Motor Industry Research Association's test track was a great help: the banked No. 1 circuit allowed the D-type to average laps of up to 150 mph and Norman Dewis covered more miles at average speeds of over 100 mph than probably anyone else of his era. Only Mercedes-Benz operated with the same disciplined thoroughness, and even then their Le Mans cars were handicapped by having been based on the smaller-capacity (3.0-litre) Grand Prix car. So while the Jaguars of the 1950s were not always the most powerful or quickest cars to start the race, they were usually the most reliable.

Below: **Heavy body roll on the 3.4 Jaguars as Hawthorn chases Sopwith at Silverstone in 1958.**

When Jaguar produced the 2.4 litre saloon in September 1955, they really invented a whole new breed of car: the luxury sporting 'compact'. Its 2.4 litre 'short stroke' engine could push the car to just over 100 mph and lent itself to tuning, but Americans were horrified - why on earth didn't Jaguar fit the great 3.4 litre engine? Alfred Momo did so for Briggs Cunningham and produced a humdinger of a sports saloon. Jaguar had intended to do the same and when the 3.4 finally arrived, in February 1957, it was a scorcher. This Jaguar saloon was faster than most sports cars of its day and was popular not only with race drivers: reformed armed robber and getaway driver John McVicar recalled how "I was an East End criminal hot-shot and I was always stealing Jaguar 3.4s. The leather seats smelled so good…"

After mixed success at its inaugural track outing at the May 1956 BRDC *Daily Express* meeting (Duncan Hamilton came third, though Ivor Bueb salvaged Jaguar's pride by winning in the Mk VII OVC 69), Paul Frere borrowed a 2.4 for the Spa Production Car Race. By this time Jaguar had catalogued a range of tuning parts for the 2.4 and Paul discovered that thanks to C-type head and carburettors, it would exceed 125 mph along the slightly downhill Masta Straight.

In practice, however, the gearbox output shaft began to seize; when Norman Dewis attempted a repair and withdrew the shaft all the gears fell into the bottom of the box! Working

Below: The new 2.4 might have seemed underpowered to the Americans, but 100 mph saloons were not common in Europe and Bill Bleakley showed that the car could win the right event. Here he takes the car through a sea-front driving test during the RAC Rally 1956, where his class win was the car's first international success.

through the night with the help of an *Ecurie Ecosse* mechanic, Dewis got the car to the grid just 15 minutes before the start.

Frere found that the 2.4 quickly left the Mercedes 220 and the Alfa 1900ti touring opposition behind - then realised the Jaguar even had the legs of the Porsches. "'To hell with it', I said to myself, 'an overall win is worth so much more than a class win'." He just caught the leading Porsche and crossed the line 100 yards ahead of it.

Above: **Sir Gawaine Baillie and Peter Jopp in their 3.4 saloon during the 1959** *Tour de France;* **they did not finish that year.**

The 2.4's first significant rally success was the class win scored by Bill Bleakley and Ian Hall in the 1956 RAC Rally. But the following year the 3.4 took over the initiative in motor sport, with the competition shop preparing a number of the already quick saloons for private entrants.

On the track, most remembered is probably Mike Hawthorn, although he raced a 3.4 only twice. The works-prepared Coombs and Tommy Sopwith's *Equipe Endeavour* 3.4s were the most active. However, one spectacular Jaguar dice in 1958 involved Hawthorn when, at the May Silverstone, he duelled with Tommy Sopwith and won in VDU 881, the tweaked 3.4 loaned to him by Jaguar. Tragically, Hawthorn could not re-enter the fray in 1959, as the Formula 1 world champion was killed on 22nd January when he lost control of VDU 881 on a wet and blustery day on the Guildford by-pass. The Coombs versus *Equipe Endeavour* battles continued however, until 1960 when the Mk 2 3.8 took over the 3.4's dominance of British saloon car racing.

Compared to these mainly short-distance events, the *Tour de France Automobile* was a different proposition altogether, a succession of races and timed hill climbs linked by often tough road sections. Inseparable from this event was Frenchman Bernard Consten, who first drove a Jaguar on the *Tour Auto* in September 1957. A brief recce drive immediately revealed that "the car had no brakes. A lot of smoke outside and a lot of smell inside, but obviously no brakes."

Nonetheless, Consten and co-owner Jack Renel were leading when an errant Citroen 2CV emerged from a crossroads. "We did some lovely skidding on the left side first, then on the roof and on the right side last, and were nicely embedded into the left-hand ditch, engine still running..." No one was hurt and the 3.4 was put back on its wheels. "The brakes worked better than ever!" Although all chances of victory that year had gone, Bernard Consten would return to the *Tour* driving the 3.8 Mk 2 - with huge success - and in 1959 da Silva Ramos triumphed in a 3.4, commencing a five-year run of victories for Jaguar. In fact, 1959 was to be the 3.4 saloon's greatest year in competition. Apart from the *Tour Auto* victory and domination of British touring car racing, Donald and Erle Morley won the Tulip Rally, and 3.4s secured the Team Prize in the Monte Carlo Rally.

Driving the D-type Jaguar

The D-type Jaguar was different in many ways from its contemporaries. John Bolster was aware of it when he tried Duncan Hamilton's OKV 1 in February 1955, commenting on the "indefinable feeling of quality that this machine imparts. I am in the lucky position to sample many successful competition cars. Although such vehicles always show high performance, it is frequently accompanied by roughness and intractability, plus some odd rattles. The Jaguar, on the other hand, gives that same air of breeding as the XK coupé possesses. It is, indeed, a new conception in sports racing cars."

Certainly, the immediate impression on driving a D-type for the first time is an overwhelming sense of solidity and quality. You almost have only to sit in a D-type to know at once why it won Le Mans so many times. This feeling of security and real comfort is far from accidental: it was part of the design brief that the driver should remain fresh and untired.

Bob Berry, who raced the car in the 1950s, wrote about this aspect of the D-type:"From my own experience I can vouch for the fact that at speeds in excess of 170 mph it was possible to sit in the cockpit, relaxed and in relative silence in an envelope of near-still air, steering the car with no more pressure than finger and thumb. Especially in the dark the effect was both uncanny and deceptive, the speed effect coming as a real shock as, on the straight, one rushed past cars of nominally similar performance."

Other sports-racing cars of the period may (or in some cases may not!) handle better than the D-type but most crash and vibrate and generally give the impression they are trying to shake themselves, and you, to bits. The D-type's rigid, semi-monocoque construction provides a wonderful feeling of being in one piece, of

tremendous strength and solidity. It is no illusion: the D-type protected its driver well in an accident and during the entire works racing programme no driver was killed or badly injured.

Performance even today is impressive, with a production D-type able to reach 60 mph in about 5.5 seconds and 100 mph in around 13 seconds. The XK engine is equally impressive when called upon to trickle the car along at 1,500 rpm in top. There are few Le Mans winners that will allow you to do that!

When it comes to handling, the more conservative side of the D-type's character emerges. There is quite strong understeer, but most drivers of the period would counter this by flicking the car into a drift on the

apex of a corner. This technique works well on smooth surfaced tracks, but on bumpy surfaces the live rear axle can hop and skitter, making the car a handful. Said Paul Frere of driving the D-type on the Nürburgring: "In places our speed was limited not so much by the convolutions of the circuit as our desire to keep the car in one piece. Along the whole stretch from Breitscheid to the Karrusel the back wheels were more in the air than on the ground, and with a full tank the suspension was bottoming frequently".

This simply brings us back to the fact that the D-type was designed for Le Mans. Jaguar tried the car with de Dion and even full independent rear suspension in the mid-1950s but at Le Mans there would have been little benefit to set against the risk of failure from a more complex suspension. And as the car won there twice more, who can argue with that?

D-type 2.4/3.4 saloons

Technical specifications

YEARS CURRENT

1954 - 1956	(D-type)
1955 - 1959	(2.4 litre saloon)
1957 - 1959	(3.4 litre saloon)

SPECIFICATION (production D-type)

Engine capacity	3,442cc
Power	250 @ 5,750 rpm
Length	12ft 10ins
Width	5ft 5.5ins
Weight:	1,904 lbs (17 cwt)
Wheelbase	7ft 6ins
Max. speed	162 mph
0-60 mph	4.7 secs
Mpg	9-14

Works D-types, with 'wide angle' cylinder head, produced up to 305 bhp and could achieve over 190 mph at Le Mans

SPECIFICATION (2.4/3.4 litre saloons)

Engine capacity	2,483cc/3,442cc
Power	112 bhp @ 5,750 rpm/210 bhp @ 5,500 rpm
Length	15ft 0.75ins
Width	5ft 6.75ins
Weight	3,024 lbs (27cwt)
Wheelbase	4ft 8.5ins
Max. speed	101 mph/120 mph
0-60 mph	14.6 secs/9.5 secs
Mpg	16-19/15-21

(manual/overdrive transmissions)

Competition results

COMPETITION RESULTS
(all D-type except where stated)

1954
Le Mans 24-Hour race, June, A.P.R. Rolt/J.D. Hamilton, 2nd
Rheims 12-Hour race, July, P.N. Whitehead/K. Wharton, 1st, A.P.R. Rolt/J. D. Hamilton, 2nd

1955
Sebring 12-Hour race, March, J.M. Hawthorn/P. Walters, 1st
International Trophy Meeting Silverstone, April, sports car race, A.P.R. Rolt, 3rd
Ulster Trophy Race, Dundrod, May, J.D. Titterington, 1st
Le Mans 24-Hour race, June, J.M. Hawthorn/I.L. Bueb, 1st, J. Claes/J. Swaters, 3rd
Goodwood 9-Hours race, August, J.D. Titterington/N. Sanderson, 2nd
Watkins Glen GP, Seneca Cup, September, S. Johnston, 1st

1956
RAC Rally, W. Bleakley, 1st in class, 2.4 litre (first 'compact' competition success)
Daily Express meeting, Silverstone, May, sports car race, R.E. Berry, 3rd; Production touring car race, 2nd, J.D. Hamilton, 2.4 litre
Spa production car race, Paul Frere, 1st, 2.4 litre (first 'compact' race win)
Rheims 12-Hour race, July, J.D. Hamilton/I.L. Bueb, 1st, J.M. Hawthorn/P. Frere, 2nd, J.D. Titterington, 3rd
Le Mans 24 hour race, July, R. Flockhart/N. Sanderson, 1st

1957
Sebring 12-Hour race, March, J.M. Hawthorn/I.L. Bueb, 3rd
Le Mans 24 Hour race, June, R. Flockhart/I.L Bueb, 1st, N Sanderson/J Lawrence, 2nd, J. Lucas/J-P Boisson, 3rd, P Frere/J. Rouselle, 4th, J.D. Hamilton/M.Gregory, 6th
Daily Express meeting, Silverstone, production car race, JD Hamilton, 1st, (3.4 litre)

1958
Daily Express meeting, Silverstone, May, production car race, J.M. Hawthorn, 1st, (3.4 litre)
Goodwood Whit-Monday meeting, production car race, J.D. Hamilton, 1st, T.E.B. Sopwith, 2nd, Sir G. Baillie, 3rd, (3.4 litre)
Brands Hatch production car race, June, T.E.B. Sopwith, 1st, (3.4 litre)
BRSCC Crystal palace meeting, June, production car race, T.E.B. Sopwith, 1st, Sir G. Baillie, 2nd, D.J. Uren, 3rd, (3.4 litre)
Snetterton, July, production car race, T.E.B. Sopwith, 1st over 3,000cc class, (3.4 litre)
Brands hatch August Bank Holiday, saloon car race, T.E.B. Sopwith, 1st over 2,700cc class, (3.4 litre)
International Brands Hatch meeting, saloon cars, T.E.B. Sopwith, 1st over 2,700cc class, (3.4 litre)
Tour de France, September, Sir G. Baillie/P. Jopp, 3rd touring category, (3.4 litre)
Snetterton One Hour saloon car race, T.E.B. Sopwith, 1st, (3.4 litre)

1959
Brands Hatch International meeting, August, touring car race, J. Sears, 1st, (3.4 litre)
Oulton Park International Gold Cup meeting, closed car race, September, R. Salvadori, 1st, (3.4 litre)

1960
Monte Carlo Rally, January, Team Prize, R. Parkes/Howarth/Senior, (3.4 litre)
Goodwood Easter Monday, saloon car race, I. Bueb, 1st, R, Salvadori, 2nd, Sir G, Baillie, 3rd, (3.4 litre)
Aintree International meeting, saloon car race, I. Bueb, 1st, R, Salvadori, 2nd Sir G, Baillie, 3rd, (3.4 litre)
Snetterton International meeting, April, saloon car race, I. Bueb, 1st, R, Salvadori, 2nd Sir G, Baillie, 3rd, (3.4 litre)
Tulip Rally, general classification, Morely/E. Morely, 1st, (3.4 litre)
Goodwood Whitsun meeting, GT and touring car race, Sir G. Baillie, 2nd (and first saloon) (3.4 litre)
Vanwall Trophy meeting, Snetterton, August, saloon and GT race, Sir G. Baillie, 1st equal, (3.4 litre)
Brands Hatch International meeting, August, touring car race, J. Sears, 1st, (3.4 litre)
Oulton Park International Gold Cup meeting, closed car race, September, R. Salvadori, 1st, (3.4 litre)
BRSCC Silverstone meeting, touring car race, A. Powell, 1st, (3.4 litre)
Brands Hatch International meeting, touring car race, J. Sears, 1st (3.8 litre), W. Aston, 2nd A. Powell, 3rd, (3.4 litre)

1961
BRSCC meeting, Snetterton, saloon car race, 1st, Peter Sargent, (3.4 litre)
Nurburgring 6-Hour race, 1st, P. Lindner/P. Nöcker, (3.4 litre)

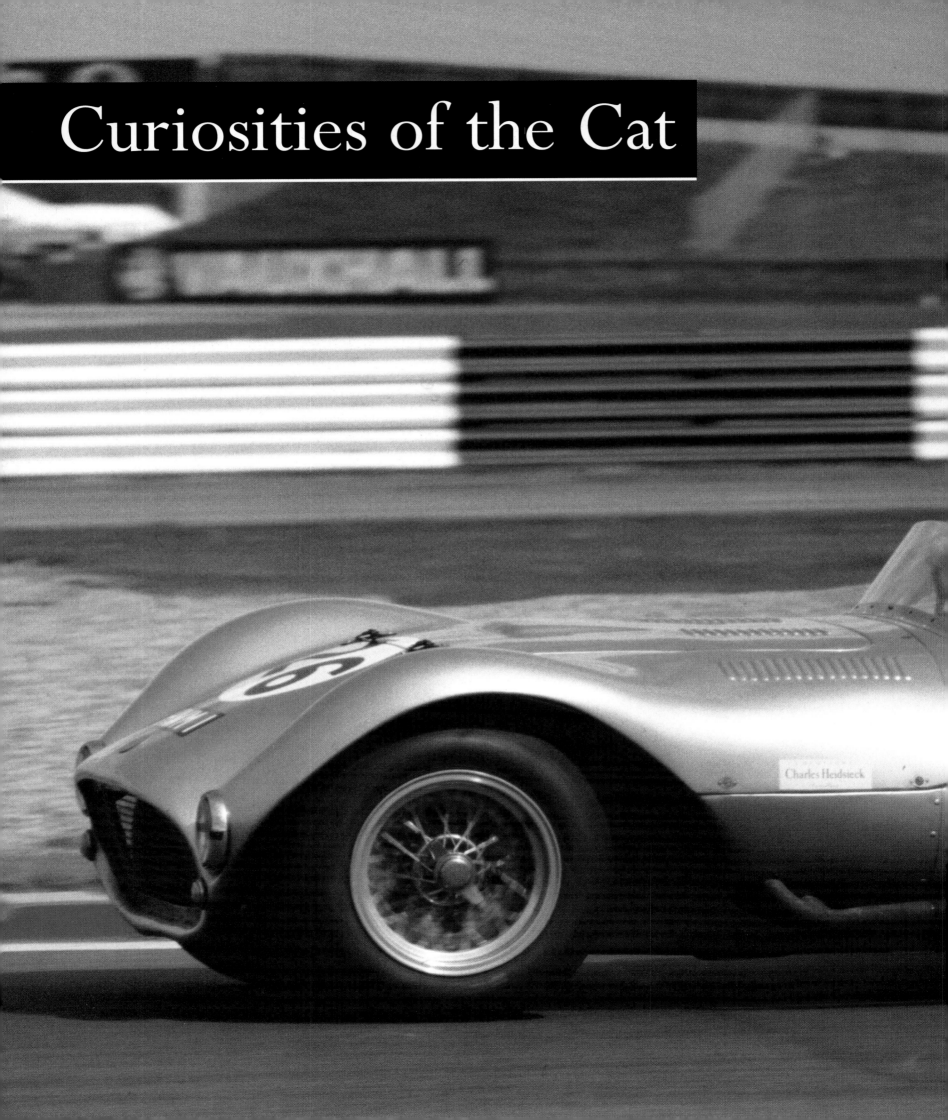

Curiosities of the Cat

The XK engine was a fantastic asset for Jaguar in the 1950s - the outstanding British production engine of its time, it was quickly pounced upon by those who wanted to utilise its power and reliability on the race track.

"THE JAGUAR ENGINE IS REALLY ONE OF THE MARVELS OF THE CENTURY."

John Bolster, Autosport

While there were some notable early 'specials' which used the original 2.5 and 3.5-litre Standard-based pushrod engines, it was the twin overhead camshaft XK power unit which proved the most tempting to private constructors.

The logic was easy to see: the XK engine was strong, reliable and, compared with other performance engines of the period (Ferrari, Maserati, Mercedes-Benz and Aston Martin), it was also obtainable and affordable. The 1950s saw four professional sports racing car constructors go down the XK route, all UK-based: HWM, Cooper, Tojeiro and Lister. Easily the most prolific of these was Lister but all usefully boosted the Jaguar XK engine's competition record.

The HWM-Jaguar

The first HWM-Jaguar was constructed by motor dealer and part-time racing driver Oscar Moore, part of whose business in the North London district of Finchley consisted of hiring out XK 120s. For the 1952 season Moore fitted his Alta-engined HWM race car with a 3.4 XK unit. The cycle-winged XMC 34, despite its somewhat antiquated appearance, finished sixth in the Dundrod TT that year; this relative success encouraged George Abecassis and his partner John Heath (owners of Hersham & Walton Motors in Surrey - and existing Formula 2 constructors) to build their own 'official' HWM-Jaguar. It was registered HWM 1 but was not their first Jaguar-powered car, as in 1951 they had installed a 3.4 XK engine in a 1949 Grand Prix Alta frame for hill-climber Phil Scragg.

HWM 1 appeared during the 1953 season, based on a prototype HWM single-seater twin-tube chassis with leaf-sprung independent front suspension. A potent ex-works C-type

Below: **The first HWM-Jaguar, the 'dual purpose' (sports/racing car) re-engined by Oscar Moore. This is the car as it first appeared, photographed at Silverstone in 1952.**

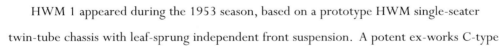

engine came from Jaguar via Lofty England. With a wheelbase of 7 ft 8 ins the HWM was more compact than a C-type Jaguar, and lighter too.

Ambitiously, the new car was entered in the Rheims 12-Hours race held in July 1953, driven by Abecassis and Paul Frere (who had previously driven F2 HWMs with success). Amongst C-types, Ferraris and Talbots, HWM 1 had gained third position when it was sidelined by rear suspension trouble.

Above: Oscar Moore and the HWM-Alta-Jaguar in later (faired-wing) form, winning a scratch race at Goodwood in July 1953; chasing him is Michael Head's XK 120. By then Moore had become the first in the UK to run a 3.8-litre Jaguar engine, boring out the 3.4 to a quoted 3,841cc.

The 1953 season produced several promising performances, including a new lap record set at Snetterton - beating Oscar Moore in the process. Then George Abecassis was holding onto third place in the Goodwood 9-Hour race when, unusually, the XK engine broke its timing chain. By this time HWM were pioneering triple Weber carburettors on the engine and John Heath loaned a set to a delighted Harry Weslake. The Jaguar works C-types were consequently fitted with Webers for Le Mans 1953: William Lyons was most grateful and in return gave HW Motors a Jaguar franchise! Two other similar cars were built for customers - VPA 9 for the Australian Tony Gaze and, later, XPA 748 for Geoff Mansell.

In 1955 the team forsook Formula 2 for sports-car racing and a second-edition HWM-Jaguar arrived. Based on a wider, purpose-designed tubular frame rather than a Formula 2 cast-off, this had forged wishbone front suspension and a coil sprung de Dion rear axle. Two cars were made, Lance Macklin and Bill Smith achieving an excellent fourth in the Goodwood 9-Hours with XPE 2. Abecassis also won twice at Goodwood and at the Castle Combe International meeting that October.

Below: John Heath in the original 'works' HWM-Jaguar, here keeping ahead of another Jaguar-powered device, the Cooper-Jaguar of Cyril Wick. The venue is Goodwood.

The second new-style car was completed in October 1955 and adopted the HWM 1 registration (the original car went to Ray Fielding, who used it for hill-climbing). Now using a D-type cylinder head, the new HWMs were quicker still, but sadly John Heath was killed racing the latest HWM 1 in the 1955 *Mille Miglia*.

George Abecassis was naturally dispirited, although he continued to drive XPE 2 with considerable success. However, 1956 saw only spasmodic appearances of the HWM team and following the September Goodwood meeting both cars were sold.

"IT CAN BE DRIVEN WITH ONE HAND AT NEARLY 150 MPH AND CURVES MAY BE ENTERED AT THIS SORT OF VELOCITY WITHOUT ANY DRAMA."

John Bolster, track testing the first HWM-Jaguar

A final competition HWM-Jaguar was built, this one for Phil Scragg; it used the later-type frame but was equipped with huge, 13-inch diameter Alfin drums within 6.5-inch wide offset Borrani wire wheels. Carrying only a very light, cycle-winged body and a full dry-sump D-type engine (the only HWM so equipped from new), SPC 982 had a frightening power-to-weight ratio, but one which Scragg used to great effect at events such as Prescott and Shelsley - hills on which he was rarely beaten in his class.

The Cooper-Jaguar

Before their involvement with the XK engine, John Cooper and his father Charles had already carved out a fine reputation building 500cc race cars, one patron being a little-known teenager by

Left: Abecassis in the revised HWM-Jaguar which appeared first at the May 1955 BRDC meeting; here, 'Abby' is on the way to second place at Goodwood Easter Monday 1956, behind Moss's DB3S.

Above: Debut race for the new T33 Cooper-Jaguar - Peter Whitehead cautiously splashed round Silverstone to ninth place at the 1954 International Trophy meeting, the car yet to be painted. Note the low 'shark nose' with splitter, behind which was an almost horizontal radiator; this was all rather ahead of its time and a more conventional arrangement soon arrived.

the name of S. Moss. In 1949 a two-seater sports car was also in production and in 1952, joining the almost invincible Formula 3 JAP-engined single seaters, were the 2-litre Bristol-powered racing cars, one of which was driven to spectacular effect by Jaguar works-driver-to-be Mike Hawthorn.

The Cooper-Jaguar came about when Peter Whitehead, co-winner of the 1951 Le Mans with Tony Rolt in the C-type, asked the Cooper Car Co. to construct a 'C-type eater' for 1954. The result was perhaps the most sophisticated of any Jaguar-powered sports-racing car. Built around a light frame of mainly curved steel tubing, the Cooper-Jaguar incorporated independent suspension all round and a C-type specification XK engine. Notably, the car even had the expensive power-assisted disc brakes used on the later works C-types - estimated at a quarter of the car's entire build cost!

Peter Whitehead first ran the Cooper-Jaguar at the *Daily Express* International Trophy meeting at Silverstone in May 1954, coming ninth in the wet, but he finished almost a lap ahead of Mike Head's C-type to win at the International Meeting at Snetterton on 24th August. After winning the final race at the Curragh circuit in Eire, Whitehead sold UBH 292 to hill climb/race enthusiast Cyril Wick - who set best sports car time at Brighton Speed Trials in September 1955, covering the standing kilometre in 25.30 seconds. Bought subsequently by Dick Steed, the car was bravely entered for the 1957 *Mille Miglia*, from which it retired.

Two other 'Mk 1' T33s were built for the 1955 season, but already a 'Mk 2' Cooper-Jaguar had been evolved, again commissioned by Peter Whitehead. A full dry-sump D-type engine and gearbox now featured, carried in an improved and simplified tubular frame.

Whitehead, with his half-brother Graham, ran the Mk 2 Cooper in the Le Mans 24-Hour

Below: Now painted and with a more orthodox air intake, the Cooper-Jaguar was driven by Peter Whitehead at Aintree in October 1954, but it was Archie Scott Brown who ran away with the sports car race in the Lister-Bristol. Note the 'Mk 1' Cooper's outboard driving position.

race in 1955, but they retired after three hours with low oil pressure. Following a modestly successful European season, Peter Whitehead tried his luck in New Zealand and Australia early in 1956. Reg Parnell took the Cooper to fifth place in the New Zealand Grand Prix at Ardmore in

January 1956, before the car was sold to Stan Jones (father of future F1 driver Alan) and taken to Australia. There, in various hands, the car enjoyed the longest competitive career of any Cooper-Jaguar, continuing to compete nationally until around 1963, including a third place for Ron Phillips in the 22nd Australian Grand Prix meeting TT race.

Cooper made two more 'T38s', a 22-year-old Tommy Sopwith, son of the aero magnate, taking delivery in 1956 of YPK 400: the car was painted dark blue and run by Tommy's team *Equipe Endeavour* (named after his father's racing yacht). Later owners continued this Cooper-Jaguar's competitive career well into 1958, making YPK 400 the most active of its type in Europe.

The final Cooper-Jaguar went to Colonel Michael Head; registered HOT 95, it finished its debut race at the March 1956 Goodwood meeting in second behind George Abecassis in the second-generation HWM-Jaguar XPE 2. Head won a ten-lap scratch race there in April, beating one of the slower Aston Martin DB3Ss, and continued to be competitive well into 1957.

The car then went to David Chamberlain, a young, 23-year-old enthusiast who bought it on hire purchase! "I swopped my XK 140 as part of the deal and ended up with the Cooper and a Beetle to use on the road." He raced the car at most of the UK circuits and found it safe and reliable. "The only near calamity was when a stub axle broke - but I found a draughtsman at

Below: The 'Mk 2' Cooper-Jaguar at Le Mans, 1955. After circulating for some three hours around 14th place, the Jaguar engine lost its oil pressure (and a great deal of its oil) and the car retired in the fourth hour.

Coopers who said, 'I'll look up the drawings - you're lucky, it's from a Wolseley 1500!'"

While the car was in the hands of Col. Head, John Bolster tested HOT 95 for *Autosport*. He was most impressed, especially as the car had been prepared for

Above: David Chamberlain obtained the ex-Michael Head Type 38 Cooper-Jaguar and had considerable fun with it. Still in Head's traditional colour of white, the Cooper is seen here at Goodwood, March 1959.

long-distance touring as well as racing (the owner was the military attaché at the British Embassy in Stockholm). Wrote Bolster: "The machine is not as light as some of its competitors, but the effective road holding, coupled with the immense power of the servo-assisted Dunlop disc brakes, renders it a highly effective racing instrument."

On the track the Cooper-Jaguar might have achieved even more had it been given the concentrated development that, for instance, the Lister-Jaguar enjoyed. And, unlike the Cambridge machine, no truly top-flight driver ever took the wheel, just wealthy and enthusiastic amateurs. However, the Cooper-Jaguar remains one of the most technically interesting of the 'independent' Jaguar sports racing cars.

The Tojeiro-Jaguar

Of all the 1950s Jaguar-powered sports-racers, John Tojeiro's cars were perhaps the most elegant. Four were built, evoking interest from Britain's leading sports car team of the period, *Ecurie Ecosse*, and enjoying the services of some of the best drivers, though they acquired something of a reputation - undoubtedly deserved - for being difficult to handle.

John Bolster, in his test of the car for *Autosport*, described its basics well: "Take a D-type Jaguar power unit and insinuate it into a very small but beautifully made multi-tubular chassis. Give it independent suspension by wishbones in front, and fit a de Dion axle at the rear, on parallel trailing arms and a bronze slider block. Cover it with an aerodynamic shell, and keep the weight down to 15 cwt including water, oil and four gallons of petrol, and you will have one of the most potent sports cars that has yet been built!"

Like the Lister-Jaguars to come, the Tojeiro-Jaguars evolved from a 2-litre Bristol-engined design. The Tojeiro-Bristol had been built by John Tojeiro in 1953 for driver Cliff Davis. Highly successful, LOY 500 so impressed AC Cars that they purchased the rights to the twin-tube frame design (and 'borrowed' the body shape too). From this emerged the AC Ace sports car which in turn gave birth to the mighty V8-engined Cobra of the 1960s.

The first Tojeiro-Jaguar arrived at the behest of XK 120 driver John Ogier. Tojeiro adapted a new spaceframe he had designed for a Bristol engine, producing a modest-size car with a wheelbase of just 7 ft 3 ins compared with a D-type's already short 7 ft 6.5 ins. Approximately 200 bhp came from a 3.4 engine in roughly C-type tune, making the very light (15.5 cwt) car highly accelerative.

John Ogier first raced 7 GNO in May 1956 but results came only when Dick Protheroe was offered the wheel. At the British Grand Prix meeting at Silverstone in July he kept ahead of Duncan Hamilton's D-type OKV 1 to take fourth place in the sports car race, and later that year he won at Crystal Palace, beating an Aston Martin DB3S. The car's straight-line speed was confirmed when Ogier achieved best time of day at the Ramsgate Speed Trials, then winning the unlimited sports car class at Brighton where he covered the standing kilometre in 25.36 seconds.

John Bolster tested the Tojeiro-Jaguar for *Autosport* in 1956 and clearly considered the Jaguar engine to be the best part of the car: "smoother, and more flexible, than the engines of many luxury limousines even when it is in race-winning tune". He proved the point by collecting the car from the Steering Wheel Club in central London and "glided into the traffic stream with only a low rumble from the exhaust to indicate its latent power".

Bolster recorded some stupendous acceleration times (standing quarter mile 13.6 secs,

Below: **John Ogier in the original Tojeiro-Jaguar, the car looking not unlike a slightly smoothed-out D-type. Ogier retired in this September 1956 race at Goodwood.**

60 mph coming up in 5.4 secs and 100 mph in 12.6 secs) but found the handling less satisfactory - "the cornering power is not up to the rest of the performance," he wrote, a typical British understatement which no doubt amused the various drivers whom the 'Toj' tried to frighten to death during its career! The problem seemed to be instant oversteer produced by the rear suspension locking up. Bolster also felt that the disc brakes could do with power assistance.

A longer, wider car emerged for 1957, the flowing body looking even more like a flattened D-type at the front. Jack Brabham drove it to fourth place at Crystal Palace and at Aintree. Graham Hill took a second place at Brands Hatch and also raced at Silverstone at the International Trophy meeting in September, although he retired after a lurid, high-speed spin. Then the car was comprehensively crashed by John Ogier at a local hill climb (the original Tojeiro had meantime been sold to Frank Cantwell in New Zealand, where it was raced for many years until returning to the UK in the 1980s).

Ecurie Ecosse, looking for a successor to their ageing D-types, arranged to borrow a new Tojeiro-Jaguar to run alongside their Lister-Jaguar. At the July 1958 British GP meeting Ivor Bueb took a good fourth place in the 'Toj' (Moss won in the works Lister) but in the Nürburgring 1000 km on 7th June Ron Flockhart went off the road avoiding a back-marker.

For Le Mans 1959 *Ecurie Ecosse* ordered a new Tojeiro-Jaguar. This, the final Jaguar-engined car from Tojeiro Automotive Developments, ran as high as fourth before the Wilkie Wilkinson-built 3.0-litre engine lost its water and seized up.

Later in 1959 the car was driven by a young Jim Clark, temporarily deserting his usual Border Reivers team. Sharing it with Masten Gregory in the Goodwood TT, Clark found the Tojeiro less impressive than his usual Lister-Jaguar: "it didn't handle nearly as well as our own Reivers car (HCH 736). Somehow it seemed to get up on tip-toe going through Madgwick and it was decidedly light to handle in places. It was quite twitchy through the chicane, too, and both

Above: The very beautiful 7 GNO in its final guise, leaping off the line at Goodwood. Ron Flockhart won this race at the Whitsun meeting with the *Ecurie Ecosse*-liveried Tojeiro. The de Dion axle was now located by a Watts linkage which did tame the beast somewhat; but it remained a tricky car to handle.

Masten and I were having a great time sliding it around the chicane on opposite lock." They held seventh place until Masten hugely stuffed the car at Woodcote, hitting the bank with such force that the Tojeiro nearly folded in half. Masten escaped, apparently, by almost getting out of the car before it hit so he was thrown clear. He escaped with a broken shoulder.

Ecurie Ecosse's association with Tojeiro then ended, the 1958 car being returned. Tony Maggs drove the car and took it to his native South Africa at the end of the year, where it performed well in the Springbok series.

On its return to the UK in 1960 the Tojeiro passed to John Coundley who was providing cars for the film *The Green Helmet*. It was rigged up to carry cameras for on-board photography and even survived a simulated crash. By 1961 it had changed hands again, and Vivienne Lewis won the Ladies Class at the Brighton Speed Trials. However, attempting the same thing two years later, she crashed fatally.

Below: 7 GNO as it is today, owned by Dick Skipworth who has a number of ex-*Ecurie Ecosse* cars. This car has largely been mastered by Barry Williams who today can sometimes beat even the quicker Lister-Jaguars - unfortunately, some 40 years too late!

This was not, perhaps, a representative end to the Tojeiro-Jaguar's active career, because although the 'Toj' may have frightened its drivers at times, it generally did not kill them. In skilled hands it could be competitive against much more expensive machinery, a remarkable achievement by the tiny Tojeiro Automotive Developments concern.

The Lister-Jaguar

When Jaguar withdrew from racing after 1956, it was primarily the green and yellow Lister-Jaguar cars from Cambridge which kept a strong Jaguar presence in top-level sports car racing. Brian Lister had been club-racing for some years (including with Cooper and Tojeiro chassis) before deciding to build his own car in 1953 - partly to demonstrate what the family light-engineering firm could do, and partly for his love of the sport. The first car was MG-engined and built, said Brian, "as virtually an experiment to see whether my ideas on chassis and chassis design generally were about right".

Below: The great team - Archie Scott Brown and Brian Lister. Together they took on the world's best on the British sports car scene.

Brian's ideas certainly were 'right'. The MG car was followed by a Lister-Bristol which became almost invincible in the 2-litre sports car class during 1955, driven by a short, mustachioed character named Archie Scott Brown - whose unformed right hand, a birth defect, originally caused the RAC to ban him from racing.

"I THINK WE WERE THE HAPPIEST TEAM IN MOTOR RACING."

Brian Lister

A Maserati A6CGS engine was used less successfully in 1956 before Lister moved up to Jaguar in 1957 - partly persuaded by Shell who were keen to sponsor another big-capacity sports car now that the D-type had become obsolete.

Built at the Lister works, the new car was simple but strong, the frame consisting of two cross-braced 3-inch diameter tubes. The design allowed the driver to sit between and not above the perimeter tubes and this, together with a low scuttle, gave the Lister-Jaguar the minimum of height and frontal area. Wishbone front suspension featured, and power came from a full dry-sump D-type engine - a coil-sprung de Dion axle at the rear transferred the horses to the wheels, helping to make the Lister-Jaguar a much quicker car than the D-type away from the smoothness of Le Mans.

As with the HWM, however, the first Jaguar-engined Lister had come from a private owner, in this case Norman Hillwood, who asked Listers to install a C-type specification engine into his Lister-Bristol.

Archie Scott Brown and the works Lister-Jaguar quickly became the combination to beat in UK sports car racing. The establishment was first shaken in April 1957 when Archie vanquished the works Aston Martins to win the British Empire Trophy race. In fact only once that year did an Aston finish ahead of the green and yellow Lister, Roy Salvadori winning at Silverstone in the 3.7-litre DBR/1. By the end of the season - Lister's most successful ever - 12 of the 14 races entered had been won. Testing MVE 303 for *Autosport*, John Bolster found the car could reach 60 mph in 4.6 secs and 100 mph in 11.2 secs and was extremely complimentary about its handling.

For 1958 Brian Lister produced an upgraded car and a 'productionised' body - this because orders were now coming in. List price was £2,750 basic with the 'D' engine, though most customers bought the car minus engine for £1,750. Major teams taking delivery included *Ecurie Ecosse*, *Equipe Nationale Belge*, and Briggs Cunningham in the United States. All found success with their cars, Cunningham driver Walt Hansgen winning the Sports Car Club of America championship in both 1958 and 1959 with Lister-Jaguars (Chevrolet engines were tried both in the US and UK but without obtaining the results of the Jaguar-engined cars).

Two works Lister-Jaguars were campaigned in 1958, both carrying the new 'knobbly' bodywork and powered by 3.8-litre D-type engines - supplied 'on loan' by a very pleased Jaguar. Local man Don Moore took care of these engines for Lister. "Don was, perhaps, in those days the most underrated engine specialist in the country," says Brian Lister - who also remembers Don as being about the only specialist who actually undercharged for his work!

Archie was now finding that his main rivals included not only Aston Martin but those 'customer' Lister-Jaguars too. The bespectacled American driver Masten Gregory in the *Ecurie Ecosse* car finally beat Archie during a scorchingly fast International Trophy meeting at Silverstone early in May. The rivalry continued at Spa later the same month. Lapping at colossal speeds, Archie was caught out by one of Spa's notoriously localised showers with tragic results.

Above: **A true moment of glory in that fantastic 'Lister' year of 1957: Archie clasps the British Empire Trophy after his win while a modestly pleased-looking Brian Lister looks on.**

Opposite: **Archie in the original Lister-Jaguar, equipped with Appendix C full-width screen, wiper and headlights required for the sports car race at the Aintree British Grand Prix meeting. But just look at those wheel tracks and the angle of the car: a graphic depiction of Archie power-sliding in the wet! He beat the Astons, of course...**

Above: **The new 1958 Lister-Jaguar, subsequently known as the 'knobbly' Lister because of its more pronounced haunches. YOB 575 began life as a new chassis kit bought by Peter Mould in 1959 for £436; he (and sometimes Gerry Ashmore, as seen here) notched up 32 awards in 39 starts up to the end of 1960.**

He crashed, the car caught fire, and he died in hospital shortly afterwards.

Brian Lister almost gave up motor racing right then. Archie had been a close friend, not just a driver. "We had a marvellous team - because Archie was a very great character... no temperament or anything like that; I think we were one of the happiest teams in motor racing ever." But there were outstanding contracts and also Lister was now one of Britain's leading hopes in sports car racing, so he soldiered on.

At Le Mans in 1958 *Ecurie Nationale Belge* and the privateers Bruce Halford and Brian Naylor entered Lister-Jaguars. Both cars had to run with the 3-litre D-type engine; but while the Belgian entry outlasted the *Ecurie Ecosse* D-types, it soon expired, though Halford and Naylor struggled on to an eventual 15th place.

The works Listers were out in force for the British Grand Prix meeting at Silverstone shortly afterwards. Determined to beat *Ecurie Ecosse*, Brian Lister (thanks to Shell) retained the best drivers: Stirling Moss backed up by Walt Hansgen. Moss did not fail, though as Masten Gregory had crashed in practice, his win was easier than it might have been.

An ostensibly more aerodynamic body designed by Frank Costin appeared for 1959 but the bulbous new shape proved less effective than expected, although Scott Brown replacement Ivor Bueb did manage the odd win. In fact the works cars were sometimes hard-pressed to equal the older versions, including HCH 736 in the hands of a young Scottish driver named Jim Clark.

Above: **The Lister-Jaguar for 1959 was given a new 'aerodynamic' body by Frank Costin but all the drivers thought the the revised car was a bit of a barge. Some were Chevrolet V8-engined.**

Clark had won three races in a row on his first appearance in HCH 736, at Mallory Park in 1959. He recalled the car fondly in his autobiography: "The Lister taught me a great deal about racing, and I had fun with that car. It was a beast of a thing, mind you, but it was more fun than any except maybe the Aston Martins I drove later."

Endurance events failed to produce results, even though Sebring, the Nürburgring 1000 km and Le Mans were all entered. None of the four Listers appearing at Le Mans finished, though Brian Lister maintained that they came very close to winning the race - the Bueb/Halford car was in fourth place when its engine failed. But competition from such as the new 2.5-litre Cooper Monaco was increasing inexorably and in August 1959, after Ivor Bueb had been killed too (in another make), Brian Lister called a halt. The cars were sold, including an unfinished prototype.

"I DON'T KNOW WHETHER MANY PEOPLE REALISE HOW NEAR WE WERE TO WINNING THAT PARTICULAR RACE"

Brian Lister, on the 1959 Le Mans

This car ran in coupé form in the 1963 24-Hour race, driven by Peter Sargent and Peter Lumsden; but it handled poorly and the clutch failed after only three hours. The same car also became the last Lister-Jaguar to compete in an international event, when John Coundley and Jack Fairman drove it at the Nürburgring in 1964. Rear suspension trouble ended their involvement.

At club level, however, various drivers - notably John Coundley, John Bekeart, Peter Mould and Gordon Lee - continued to keep the Lister-Jaguar competitive in lesser events well into the 1960s, while Phil Scragg dominated his class in hill climbs around this period.

The Lister-Jaguar was certainly one of Britain's quickest sports-racing cars, and Brian Lister's contribution to the Jaguar competition story is considerable. Nor did it end there: the name Lister returned to sports car racing some 30 years later...

Left: **Lister swan-song: Peter Lumsden and Peter Sargent ran the final, space-frame, Lister-Jaguar in coupé form in the 1963 Le Mans, where it retired; it also ran in the 1964 Nürburgring 1000 km but failed to achieve success.**

Jaguar at Le Mans 1950-1997

A COMPLETE LISTING OF ALL THE **J**AGUARS THAT HAVE RUN AT **L**E **M**ANS, FROM 1950 TO 1997

YEAR	TYPE/CAPACITY	RACE No	CHASSIS No.	DRIVERS	POSITION
1950	XK 120/3442cc	15	660041	Clark/Haines	12th
	XK 120/3442cc	16	660042	Whitehead/Marshall	15th
	XK 120/3442cc	17	660040	Johnson/Hadley	Retired 23rd hour
1951	C-type/3442cc	20	XKC003	Whitehead/Walker	1st
	C-type/3442cc	22	XKC002	Moss/Fairman	Retired
	C-type/3442cc	23	XKC001	Johnson/Biondetti	Retired
	XK 120/3442cc	21	660449	Lawrie/Waller	11th
1952	C-type/3442cc	18	XKC001	Rolt/Hamilton	Retired 4th hour
	C-type/3442cc	17	XKC011	Moss/Walker	Retired 3rd hour
	C-type/3442cc	9	XKC002	Whitehead/Stewart	Retired 1st hour
1953	C-type/3442cc	18	XKC051	Rolt/Hamilton	1st
	C-type/3442cc	7	XKC053	Moss/Walker	2nd
	C-type/3442cc	19	XKC052	Whitehead/Stewart	4th
	C-type/3442cc	20	XKC047	Laurent/de Tornaco	9th
1954	D-type/3442cc	14	XKC402	Rolt/Hamilton	2nd
	D-type/3442cc	5	XKC404	Whitehead/Wharton	Retired 13th hour
	D-type/3442cc	12	XKC403	Moss/Walker	Retired 12th hour
	C-type/3442cc	16	XKC012	Laurent/Swaters	4th
1955	D-type/3442cc	6	XKD505	Hawthorn/Bueb	1st
	D-type/3442cc	10	XKD503	Claes/Swaters	3rd
	D-type/3442cc	7	XKD506	Rolt/Hamilton	Retired 16th hour
	D-type/3442cc	8	XKD508	Beauman/Dewis	Retired 11th hour
	D-type/3442cc	9	XKD507	Spear/Walters	Retired 7th hour
	Cooper-Jaguar	11	CJ/1/55	P&G Whitehead	Retired 5th hour
1956	D-type/3442cc	4	XKD501	Flockhart/Sanderson	1st
	D-type/3442cc	5	XKD573	Swaters/Rouselle	4th
	D-type/3442cc	1	XKD605	Hawthorn/Bueb	6th
	D-type/3442cc	2	XKD603	Frere/Titterington	Retired 1st hour
	D-type/3442cc	3	XKD602	Fairman/Wharton	Retired 1st hour
	XK140/3442cc	6	S804231	Bolton/Walshaw	Excluded 21st hour
1957	D-type/3442cc	3	XKD606	Flockhart/Bueb	1st
	D-type/3442cc	15	XKD603	Lawrence/Sanderson	2nd
	D-type/3442cc	17	XKD513	Lucas/Brussin	3rd
	D-type/3442cc	16	XKD573	Frere/Rouselle	4th
	D-type/3442cc	4	XKD601	Hamilton/Gregory	6th
1958	Lister-Jaguar	10	BHL5	Halford/Naylor	15th
	D-type 2987cc	8	XKD601	Hamilton/Bueb	Retired 19th hour
	D-type 2987cc	11	XKD513	Brussin/Guelfi	Retired 7th hour
	Lister-Jaguar	9	BHL105	Rouselle/Dubois	Retired 4th hour
	D-type/2987cc	57	XKD502	Charles/Young	Retired 3rd hour
	D-type/2987cc	6	XKD603	Fairman/Gregory	Retired 2nd hour
	D-type/2987cc	7	XKD606	Sanderson/Lawrence	Retired 2nd hour
1959	Tojeiro-Jaguar	8	4th car	Flockhart/Lawrence	Retired 12th hour
	Lister-Jaguar	1	BHL2/59	Bueb/Halford	Retired 9th hour
	D-type/2996cc	3	XKD603	Ireland/Gregory	Retired 7th hour
	Lister-Jaguar	2	BHL3/59	Hansgen/Blond	Retired 5th hour

Year	Type/Capacity	Race No	Chassis No.	Drivers	Position
1960	D-type/2997cc	5	XKD603	Flockhart/Halford	Retired 14th hour
	E2A/2996cc	6	E2A	Gurney/Hansgen	Retired 10th hour
1962	E-type/3781cc	10	860630	Cunningham/Salvadori	4th
	E-type/3781cc	9	850009	Lumsden/Sargent	5th
	E-type/3781cc	8	860458	Charles/Coundley	Retired 4th hour
1963	E-type/3781cc	15	S850659	Cunningham/Grossman	9th
	E-type/3781cc	16	S850666	Salvadori/Richards	Retired 6th hour
	Lister-Jaguar	17		Lumsden/Sargent	Retired 4th hour
	E-type/3781cc	14	S850664	Hansgen/Pabst	Retired 1st hour
1964	E-type/3781cc	16	S850662	Lindner/Nöcker	Retired 16th hour
	E-type/3781cc	17	S850663	Lumsden/Sargent	Retired 8th hour
1984	XJR-5/6000cc	40	008	BallotLena/Watson/Adamowicz	Retired 15th hour
	XJR-5/6000cc	44	006	Tullius/Redman/Bundy	Retired 20th hour
1985	XJR-5/6000cc	44	008	Tullius/Robinson/Ballot Lena	13th
	XJR-5/6000cc	40	006	Redman/Adams/Haywood	Retired 11th hour
1986	XJR-6/6500cc	52	186	Redman/Haywood/Heyer	Retired 6th hour
1986	XJR-6/6500cc	53	385	Brancetti/Percy/Haywood	Retired 10th hour
	XJR-6/6500cc	51	286	Warwick/Cheever/Schlesser	Retired 17th hour
1987	XJR-8LM/6900cc	4	387	Cheever/Boesel/Lammers	5th
	XJR-8LM/6900cc	5	286	Lammers/Watson/Percy	Retired 11th hour
	XJR-8LM/6900cc	6	186	Brundle/Nielsen	Retired 16th hour
1988	XJR-9LM/7000cc	2	488	Dumfries/Lammers/Wallace	1st
	XJR-9LM/7000cc	22	188	Cogan/Daly/Perkins	4th
	XJR-9LM/7000cc	21	186	Cobb/Jones/Sullivan	16th
	XJR-9LM/7000cc	1	588	Brundle/Nielsen	Retired
	XJR-9LM/7000cc	3	287	Boesel/Pescarolo/Watson	Retired
1989	XJR-9LM/7000cc	1	588	Lammers/Tambay/Gilbert-Scott	4th
	XJR-9LM/7000cc	2	688	Nielsen/Wallace/Cobb	Retired
	XJR-9LM/7000cc	3	288	Jones/Daly/Kline	Retired
	XJR-9LM/7000cc	4	287	A.Ferte/M.Ferte/Salazar	8th
1990	XJR-12LM/7000cc	1	990	Brundle/A.Ferte/D.Leslie	Retired
	XJR-12LM/7000cc	2	290	Lammers/Wallace/Konrad	2nd
	XJR-12LM/7000cc	3	1090	Nielsen/Cobb/Salazar/Brundle	1st
	XJR-12LM	4	190	Jones/Sala/M.Ferte	Retired
1991	XJR-12/7400cc	33	891	Warwick/Nielsen/Wallace	4th
	XJR-12/7400cc	34	991	Fabi/Wollek/Acheson	3rd
	XJR-12/7400cc	35	990	Jones/Boesel/M.Ferte	2nd
	XJR-12/7400cc	36	290	Leslie/Martini/Krosnoff	Retired
1993	XJ220C/3500cc	50		Brabham/Nielsen/Coulthard	15th
	XJ220C/3500cc	51		Hahne/Percy/Leslie	Retired 1st hour
	XJ220C/3500cc	52		Belmondo/Cochrane/Fuchs	Retired 14th hour
1995	XJ220C/3500cc	58	TWR 003	Percy/Jacobelli/Thuner	Retired 126 laps
	XJ220C/3500cc	57	TWR 001	Needell/Piper/Weaver	Retired 135 laps
1996	Lister Storm 6996cc	11	053115	Needell/Lees/Reid	19th/11th GT1
1997	Lister Storm 6996cc	45	053211	Lees/Needell/Fouche	Retired
	Lister Storm 6996cc	46	053214	Bailey/Erdos/Skaife	Retired

The career of the E-type Jaguar in competition was an honourable one - although designed purely for road use, it proved to be one of the few cars able to offer a credible challenge to the mighty GTO Ferrari.

"THE E-TYPE JAGUAR HAS MADE ITS ELECTRIFYING APPEARANCE, AND AT ONE STRIDE BRITAIN TAKES THE LEAD IN THE GRAND TOURING MARKET OF EUROPE." Autosport *magazine, reporting from the Geneva Salon*

Geneva, March 1961 - a spectacular new sports car makes its entrance. The arrival of any new Jaguar is an occasion but the appearance of the E-type in Switzerland was an epochal event in the history of the sports car which reverberates to this day.

Even 40 years or more later, nearly everyone recognises an E-type Jaguar. It is the epitome of the British sports car - and it captured the true spirit of Britain in the 1960s: optimistic, ever more liberated and soon to produce the Beatles and George Best.

The new sports car, together with the big Mk X announced in October 1961, contributed to Jaguar's wonderful model line-up of the early 1960s. Already in production since 1959 was the Mk 2 saloon, the125 mph 3.8-litre engined version of which was, by the time the E-type arrived, already dominating British touring car racing. It would achieve even more than that over the following couple of years.

The E-type also quickly established a formidable reputation in competition. On the British club racing scene it remained almost unbeatable for many years and, in the US, Bob Tullius and Group 44 rounded off the car's successful career in SSCA racing by winning a national championship as late as 1975.

Below: **XKE 101 (usually known as E1A) was the first step towards a D-type replacement. However, the project ended up as the E-type road car. It is shown here while on secret loan to Christopher Jennings, editor of** *The Motor,* **in 1958.**

Nevertheless, the E-type racing story is also about what might have been. In 1961, when the car received a spectacular reception at the Geneva Motor Show, there was still the vestige of a competition department at Browns Lane which, headed by Michael MacDowel, supported private entrants as best it could. But almost five years had passed since the factory had last competed officially and the need for a return to Le Mans to boost sales was decreasing: the Mark 2 saloon was selling like hot cakes, while demand for the new E-type was far outstripping Jaguar's projections. So competition matters had assumed a fairly low priority and this was to be reflected in the company's attempts to make the E-type a race winner. The E-type's design origins certainly lay firmly in

Right: Now in Briggs Cunningham's colours, E2A awaits the start at Le Mans 1960 alongside a Chevrolet Corvette. The car's 3-litre engine produced the magic 100 bhp per litre, the highest specific output of any factory XK engine.

racing, though, as they can be traced back to a 2.5-litre sports-racing prototype built in 1957 - chassis no. XKE 101 but usually known by its body number, E1A (the 'A' stood for aluminium, the material used in its construction). It was built primarily as a successor to the D-type at Le Mans, where the maximum engine capacity was soon to be 3-litres; though smaller, it looked much like the D-type but had the important advance of independent rear suspension.

Yet with resources diverted into re-starting production after the big fire of February 1957 (which destroyed nearly a third of the Browns Lane assembly plant), and the urgent need to develop new road cars, a return to Le Mans had to be postponed. It was Sir William's idea to use a slightly larger version of E1A as the basis for the replacement of the increasingly old-fashioned XK 150 sports car. So the E-type was born, visually and technically similar to the D-type.

Below: E2A takes the Esses at Le Mans 1960; it did not complete the 24 hours, being let down by its engine.

The E-type's major advance over the D-type was its all-new independent rear suspension which gave much better ride and handling qualities. This had been designed by Bob Knight and his team - Knight being described by Charles Bulmer, former editor of *Motor* magazine, as "far ahead of his contemporaries...probably the only senior British engineer who was then able to master the very difficult suspension and handling theory which was being developed in the USA and put it into practice together with the Peugeot compliance theory for noise suppression". This last phrase refers to the way the suspension was carefully insulated from the body to minimise noise.

A similar suspension had meanwhile been used in another, later, Le Mans prototype; code-named E2A, this was much more of a full-size, updated D-type complete with tail fin. Briggs Cunningham persuaded Jaguar to let him run the sole car built in the 1960 Le Mans, but while fast - it reached a calculated 190 mph on the Mulsanne straight - after 89 laps its aluminium block 3-litre engine failed, causing it to retire.

But with the arrival of the E-type in 1961, Jaguar's interest had swung away from sports-prototypes like E2A because that year the FIA (then as now motor sport's governing body in Europe) had launched a new, heavily-promoted World Championship for Grand Touring cars. This category was for ostensibly series-built production sports car with no capacity limit. The E-type fitted beautifully into this - and it used the 3.8-litre XK engine which had long been developed into a powerful and reliable racing unit. So Jaguar were tempted into a competition

programme with the car which had never been originally envisaged as a racing car - a factor which ultimately would make it hard to turn the E-type into an international GT race winner.

The car made its competition debut on 16th April 1961, at Oulton Park amid much excitement. Two works prepared cars were

Above: **Graham Hill sets the E-type up for a power slide at Silverstone in the 1962 version of the car, still steel-panelled.**

entered, by John Coombs and Tommy Sopwith - favoured by Jaguar because of their successes with the Mk 2 saloon. The right result was certainly obtained as Graham Hill in Sopwith's ECD 400 won ahead of Innes Ireland's Aston Martin DB4GT. Roy Salvadori in Coombs' BUY 1 had led initially but brake fade dropped him back to an eventual third. Significantly - so it seemed - the 250GT Ferraris were well out of contention in fourth and fifth places. It was Salvadori who beat them again on 21st May at Crystal Palace, London; but it was to be something of a false dawn for the E-type in motor racing - tougher events and Enzo Ferrari's answer were on the way...

Above: **Briggs Cunningham entered this works-prepared fixedhead in the 1962 Le Mans race. About to see it off to France are Bob Penney and Frank Rainbow, who prepared it.**

In the meantime other selected private owners were receiving E-types, the first eight or nine right-hand drive roadsters being built to a mild competition spec. But they were then largely on their own - major works support was reserved for the Coombs E-type, soon re-registered 4 WPD, which played the role of the works race development car. Graham Hill became its regular test and race driver, having been tempted away from Tommy Sopwith's *Equipe Endeavour* team by a larger retainer!

Several wins followed during the rest of 1961, although on the car's international debut at Spa-Francorchamps in May 1961, ECD 400 and Mike Parkes came a far from disgraceful second behind the latest 250 GT Berlinetta Ferrari, very light and with 290 bhp against the E-type's 275 bhp.

The Ferraris might not have had it so relatively easy. During 1962 Jaguar's experimental and competition departments had secretly built a special version of the E-type. Chassis no. EC 1001 had an alloy-block, fuel-injected 3.8-litre engine and a lightened (steel) body no heavier than most 250 GTs, with a flowing aluminium top and augmented by a longer, more penetrative nose - all seemingly allowable under GT rules which permitted bodywork variations. This handsome, Malcolm Sayer-designed car, usually called the 'low drag coupé', was one of an intended batch of six.

But the project was then shelved and it was not until 1963 that a true 'competition' E-type emerged. Why was the low drag coupé sidelined? Roger Woodley, a Jaguar apprentice at the time, speculated that it was "abandoned in favour of the later aluminium lightweights due to two factors - test driver Graham Hill had difficulty accommodating his helmeted head in the low drag style roof, and Ferrari were cheating Appendix J something rotten and, on the basis of what they were doing, it was clear that a full 'ally' car would be acceptable in the then Group 3 GT class".

Meanwhile the 1961 Le Mans saw no Jaguars entered, for the first time in 11 years. Three E-types contested the 1962 race, however: a factory-prepared fixedhead entered by Briggs Cunningham; a modified roadster with a fastback top entered and driven by Peters Lumsden and Sargent; and another fixedhead entered by Maurice Charles, co-driven by John Coundley.

The latter car was delivered barely five weeks ahead of the race, so Maurice Charles had little time for preparation. In France, things were fraught from the start, as Andrew Whyte recounted: "There had been some exasperation even during practice, when the team had difficulty in obtaining the use of a works engine. 'Mr Charles, please put Mr MacDowel down,' Lofty had been heard to say in his usual quietly authoritative way."

The car, now with its borrowed works engine, initially went quite well. "I made a fantastic start," says Maurice, "and I must have been about the third or fourth car under the Dunlop bridge. Innes Ireland was in a GTO in front and I just walked by him going down the Mulsanne straight. Only Bruce McLaren in the Maserati 151 and someone in a Ferrari prototype got past on the first lap. I was streets ahead of the other E-types." But after three hours Charles and Coundley were out with bearing failure (debris from the original engine blow-up was thought to have lodged in the oil cooler).

Lumsden and Sargent had gearbox problems. Recalls Peter Sargent: "We would have been third without a doubt because there was an ailing Ferrari in front of us, which in the end we couldn't catch, and then the Cunningham car passed us." So the American-entered car came fourth while Lumsden and Sargent soldiered on in top gear only to finish fifth.

Below: The Kjell Qvale - entered Leslie/Morrill car was bought shortly after Sebring by former WW2 fighter ace Howard Gidovlenko, who almost immediately mothballed it at his suburban Los Angeles home. It lay there untouched for some 35 years until sold and revived in 1998. Here it emerges from its long hibernation.

Meanwhile development of Coombs' 4 WPD continued; for 1962 it acquired a lighter (but still steel) body and more power. Graham Hill secured a few second and third places but by now the Ferrari GTO had appeared and suddenly things had become much hotter for the Jaguars.

"FIGURES ARE ALL VERY WELL, BUT THESE ALMOST INCREDIBLE TIMES ARE RECORDED IN A SILKY SILENCE THAT HAS HITHERTO BEEN UTTERLY FOREIGN TO THE SPORTS CAR." *John Bolster on road testing the new E-type*

The Ferrari 250 GTO ('0' for 'Omologato') had been built more or less in response to the E-type, a compliment indeed from Modena! Its specification was arrived at after careful examination of the *Gran Turismo* regulations: these required a minimum quantity of 100 cars to be made, but allowed alternative coachwork. The handful of GTOs built managed to qualify as differently-bodied 250 GTs.

Sauce for the goose... Jaguar cited its all-aluminium roadster as a 'special-bodied' version of the production E-type (of which thousands had by then been built), and in fact that was exactly how they were sold: there was one invoice for the new car, and another for all the 'modifications'.

In reality, all 12 'lightweight' roadsters (except 4 WPD which was rebuilt to this spec for 1963) were manufactured as such from scratch. A pair of lightweights marked the type's debut at Sebring in March 1963, where one of the cars - driven by Ed Leslie and Frank Morrill - finished seventh, and won its class. That was to be the best result the 'lightweight' E-type would ever score in an endurance classic; and even then, GTOs were far ahead in fourth, fifth and sixth places, behind the Ferrari prototypes. Following

Above: Now transformed into a true 'lightweight', 4 WPD was usually driven by Graham Hill, the most successful driver of the type in the UK. This is Hill winning at Silverstone in May 1963.

the race, Leslie drove the E-type back across the featureless Florida plains to Miami for its flight to San Francisco, with racing numbers, open exhausts and a suitcase strapped onto the trunk lid!

Graham Hill won four times in the reborn 4 WPD during the 1963 season, finding that on short British circuits the generous torque of the 3.8 injected engine could haul the E-type out of slow corners quicker than the 3-litre V12 in the Ferrari GTO. But when pitted against Ferrari in long distance events the Jaguar wilted, as Peter Lindner found when he entered his brand-new car in his 'home' Nürburgring 1000 km.

He started well, as *Motor* magazine reported: "Lindner's silver car leapt away at the start and led as the cars burst out of the south curve, rushed back behind the pits in a glorious howl of sound and disappeared beyond the north curve on the first of 44 laps of the long, winding and wearing 14.1-mile circuit." Lindner was still leading as the cars streamed onto the pits straight at the end of the first lap, and continued to lead the GT class and hold fourth overall for some while. Then the alloy-block engine expired...

Lindner, Jaguar's German importer, had begun racing and rallying Jaguars with a 3.4 saloon in the late 1950s, though it was while driving his Aston Martin DB4GT (he also sold Astons and Lotuses) that a meeting with Peter Nöcker began a famous Jaguar driving partnership. A successful campaigner with his own 250 GT Ferrari, Nöcker had won the 3-litre GT class in the 1961 Nürburgring 1000 km, even collecting points for Ferrari in the GT championship! An impressed Lindner asked him to share his (works-supported) 3.4 saloon in 1961; they then moved on to the Mk 2 3.8, and in 1963 the E-type joined the team.

The Lindner car became the most developed of the works-prepared competition E-types, but Peter Nöcker does not remember it as an easy car to drive. "The E-type was a difficult car, never neutral, always understeering or oversteering, mostly understeering. We tried many things but it was always like driving on snow, then in the last part of the curve it would suddenly oversteer." At Goodwood during practice for the 1964 Tourist Trophy, Nöcker invited Peter Sutcliffe to drive his car. He crashed it quite badly, but Nöcker was not surprised. "It was always a problem with the Lindner car."

Lindner and Nöcker did not compete at Le Mans in 1963 (they were at the Nürburgring, contesting the first round of the new European Touring Car Championship in the Mk 2) but

Previous spread: **Roy Salvadori and 86 PJ (then owned by Tommy Atkins) at Mallory Park in July 1963.**

Right: **Drama. Le Mans 1963! No. 15 limps into the pits having thoroughly bent its front end. But after heroic efforts in the pits, the front of the bonnet from another car was grafted on, to allow a ninth place to be secured.**

Above: **Roy Salvadori flies in Tommy Atkins' 86 PJ but the lightweight had to give best to the GTO Ferraris at the 1963 TT. This profile shot shows the lightweight's characteristic hardtop and trunklid vents well.**

Briggs Cunningham entered three lightweights, his Sebring car being joined by two new roadsters. Walt Hansgen and Augie Pabst went out in the first hour (with a broken gearbox), and the Richards/Salvadori car spun on oil and crashed with such force that Salvadori was flung out of the rear window - yet escaped with only bruising.

The remaining E-type, driven by Bob Grossman and Cunningham himself, looked set to finish well up in the top ten when Grossman had the horrifying experience of the brake pedal pin shearing at the end of the Mulsanne straight. The brakeless E-type hit the straw bales in the escape road, heavily deforming the front end, although Grossman managed to limp the car back to the pits.

The position looked hopeless but Cunningham was, as usual, determined to finish. Lofty England, on unofficial duty in the pits, sent for the bonnet from the retired, undamaged, E-type. The car also needed new front brakes, radiator and two front wheels. "I got it all nicely organised," said Lofty. "We'd take the damaged bonnet and we'd carry it through the pit and then by some miracle we'd suddenly appear with a 'repaired' bonnet - which as you can imagine was from the other car."

But Briggs played by the rules and checked with the course director. "Oh no, Mr Cunningham, that's contrary to race regulations, but we'd like to see you finish so cut the old bonnet in half and cut the new bonnet in half and bolt it together." This was duly done and the car finished ninth! Not only was this the best performance ever by a lightweight E-type at Le Mans but it also proved to be the last Jaguar to complete the race for 22 years.

Above: 'The Peters' (Lumsden and Sargent) dramatically re-shaped their car in 1964 with more aerodynamic nose and tail, and 49 FXN became one of the quickest E-types.

One of the E-type's few genuinely significant successes at top level came shortly after Le Mans, but not thanks to a lightweight. Dick Protheroe had bought the low-drag coupé from Jaguar to replace his previous (second) fixedhead and chose a 25-lap GT and sports car race at Rheims as his first event.

He barely put a foot wrong and led the very competitive GTO of Bianchi and Noblet to the chequered flag, winning the GT class by just one second and finishing second overall to a front-engined *Testa Rossa*. This clearly demonstrated that, given the right event, the E-type could deliver the goods - provided it lasted the distance. If a team of low-drag coupés had been prepared in 1961, and properly developed thereafter, the GTO Ferrari might not have achieved the dominance it did.

Wider wheels, higher lift camshafts and stiffer suspension featured on the works-prepared 4 WPD for 1964, though in February testing Derrick White recorded that Graham Hill was still complaining that the car understeered and that "the response of the GTO Ferrari was much quicker and more predictable than that of the competition E-type".

At the suggestion of Lofty England, a June 1964 test session at Silverstone featured a Formula 3 driver, who commented that 4 WPD's brakes were a little spongy and felt that less understeer would be desirable, but otherwise seemed happy. After ten warming-up laps using 6,100 rpm, he went out again using 6,300 rpm. The fourth lap was covered in 1 min 41.9 secs, the best any competition E-type had achieved at Silverstone.

Lofty England reported back to Sir William and Bill Heynes. "It is interesting to note," he wrote, "that this driver, who had not previously driven a lightweight E-type, put up a better time on a not completely dry circuit than that achieved by anyone else with this type of car."

That driver was Jackie Stewart, who within six years would be Formula 1 World Champion. In fact Jackie already had some small experience with an E-type, as north of the border he had raced a mildly-tuned roadster - a car which doubled as the family Jaguar dealership's E-type demonstrator! A win with it in 1963 caught the eye of David Murray, who signed Jackie for *Ecurie Ecosse* - the first big break in his motor racing career.

Stewart raced 4 WPD after his Silverstone test and recalled when speaking to David Tremayne recently how he was somewhat in awe of John Coombs himself - "He was always immaculate and apparently a scary figure of authority". But he loved the E-type "because it was very easy to drive. It wasn't vicious but, of course, it

was powerful and well-balanced. I really loved it, and actually at the time I would have been perfectly happy to go no further than driving for John Coombs. I felt I'd really arrived!"

Above: **Bob Jane came a long way to race his new competition E-type in the UK, before taking it back to Australia (where he also ran it as a road car, equipped with bumpers). This is the car at the British Grand Prix meeting in 1964.**

But even the Stewart talent could not make the competition E-type a significant achiever in 1964, especially as Carroll Shelby had now fully sorted the 4.7-litre AC Cobra - a car which beat Stewart and 4 WPD at the Brands Hatch GP meeting (and which went on to take the GT championship in both 1964 and 1965), even if Jackie finished ahead of the formidable Parkes/GTO combination.

The Peter Sargent and Peter Lumsden competition E-type (49 FXN) was now one of the fastest 'independents' thanks to their Costin-influenced version of a low-drag body, plus careful engine and suspension development by Playfords. Peter Sutcliffe's car retained the standard shape but produced the best E-type results of 1964, winning the *Coupe de Paris* GT race at Montlhéry in May, with further successes at Zolder and during a South African tour.

The 1964 Le Mans race was the last to be entered by a Jaguar until 1984 and served only to show that the E-type was falling further behind in the GT stakes. Lindner and Nöcker, experiencing their first Le Mans, found both the Daytona Cobra coupés and the Ferrari GTOs much faster, despite having the most powerful XK engine to date - giving over 340 bhp. The E-type expired during the 15th hour, while in 29th place, with a failed head gasket.

It was during practice for that year's Goodwood Tourist Trophy that the Lindner car was crashed by Peter Sutcliffe, after which it was rebuilt by the factory. Lindner then ran the E-type in the Montlhéry 1000 km race, but aquaplaned at high speed and crashed. The German was killed, a sad end for someone who had put so much into promoting Jaguar.

"NO ONE EVER SAID THE E-TYPE WOULD GO MOTOR RACING."

Norman Dewis, chief development driver

For 1965, 4 WPD reverted to Coombs and although the company still provided help and parts to private entrants, Jaguar ceased to develop the E-type. But the E-type had always attracted enthusiast-drivers who, from the early 1960s, developed their own cars and did extremely well away from the big international GT races. Dick Protheroe bridged the gap between the works or big-money teams and these keen amateurs, although the latter could sometimes give the 'professional' drivers quite a hard time when their paths crossed.

Ken Baker was one, who between 1961 and 1966 developed his roadster (7 CXW) into a very formidable machine; in 1962 his usual sparring-partner was Robin Sturgess, the Leicester

Below: **If this E-type wasn't successful in rallying, the owners can't be accused of not trying! The fixedhead displays many modifications including a multitude of extra lights.**

Jaguar dealer, who was running (unusually) the fixedhead E-type.

Sturgess recalls, though, the gulf between the big names and enthusiasts like himself. "I was actually paid to start in the *Daily Express* meeting at Silverstone in 1962 - I was invited to run the E-type after I'd won three races in a row just before. I was very flattered.

"Of course, the fast boys in the works cars absolutely wiped the floor with me. Graham Hill lapped me - and this was a Grand Prix circuit - and I thought to myself, 'Come on...!' So I tried to stick with him for a lap, and kept within about 50 yards, but at the end of the lap I was scared witless, and the sweat was just pouring off me.

"I did 22 meetings with that car in 1962. You have to bear in mind that it was doubling as a demonstrator - every weekend we'd change the diff from 3.31 to 3.54 or what was appropriate for the circuit

Right: The era of the wide tyre arrived towards the end of the 1960s and in the UK, the E-type so equipped cleaned up in the 'modified' sports car events in the UK. John Quick was one of the most successful; here he keeps John Brittan's Midget at bay coming into Druids at Brands Hatch, August 1969.

we were going to." Looking back some 40 years later, Robin Sturgess also observes: "You forget how seriously dangerous it all was - you rolled your trousers up, put on your helmet and a pair of string-backed gloves, and got on with it!"

On the UK club racing scene, the E-type competed in the various classifications of sports car racing including 'Production Sports' which began in 1968 and introduced wide slick tyres, and 'Modified Sports' which brought in wildly flared bodywork in 1970. Although fiercely competitive in any guise, 'Prod Sports' proved to be the E-type's golden era. "Races involving the E-types were often the best of the day," says Mike Cotton, then a staffer on *Motoring News* and a great friend of leading exponent John Quick.

"THE BIG ADVANTAGE THE E-TYPE HAD OVER THE GTO WAS ITS TORQUE - WE COULD LEAVE THE FERRARIS OUT OF SLOW CORNERS." *Roy Salvadori*

In the United States Merle Brennan and his Huffaker-prepared fixedhead was the outstanding combination in club racing. During 1964 and 1965 his white fixedhead, provided by Kjell Qvale of British Motors, San Francisco, won 39 out of the 42 events entered. So disbelieving were some of the Corvette Stingray drivers that the Jaguar was dismantled twice and weighed seven times! But it was always found to be legal... Brennan secured the SCCA's B-production championship in 1964 and in 1965 again made it to the finals at Daytona, but couldn't defeat the Mustang GT350s.

The E-type continued winning again in the 1970s. The Series 3 E-type of 1971 had introduced Jaguar's magnificent new all-aluminium V12 engine, but the car's basic design was ageing and as the decade wore on, V12 E-types were becoming harder to sell (in 1970, 70 per cent of all Jaguars sold in America were E-types; by 1974 that model accounted for less than 50 per cent). Mike Dale, vice-president of Jaguar North America, obtained the backing of his president, Graham Whitehead, and British Leyland to sponsor - with Goodyear Tyres and Quaker State Oil, - a racing programme to perk up sales. This set a new pattern for Jaguar in competition: that of retaining outside concerns to race the cars in place of in-house preparation.

There followed a two-pronged attack on the SCCA's B-production class. On the East coast was Bob Tullius's Virginia-based Group 44 team, legendary for its professionalism and standard of preparation. On the West coast, Joe Huffaker

Above: **Bob Tullius takes much of his Group 44 team with him on a victory lap at Summit Point, West Virginia in August 1974. Beside Tullius is partner/engineer/co-driver Brian Fuerstanau, and next to him is Mike Dale of Jaguar Cars; with arm raised is Lawton Foushee, crew chief and designer.**

in San Rafael near San Francisco was retained, his track record with Kjell Qvale's E-types going back to 1962 and Merle Brennan. With these two teams, Jaguar had the best in the business.

Neither disappointed, despite starting midway through the 1974 season. Lee Mueller in the Huffaker V12 won the SCCA B-production North Pacific Division Championship and Bob Tullius the North East equivalent. When the two E-types went to Road Atlanta for the national finals, Mueller was sidelined by a puncture and Tullius lost by under a second to Bill Jobe's Corvette.

Both teams completed the full 1975 season, Tullius winning six races and Mueller four to make them runners-up in their regional categories. At Road Atlanta, the national championship decider, Lee Mueller again suffered ill-luck when the differential carrier broke, but Tullius in the gleaming white and green 450 bhp V12 took a convincing win over Corvette and Porsche

Above: The V12 E-type was still winning races at club level into the new century thanks to the efforts of Robin Hamilton with his Rob Beere-prepared 600 bhp monster.

Right: The E-type might have been developed into a successful international rally car during the early sixties, before the really rough special stages arrived; but Jaguar were not interested in doing so and relatively few private entrants tried, so the car's potential was never really explored. This roadster is competing in the 1962 Monte Carlo rally.

Carrera opposition to become national B-production champion. It was a climactic end to the E-type's 'professional' racing career, reinforcing the sporting side of Jaguar's image generally, quite apart from shifting all remaining cars lingering at the dealerships...

All was not quite over for the E-type in the United States. Enter the tiny but determined *Gran Turismo* Jaguar concern of Eastlake, Ohio. Through sheer consistent, painstaking development they produced a six-cylinder E-type which scored more wins in SCCA racing than any other. Although the car was raced for a long time afterwards, perhaps most remembered is Freddy Baker's victory in the SCCA national C-Production class in 1980 against the might of the Datsun 240Z works-backed teams (whose drivers included film star Paul Newman). In the mid-1970s some SCCA competitors were grumbling about 'professional' teams invading their sport. In 1980 the Datsun drivers complained about an amateur team denying them the commercial benefits of a championship win!

Today, like most other sporting Jaguars, the E-type is highly active in club racing (in which Malcolm Hamilton's intimidating 7-litre V12 beat all comers in 1998) and in historic motor racing - where perhaps it vanquishes the GTO Ferrari more often than it ever used to.

The early 1960s saw a golden age of Jaguar saloon car racing. Powered by the potent 3.8-litre XK engine, the compact Mk 2 replaced the 3.4 as about the quickest four-door car you could buy. That same power/weight ratio made it an equally successful track car: the Mk 2 won the first ever European Touring Car Championship, dominated the *Tour de France Automobile* for several seasons, and even when its competitive career in Europe ended after 1963, remained the car to beat in Australian and New Zealand touring car racing for a year or so. Only after 1966 did the Mark 2 honourably retire.

Even though the car won more races than any other saloon in the UK between 1960 and the end of 1963, no Mk 2 driver became British saloon champion. This was because wins (and points) were split between the Coombs and *Equipe Endeavour* teams. Their rivalry made the racing great fun to watch, though, especially as many more circuits (Brands Hatch, Goodwood, Oulton Park and Aintree included) had joined Silverstone in running touring car races. Roy Salvadori was the regular Coombs driver, with the dark blue Sopwith car initially being handled by Mike Parkes

Previous spread: **The ex-Coombs 3.4 saloon driven by Grant Williams at the Goodwood Revival Meeting in 1999.**

Below: **Nemesis postponed: the big Ford Galaxies, perhaps handicapped by the wet conditions, failed to win the *Motor* 6-Hours race at Brands Hatch in 1963. But their time was not long off...**

Above: **In his only Mk 2 drive, Stirling Moss came second to Roy Salvadori's 3.8 in the saloon car event at the International Trophy meeting, Silverstone, in 1960.**

and Graham Hill; by 1962 Hill was driving for Coombs and Jack Sears took his place.

Other notable Mk 2 drivers included Stirling Moss; in a one-off drive for Tommy Sopwith, he came second at Silverstone to Roy Salvadori in John Coombs' car. It had been some time since he had raced a saloon and Moss was not particularly enamoured by his brief experience of the Mk 2. "It was quite competitive," he told Doug Nye, "but it seemed much more nervous than the old Mk VII and nowhere near as forgiving." Moss was quickest in practice and led the race until he was baulked, allowing Salvadori to nip by at Stowe. "I would never seriously race a Jaguar again," said Moss.

The Mk 2s were challenged early on by the big American machines but these took a surprisingly long time to displace the Jaguars. As early as the May 1961 Silverstone meeting Dan Gurney's Chevrolet Impala headed a pack of Mk 2s and probably would have won had a wheel not collapsed. A renewed V8 attack came in 1962 when this time the Alexander Engineering prepared Chevy IIs offered a successful challenge. Charles Kelsey made a good start at the Brands Hatch May meeting and just kept Roy Salvadori's Mk 2 at bay. But Salvadori beat the Chevrolet at Crystal Palce two weeks later.

It was 1962 that saw the first of Motor magazine's Six Hour races at Brands Hatch; it was won by Mike Parkes and Mike Salmon for Coombs after the Sopwith car retired; Peter Nöcker and Peter Lindner came third.

For 1963 Graham Hill drove Tommy Atkins' Mk 2 (as well as his lightweight E-type) though was beaten on occasion by Roy Salvadori. But none of the Mk 2s could hold off the Ford Galaxie and it was Jeff Uren in the Willment prepared car who that year finally broke the Jaguar saloons' monopoly at Silverstone, held since 1952.

The big Fords appeared set to take over altogether but the Motor Six Hour race that year resulted in a Jaguar victory. Run in pouring rain, the nimbler Jaguars got the better of the Galaxies of Baillie/Jopp and Jack Brabham/Dan Gurney. Surprised winners were Denny Hulme and Roy Salvadori, after the Salmon/Sutcliffe Mk 2 was disqualified for having oversize inlet valves. Lindner and Nöcker were accordingly elevated into second.

Although the sun was setting on the Mk 2's dominance on British circuits (the Lotus Cortinas were the final nail in the car's coffin), 1963 did see the car win the first European Touring Car championship, thanks to Peter Lindner and Peter Nöcker. Lofty England had agreed to support the German importer and three factory-prepared Mk 2s duly arrived (part of a batch - four more went to Charley Delecroix in France for selected French rally drivers).

The German-organised championship awarded points to drivers, not cars, and there was a choice of qualifying events. The first was the Nürburgring 1000 km, Mercedes-Benz' home

Left: John Coundley ploughs through the wet at Brands Hatch during the 1963 *Motor* 6-Hours race. The event was won against the odds by Denny Hulme and Roy Salvadori in another 3.8 - the Galaxies started firm favourites.

circuit. But Lindner also knew it well, lapped fastest in practice, and won, beating Eugen Bohringer's 300SE Mercedes by half a lap. This early success somewhat demoralised the Mercedes camp which had hoped to win both the rally and touring car championships that year.

Next up for Lindner and Nöcker was the *Motor* 6-Hours at Brands Hatch. Here, as related, they finished second but collected full points, because the winning Mk 2 had not entered the championship. Then at Zolder in Belgium Nöcker collected a win after Lindner's Mk 2 was involved in an 'off' with the second Mk 2.

This incident caused a change of plan, as Peter Nöcker relates: "Peter Lindner said to me in the 1963 year, 'You make the German Championship on the touring cars and I make the European Championship'." But Nöcker was now some points ahead of Lindner who told him: "I have no chance to win, Peter, so you must drive both championships together." From then on Lindner played a supporting role, including the final round in Budapest where all three of Lindner's Mk 2s ran. Nöcker won, Lindner was third and Tilo Schadrack was ninth.

Nöcker had also made best saloon time at the Timmelsjoch hillclimb in Austria - one such event was mandatory in the championship. Together it was enough to make Peter Nöcker the first European Champion - and, shortly afterwards, German touring car champion as well.

That ETC win was an important milestone in Jaguar's racing career but it was not given the coverage it deserved. Said Andrew Whyte, who was in Jaguar's PR department at the time: "I always felt that we could have made more publicity out of that particular achievement than we did. The Lindner/Nöcker team did much for Jaguar's sales and reputation in Germany, but was hardly noticed elsewhere."

What coverage there was also tended to revolve around the dashing, publicity-conscious Lindner anyway. Peter Nöcker wryly remarks, "It was always Lindner/Nöcker, never the other way, and when I won the European Championship, one paper carried the headline 'Peter Lindner wins the European championship - driver Peter Nöcker'."

Outside Europe, the Mk 2's greatest achievements were in Australia where Bob Jane's exploits became legendary. Jane began racing his car in 1961 and as local regulations allowed more changes than did the FIA in Europe, his Mk 2 was soon running with triple Weber carburettors, larger valves and locally machined camshafts - producing well in excess of 300 bhp. "A great deal of work was done on the suspension and brakes," said Jane. "This, I think, was the car's best point as it could outbrake any touring car."

The Jane Mk 2 was fully sorted out by 1963 and in Australia's famously rough and tough saloon car races, almost always won against locally made Holdens and imported Impalas. Jane continued to win throughout 1964 despite the appearance of a Holman & Moody-powered Ford Galaxie. Only the arrival of the Mustangs in 1965 forced Bob Jane to give up and sell the car.

The final major endurance win for the Mk 2 took place in New Zealand, when Ray Archibald and Tony Shelly won the 1966 Pukekohe 6-Hours event (the 3.8 had, in fact, won this race twice before).

In rallying, the Mk 2 Jaguar was not a significant player, even in Europe, where the XK had done so well in the 1950s. There was one exception though as it included timed hill climbs and, especially, circuit races, the *Tour de France Automobile* was more than 'just' a rally. The 3.4 saloon had

Above: **In terms of outright speed, Bob Jane's Mk 2 was probably the fastest of its time, local Australian regulations allowing Weber carburettors and, ultimately, 4.2-litre capacity. The 300+ bhp car was still competitive - against Impala and even Mustang opposition - into 1965.**

proved that this format suited the Jaguar saloon well and the company provided (by its standards) a high level of support to selected *Tour* entrants. One man in particular took advantage of this - Bernard Consten.

As recorded earlier, Consten and his co-driver Jack Renel had led but then eventually retired from the 1957 event in their 3.4. In 1960 they returned with a Jaguar-prepared 3.8 Mk 2 to win the 'touring' classification (the Ferrari 250 GT usually mopped up the GT category), a feat repeated in 1962 when Consten had to fight off a strong challenge from the similar cars of Sir Gawaine Baillie and Peter Jopp, and Jack Sears and Claude Lego. But both the British-entered 3.8s crashed.

Above: One of the greatest Jaguar partnerships of all time - Jack Renel and Bernard Consten. The incomparable Consten (right) won the *Tour* four times in succession, from 1960 to 1963.

In 1963 it looked very much as if the new influx of 'big banger' American machinery would end the Mk 2's dominance of the *Tour*, just as they were doing in touring car racing. Three 7-litre Ford Galaxies challenged Consten, who responded by making best time at the *Les Trois Epis* hill climb immediately after the start! At the Nürburgring and on the fast Spa, Rheims and Le Mans circuits, the Frenchman avoided stressing his Jaguar and let the Galaxies bellow off; but as the 3,600-mile event brought the cars into wetter weather and tighter roads, Consten pressed hard and the Galaxies began to suffer problems. Only Greder's remained for the final hill climbs.

On these Consten posted the quickest times and so won the 1963 Tour with apparent ease. To further emphasise the Mk 2's success, second place was taken by Annie Soisbault and Louisette Texir in their 3.8. Paddy Hopkirk and Henry Liddon in their works Mini finished third of the 11 cars (out of 61) which finished. This had been the fourth consecutive *Tour de France* win for Consten and Renel, and Jaguar's fifth. In 1964 Consten had to contend not only with the Galaxie but with the Ford Mustang too. Despite this, the 3.8 Mk 2 still won the Mountain Championship for best aggregate performance in the hill climbs. Overall, though, the Mustang of Andrew Cowen and Peter Proctor finally prevailed; Bernard Consten - hailed by Andrew Whyte as "one of the greatest, yet relatively unsung, long-distance rally drivers of his time" - and the 3.8 Mk 2 had finally met their match.

There is a postscript, however. After 1964 the *Tour* was dropped (it was an expensive event to promote) but Bernard Consten, after becoming president of the French motor sport federation in 1969, assisted the *Automobile Club de Nice* in reviving the event. By then there were no sporting Jaguar saloons in production; Porsche was the successful make.

"THE CAR DID VERY WELL, LAPPING MIRA AT 161MPH AND DOING 175MPH DOWN THE STRAIGHT."

Lofty England on the XJ13 in 1967

The XJ13 was Jaguar's first and only mid-engined car, an exotic, four-cam V12-powered machine clothed in an exquisitely beautiful Sayer-designed aluminium body. Built for Le Mans in the mid-1960s, circumstances conspired to ensure that it never raced. It also stands as Jaguar's final in-house competition car. When the name did return to the 24-Hour race, it would be on cars designed and constructed entirely by outside specialists.

As the D-type passed into obsolescence in 1956, the far-sighted Bill Heynes instructed Malcolm Sayer to lay out proposals for a mid-engined Le Mans sports prototype as part of an investigation into Jaguar's next Le Mans car. It would probably have been powered by a highly developed 3-litre version of the XK engine, which engineer George Buck recalls suggesting to

Below: **A 1990s shot of the rebuilt XJ13 at the Goodwood Festival of Speed.**

Sayer might be mounted crosswise. The project got as far as a mock-up but no further; had it appeared in, say, 1957 it would have been years ahead of its time - a mid-engined car did not win Le Mans until 1962.

Heynes also made sure that he had a suitable big-capacity engine on the drawing board should Le Mans regulations allow one, and Tom Jones had drawn a V12 as far back as 1951. These advanced concepts finally became a reality in the 1960s, thanks to a change in Le Mans regulations which allowed sports prototypes to use unlimited capacity engines from 1963. Bill Heynes could see that his 5-litre V12, by then under development as a dual purpose road-car/racing unit, finally had a relevance. In 1964 he received the go-ahead to build a new Le Mans Jaguar.

On the design side, the Lola-Ford of 1963 and its Ford GT40 offspring, which ran at Le Mans

in 1964, pointed the way ahead, and in 1965 the building of the new car - code named XJ13 - began. Construction followed D-type principles except that the engine was suspended from the

Above: **The sad state of the XJ13 after its roll into the mud. Norman Dewis escaped unscathed and the car remained rebuildable.**

rear of aluminium monocoque and itself carried some of the rear suspension loads.

For a racing project the car took a tortuously long time to appear, not running under its own power until March 1967. All sorts of factors were responsible for the delay, including pressure to develop new models like the XJ6 saloon and the merger of Jaguar with BMC in July 1966.

Meanwhile the Ford GT40, now in 7-litre Mk IV form, gained its second Le Mans victory in 1967. While XJ13 probably would have been highly competitive against the original 1966 GT40, in terms of tyre width, power and weight it had now been well and truly overtaken. Moreover, for 1968, sports-prototypes were to be restricted to 3 litres, ruling out Jaguar's big V12 anyway. XJ13 was obsolete with less than a thousand miles of secret testing on the clock.

Norman Dewis, in a series of discreet Sunday morning sessions at MIRA, continued to sort the car out, however. David Hobbs was also called in to try the car, and both he and Norman circulated MIRA's banked circuit in 1967 at 161.6 mph - a great increase over the D-type's best of around 151 mph. When the XJ13's speed was released it remained in the *Guinness Book of Records* for many years as the fastest lap of an enclosed circuit in the UK.

While XJ13 never raced, it was certainly involved in drama. After being mothballed at

Coventry for several years, it was brought out of retirement on 20th January 1971 for the making of a film to promote the forthcoming Series 3 V12 E-type. Norman Dewis once again settled down in XJ13's snug cockpit and completed a number of quite high-speed laps for the cameras.

"I was on my final lap," remembers Dewis, "on the banking and thinking, good, this is nearly finished, when there was a sudden bump from the rear end (a rear wheel had collapsed). I was already high up on the banking and the car was suddenly aiming for the wire safety fence at the top, which it hit. That sprung me down across the banking, the car doing almost a complete loop.

Above: **XJ13 during repair at Abbey Panels, clearly showing the construction, the engine supended from an aluminium monocoque - all rather like a rear engined D-type!**

"As it came off the track at the bottom it was at an angle of 45 degrees across the track, and it hit one of the red and white marker barrels there. That pushed in the screen pillar and put a hole in my helmet - but it didn't touch my forehead!

"I was now going across the infield, which was soft and muddy, so I switched off and got down under the scuttle, and it did two nose and tails and three side rolls. I could see the sky as we went over. It was as if we were being catapulted. The speed of it - it seemed ages and ages before it stopped. But it landed on its wheels, I was OK and got out just a bit bruised!"

It was a monumental hum-dinger of a high-speed accident, but the indestructible Norman Dewis walked away with nothing worse than a wrenched neck. The mud-encrusted car looked like a total write-off (though in fact the main structure had survived remarkably well) and the disconsolate party returned it to Browns Lane.

There, XJ13 lay under a cover until Lofty England - who in 1972 succeeded Sir William as Jaguar's chairman and chief executive - decided it should be restored. He leaned heavily on Abbey Panels, who had built the car's original body, to assist, and with the aid of the body jigs which had been preserved, the difficult and expensive task of rebuilding the car commenced.

The job was finished in 1973 and the British Grand Prix meeting at Silverstone saw the XJ13 in action publicly for the first time ever - Lofty driving. Since then this magnificent car has appeared many times and no one who has heard the sound of its musically raucous 500 bhp V12 engine will ever forget it.

Driving the E-type

The E-type has a very special feel to it. Even getting into the car is an experience - you have to guide your legs under the big, wood-rim steering wheel and then lever your body over the wide sill before plopping down onto the diminutive bucket seat. You sit really low, too, between that big sill and a high transmission tunnel. But the view is simply wonderful - directly ahead are the big, black-faced speedometer and tachometer, and beyond them the bonnet, with its characteristic power bulge in the centre, stretches way out ahead. It curves down out of sight, in fact, and first-time drivers have to be careful not to dent that beautifully rounded snout because the front 18 inches are obscured.

Turn the ignition key and press the round starter button and the starter motor engages with an echoing 'clang'; the engine fires and idles smoothly with a slight hum which can be felt as well as heard. Select first gear (it might take a second try - and avoid getting reverse by mistake as it is very close on the gate), let the clutch in and ease away. Fine; treat the long-travel accelerator lightly and the E-type is as docile as a Mini. Floor it and the nose lifts, you are pinned back in your seat, and the car launches itself towards the horizon. You need to get into second almost at once, and a snick-free change is difficult for the uninitiated - synchromesh is not this gearbox's strongest suit. Not many seconds later and you'll be in third gear: that will pull you to well over 110mph and, when you do change into top, that wonderful surge continues, appearing to lose force only beyond 135mph. Given a little space, 145 or even more will appear on the speedo.

Just as impressive is the E-type's top-gear performance. It takes the same amount of time to get from 10 mph to 30 mph as it does to gain 100 mph from 80 mph - around 5.7 seconds. That is genuine flexibility.

Race-prepared E-types are all this and more, of course. A fully-modified car will reduce the 0-100 mph time from around 16.5 seconds to around 12 and push the maximum speed to upwards of 170 mph.

Handling? The independent rear end with its limited slip differential is brilliant at putting the power down. You would not expect it, but the E-type is great in the snow, the traction is so good. When it comes to modified cars, though, it can be very different. A wide-tyred racing E-type is easy to drive at eight-tenths. At nine or nine-and-a-half tenths

of its maximum cornering capability, it can be very difficult - on a knife-edge, in fact, requiring determination and strong nerves as, depending on how the suspension has been set up, the transition from understeer to oversteer can be very, very sudden. But when you get it right, the feeling is highly satisfying.

E-type and Mk2

Technical specifications

YEARS CURRENT
1961 - 1964	(3.8 litre E-type)
1963 - 1964	(competition E-type)
1971 - 1975	(Series 3 V12 E-type)
1959 - 1967	(Mk 2 3.8 litre saloon)

SPECIFICATION (3.8 E-type/Mk 2 saloon)
Engine capacity	3,781cc
Power	265 bhp @ 5,500 rpm/220 bhp @ 5.500 rpm
Length	14ft 7.5ins/15ft 0.75ins
Width	5ft 5ins/5ft 6.75ins
Weight	2,699 lbs (24.1 cwt)/3,360 lbs (30 cwt)
Wheelbase	8ft/8ft 11.25ins
Max. speed	147 mph/125 mph
0-60 mph	67 secs/8.8 secs
Mpg	18-20/16-19

SPECIFICATION (Series 3 V12 E-type open two seater)
Engine capacity	5,345cc
Power	272 bhp @ 5,850 rpm
Length	15ft 4ins
Width	4ft 1ins
Weight	3,225 lbs (28.8 cwt)
Wheelbase	8ft 9ins
Max. speed	146 mph
0-60 mph	6.5secs
Mpg	14-17

(manual transmission)

COMPETITION RESULTS
E-type and 3.8 litre Mk2

1960
BRSCC meeting, Snetterton, touring car race, Sir G. Baillie, 1st, Mk 2
Tulip Rally, April, J. Boardman/J. Whitworth, 1st improved production touring cars, Mk 2
Daily Express Trophy meeting, Silverstone, May, R. Salvadori, 1st, S. Moss, 2nd, G. Hill, 3rd, Mk 2
International Alpine Rally, July, J. Behra/R. Richard, 1st touring car category, 3rd overall; Coupes des Alpes, R. Parkes/G. Howarth, 3rd touring car category, Mk 2
Brands Hatch International meeting, touring car race, J. Sears, 1st, Mk 2
Tour de France, September, B. Consten/J. Renel, 1st touring category, P. Jopp/Suir G. Baillie, 2nd, Mk 2
British Empire Trophy meeting, Silverstone, October, saloon car race, Sir G. Baillie, 1st, D. Taylor, 2nd, Mk 2
US Grand Prix meeting, Riverside, November, compact car race, W. Hansgen, 1st, A. Pabst, 2nd, Mk 2
Brands Hatch Boxing Day meeting, December, touring car race, Sir G. Baillie, 1st, Mk 2

1961
Oulton Park GT Trophy race, April, G. Hill, 1st, R. Salvadori, 3rd (the E-type's first race)
Goodwood Easter Monday meeting, saloon car race, M. Parkes, 1st, Mk 2
Spa GT race, cars over 2,000cc, May, M. Parkes, 2nd, E-type (first race overseas for the E-type)
British GP meeting, Aintree, GT race, July, J. Sears, 2nd, E-type
British Empire Trophy meeting, Silverstone, touring car race, M. Parkes, 1st, G. Hill, 2nd, Mk 2
August Bank Holiday meeting, Brands Hatch, August, GT race, B. McLaren, R. Salvadori, 1st, E-type; touring car race, M. Parkes, 1st, R. Salvadori, 2nd, J. Sears, 3rd, Mk 2
Coupe du Salon meeting, Montlhery, touring car race, B. Consten, 1st, C. de Guezac, 2nd, Mk 2

1962
BRSCC Snetterton meeting, GT cars, R. Sturgess, 1st, E-type, P. Sargent, 1st Mk2
BARC Oulton Park, GT Race, G. Hill, 2nd, E-type
Snetterton Saloon Car Race, M. Parkes, 1st, Mk2
Goodwood Saloon Car Race, over 3,000cc, G. Hill, 1st, Mk 2
Aintree '200' Saloon Car Race, over 3,000cc, G. Hill, 1st, Mk2
Silverstone International Trophy, Production Cars, G. Hill, 1st, Mk 2
Hockenheim Races, 56 km Race, J. Neerpasch, 2nd, E-type, Ruthardt, 3rd, E-type; Saloon Cars, P. Nöcker, 2nd, Mk 2
Crystal Palace, Saloon cars over 3,000cc, R. Salvadori, 1st, Mk 2
Mallory Park GT Race, G. Hill, 2nd, E-type
Goodwood Whitsun Saloon Car Race, P. Woodroffe, 1st, Mk 2
Le Mans 24 Hours, B. Cunningham/R. Salvadori, 4th, E-type fixedhead
Nürburgring 6-Hour Touring Car Race, P. Lindner, 1st, Schadrack, 2nd, Kreft, 3rd, Mk 2
Nürburgring 12-Hour Touring Car Race, P. Lindner/H.J. Walter, 1st, Mk 2
British Grand Prix Aintree, Saloon Car Race, J. Sears, 1st, Mk2
Nürburgring GT Race, Sir J. Whitmore, 3rd, E-type
Crystal Palace GT Race over 2,600cc, R. Protheroe, 1st, E-type
Tour de France Touring Car Class, B. Consten/J. Renel, 1st
Silverstone Clubman's Meeting, GT and Sportscars, P. Sturgess, 1st, E-type, P. Woodroffe, 1st, Mk 2
Brands Hatch International 6 Hour Saloon Car Race, M. Parkes/J. Blumer, 1st, P. Lindner/P. Nöcker, 2nd, Mk 2
Geneva Rally, Touring Cars over 2,001cc, C. Craft, 1st, Mk 2
Brands Hatch Boxing Day Race, K. Baker, 1st, E-type

1963
Snetterton Touring Car Race, B. McLaren, 1st, Mk 2
Snetterton International Trophy Meeting, Sports Cars over 2,000cc, G. Hill, 1st, E-type, Saloon Cars over 2,000cc, R. Salvadori, 1st, Mk 2
Monza, March, International Class C speed records, 3 days at 107.023 mph, 4 days at 106.622 mph, 15,000 km at 106.615 mph, 10,000 miles at 106.58 mph, Mk 2
BARC National Meeting, Oulton Park, Touring Cars Over 2,000cc, G. Hill, 1st, Mk2
Goodwood Easter Meeting, Touring Cars, G. Hill, 1st, R. Salvadori, 2nd,

Competition results

M. Salmon, 3rd, Mk 2s. GT Cars Race, G. Hill, 1st, R. Salvadori, 3rd, E-types
Mallory Park Easter Meeting, GT cars over 2,500cc, K. Baker, 1st, E-type
Aintree '200' Saloon Cars over 2,000cc, G. Hill, 1st, Mk 2
Silverstone International Trophy, GT cars, G. Hill, 1st, R. Salvadori, 2nd,
R.Protheroe, 3rd, Saloon Cars Race, R.Salvadori, 2nd, P. Dodd, 3rd, Mk2s
Japanese International Meeting, Suzukaa. GT Race, Yokoyama, 1st, E-type
Crystal Palace Whitsun Meeting, Touring Cars, R. Salvadori, 2nd, G. Hill,
3rd, Mk 2
Goodwood Whitsun Meeting, Saloons Race, M. Salmon, 1st, Mk 2
Nürburgring 12-Hour Touring Car Race, P. Lindner/P. Nöcker, 1st, Mk 2
Brands Hatch 6-Hour Production Car Race, R. Salvadori, 1st,
P. Lindner/P. Nöcker, 2nd, Mk 2
Zolder, Belgium, touring car race, P. Nöcker, 1st, J. Sparrow, 2nd, Mk 2
Silverstone, Saloon Cars over 3,000cc, M.Aston, 1st, Mk 2
Mallory Park GT Race, G. Hill, 1st, R. Salvadori, 2nd, E-type
Snetterton, National Meeting Saloon Car Race, M. Salmon, 2nd,
M.Aston, 3rd, Mk 2s, Touring Car Race, X. Adams, 2nd, M. Pendleton,
3rd, GT Race, P. Sutcliffe 1st, K.Baker, 2nd, E-types
British GP, Silverstone, Touring Car Race, M. McDowell, 3rd, Mk 2, GT
Race, R. Protheroe, 3rd, E-type
Budapest, Hungary, touring car race, P. Nöcker, 2nd, Mk 2
BRSCC Mallory Park, GT Cars over 2,500cc, Wakup, 1st, E-type
BRSCC Aintree, GT Race, R. Mac, 1st, T. Dean, 2nd, E-types, R. Beck,
3rd, XK120
Brands Hatch Trophy Meeting, Saloon Cars Race 'A', A. Powell, 2nd, Mk
2. Race 'B', G. Hill, 2nd, R. Salvadori, 3rd, Mk 2
Goodwood Tourist Trophy, R. Salvadori, 3rd, E-type
Tour de France, Touring Car Class, B. Consten/J. Renel, 1st, Mk 2,
Coupe de Dames, Mlle Soisbault/Mlle Texier
Bridgehampton 500 km Race, W. Hansgen, 3rd, E-type
Pukekohe 6-Hour Touring Car Race, New Zealand, T. Shelly/R.
Archibald, 1st, Mk2
Brands Hatch Boxing Day, GT Cars over 2,500cc, T. Dean, 1st, E-type

1964
Coupe de Paris Montlhery, GT Race, P. Sutcliffe, 1st, E-type
Brands Hatch European Grand Prix, GT Cars, J. Stewart, 1st, E-type
Limburg Grand Prix, GT Cars 2.5 litres, P. Sutcliffe, 3rd, E-type
Snetterton 3-Hour GT Race, R. Mac, 2nd, E-type

1965
Brands Hatch GT Race, W. Pearce, 1st, E-type
Brands Hatch 1000 Mile Production Sports Car Race, J. Oliver/C. Craft,
3rd, E-type
Spa Cup, Touring Car race, J. Sparrow, 2nd, Mk 2

1966
Pukekohe, New Zealand 6-Hour Touring Car Race, R. Archibald/T.
Shelly, 1st, Mk 2

The E-type gained many club victories in UK production and modified
sports car racing, too numerous to include here

SERIES 3 V12 E-TYPE

1974 (UK)
Peter Taylor becomes British Production Sportscar Champion in Series
3 V12 coupe

1974 (USA)
Huffaker Engineering car:-
Seattle, Washington state, August, Lee Mueller, 1st
Ontario, California, Lee Mueller, 1st
Portland, Oregan, Lee Mueller, 1st
Sears Point, California, Lee Mueller, 2nd

GROUP 44 CAR
Summit Point, W. Virginia, Bob Tullius, 1st
Gainsville, Florida, Bob Tullius, 1st
Bryer, New Hampshire, Bob Tullius, 1st
Nelson Ledges, Ohio, Bob Tullius, 1st
Road Atlanta, SCCA B-production finals, Bob Tullius, 2nd

1975
Huffaker Engineering car:-
Portland, Oregan, Lee Mueller, 1st
Westwood, Brittish Columbia, Lee Mueller, 1st
Portland, Oregan, Lee Mueller, 1st
Phoenix, Arizona, Lee Mueller, 1st

GROUP 44 CAR
St Louis, Missouri, Bob Tullius, 1st
Summit Point, Virginia, Bob Tullius, 1st
Brainerd, Minnesota, Bob Tullius, 1st
Nelson Ledges, Bob Tullius, 1st
Lime Rock, Connecticut, Bob Tullius, 1st
Indianapolis Raceway, Bob Tullius, 1st
Road Atlanta, SCCA B-production finals, Bob Tullius, 1st and National
Champion

1976
Bob Tulluis scored three victories with the Group 44 E-type as an
interim measure until the replacement XJ-S was ready

Thundering elegance

If Bentley hadn't invented the phrase "the silent sports car"
it could well have been adopted by Jaguar to describe the
XJ-S GT when it appeared in 1975. The refinement of
the new coupe´, however, belied its supercar performance.

"THE BEAUTY OF JAGUAR IS THAT IT IS ACCEPTED ANYWHERE IN THE WORLD AND YOU ARE MADE TO FEEL GOOD." *Win Percy, Group A XJ-S driver*

Jaguar's new XJ-S coupé combined all the speed of the outgoing V12 E-type with the world-renowned ride, handling and refinement of the XJ12 saloon.

But it was not really a sports car. The XJ-S had drifted away from the original E-type concept of a lithe two-seater. The expensive, luxury Grand Tourer was far removed from the new Jaguar sports car many were eagerly anticipating, both in size and in styling. It was hard to believe that the same man, Malcolm Sayer, had designed both the E-type's curves and the flat-bonneted, flying buttressed XJ-S.

This discrepancy and the car's 16 mpg thirst interacted with a slice of plain bad luck: the arrival, virtually coincident with its launch, of the 'oil crises' of the mid-1970s which suddenly made big cars unfashionable. On top of all this, the XJ-S was afflicted by quality problems at

Browns Lane, where morale was at an all-time low due to the inept management of Jaguar's owners, British Leyland.

No wonder the XJ-S needed all the support it could get in the marketplace. And in North America, Bob Tullius and Group 44 were obviously the people to help boost the car's image by racing it.

But it was not only Group 44's record of winning with the E-type that attracted Jaguar's

Above: The Group 44 XJ-S coupé photographed in action during the 1977 season which began in May. Jaguar was still enmeshed within British Leyland at the time and as they were paying a lot of the bills, that name received the best decal places!

Right: The original 1976 Group 44 XJ-S, during the 1976 SCCA run-offs at Road Atlanta. Bob Tullius is leading a Porsche which, along with Corvette and Camaro, made up the usual opposition in Trans-Am.

Mike Dale and Graham Whitehead at Jaguar's North American headquarters. Equally important was the team's professionalism. Not only was the team always immaculately turned out, it was also the first such organisation to employ a full-time PR person, who, for example, would spend time in the weeks leading up to each race briefing the local media and distributing information.

The championship target this time was the more professional Trans Am series, as opposed to the SCCA's more amateur events which Group 44 had targeted with the V12 E-type. Bob Tullius relished the challenge although he joked that "it was a matter of propagating our existence! When the E-type was no longer available we had to race something". At top level, that is - Group 44 were still fielding MGs and Triumphs for what had become the Jaguar Rover Triumph group.

The XJ-S's first season in racing - in 1976 - was a period of exploration as the team tested their modifications and assessed the opposition (the XJ-S ran in the over 2.5-litre Category 1 against cars like the Corvette and Porsche 911S). Group 44 engine builder, and co-founder of

Group 44, Brian Fuerstenau kept as many power unit parts standard as possible, which, combined
with a dry-sump lubrication system, avoided the oil surge problems that Broadspeed were having
with the big Jaguar XJ12 coupés in Europe. With six Weber carburettors the 5.3-litre V12 now
put out 475 bhp, some 90 bhp more than standard, and a later *Road & Track* test showed that it
could reach 100 mph in 10.3 secs.

"AT DAYTONA I COULD DRIVE UP AND DOWN THE BANKING AT 180 MPH

QUITE EFFORTLESSLY." *Bob Tullius*

The first race for the car was on 22nd August 1976 at Mosport in Canada, but Tullius retired
the car with high oil temperature when leading his class. At Lime Rock, Connecticut, though,
the XJ-S scored its first Trans Am win, and although the next two races - at Road Atlanta and
the IMSA Camel event at Daytona - failed to produce results, it was enough to demonstrate that
the car had real promise.

The fruits of the Trans Am project emerged over the next two seasons. In 1977 Tullius won
his category at Seattle on 29th May, and across the ten races entered - sometimes with Fuerstenau
co-driving in the longer events - the XJ-S ended the season with five wins, two second places
and one third. One of those wins was at Mosport, where the race duration of six hours gave
Jaguar its first long-distance victory since the 3.8 Mk 2 had won in far-away New Zealand in
1966. It was all enough to give Bob Tullius the driver's championship in Category 1 - again, the
first championship for a Jaguar in many years.

Group 44 had worked hard on the car's handling which, combined with good preparation and the best drivers available, produced the results: Jaguar used them to good effect in promoting the XJ-S, linking the 'racer' with the svelte road car by the phrase 'Thundering Elegance'.

For 1978 a new, lighter car had been built, backed up in some events by the original car suitably upgraded. The series started at Sears Point, California, and the ten rounds included a six-hour endurance race at Watkins Glen, New York State, before ending exotically at the Ricardo Rodriguez Autodrome in Mexico City. Seven wins in Category 1 provided Bob Tullius with his second Trans Am title and, this time, gave Jaguar the manufacturer's championship.

Apart from one trip to Daytona, the XJ-S did not race in 1979 or 1980, although Group 44 were busily occupied with the TR8. It was left to Gran Turismo Jaguar to keep the marque in the headlines, which Englishman Freddie Baker did most successfully, breaking the Datsun 'Z's ten-year monopoly on the SCCA C-production championships with his venerable E-type - which was circulating faster than the Group 44 V12 E-type had done five years earlier!

Above: **Bob Tullius was already a five-times SCCA championship winner at the start of the Trans-Am campaign. His dedication brought Jaguar great results in North America.**

The white and green machines were back in 1981. Sir Michael Edwardes, in his far-reaching sort-out of the British Leyland empire, had installed John Egan at Jaguar in April 1980. Within months the whole atmosphere at Jaguar had changed for the better, making it easier for Mike Dale and Graham Whitehead to retain the Group 44 team for another assault on the Trans Am series.

Rule changes meant that the XJ-S could now run with a tube frame 'chassis', to which were fastened detachable, lightweight glass fibre XJ-S shape body panels. The V12 engine now provided 525 bhp and was installed 7.5 inches further back, driving through a Franklin quick-change differential. All these changes produced a much faster car.

"WE GOT COMPLAINTS BECAUSE WE PASSED ON THE OUTSIDE AND IN PLACES PEOPLE THOUGHT WERE IMPOSSIBLE."

Lanky Foushee, Group 44 crew chief and designer

This allowed the XJ-S to compete for outright wins - always more valuable than category successes. Group 44 did not disappoint. After problems in practice in Round One at Charlotte, North Carolina, Tullius started mid-field but finished second. He then won at Portland, Oregon, and at Brainerd, Minnesota and Mosport; but elsewhere the spoils were divided amongst Porsche,

Above: **Interior of the standard-shelled 1976-built XJ-S, stripped of all the usual Jaguar luxuries and well braced by an extensive roll cage.**

Camaro or Corvette. Eppie Wietze (Corvette) took the championship, with Tullius an impressive runner-up.

There might have been a second full season for the tube-frame car if driver Gordon Smiley, who had arranged sponsorship for himself, had not been killed when his March Indycar crashed during Indianapolis qualifying.

The XJ-S was to race once in 1982 however, though strictly in the cause of the brand new XJR-5 sports prototype: this was to be the first mid-engined car ever to race under the Jaguar name. The chosen event was the Daytona 24 Hours early in the year. Bob Tullius explains: "The only reason we ran that race was to run the engine for 24 hours…

"You can run a pretty good programme to simulate a 24-hour race on a dyno but it's still not like using the race track. Goodyear wanted us to do the race on street tyres, which worked out well because all we did was to ride around for 24 hours and use the engine as much as possible.

"We obtained a speed of 194.46 mph - on street tyres. It was staggering to me when I ound out how fast I was going on those tyres!"

The exercise paid off when Group 44 came to design, build and race the first XJR, a story to be told in the next chapter.

Below: **Group 44 continued to run a steel-shelled XJ-S in 1981; this is the car in the Lime Rock paddock, 1981.**

Meanwhile, in Europe, the XJ-S had taken longer to reach the race track. First came the ill-starred BL (not Jaguar)-endorsed Broadspeed racing programme in 1976/77, when the enormously quick but hopelessly unreliable XJ12Cs would usually smash the lap record in practice, lead by miles for a few laps, and then almost

Above: The first Group A XJ-S, with Tom Walkinshaw, the architect of the project to return Jaguar to the race tracks in Europe.

Previous spread: **Winning year: the all-conquering 1984 XJ-S won the European Touring Car Championship in 1984 but not this race at Silverstone - off come the 'slicks', on go the treaded 'wet' tyres, but not soon enough and TWR lost the race to BMW.**

inevitably break down. One of the most irritated observers of the debacle had a particularly close-up view.

"I had been racing BMWs in the 1970s when they were annihilating the Jaguars," explains one Thomas Dobbie Thomson Walkinshaw. "They were beating them too easily because the Jaguars were making such a mess of it. I thought that Jaguar should be winning races, really, and decided to do something about it."

That was the spur which ultimately resulted in Jaguar not only regaining the European Touring Car Championship with the XJ-S but also its Le Mans crown with the XJR sports prototypes that followed.

Tom Walkinshaw had long been a Jaguar admirer. "My father was a Jaguar fan and I had been ever since I was knee-high," he told Mike Cotton in a *Jaguar World* interview. Tom had entered motor racing with a Lotus 51 tuned by former Ecurie Ecosse D-type mechanic Stan Sproat, then won the Scottish Formula 3 championship before driving professionally for first Ford and then BMW. At the same time he was developing his own race car preparation and motor sales businesses which would form the foundations of the multi-million pound TWR Group.

"IF YOU WERE NOT CONFIDENT, IF YOU SHILLY-SHALLIED, YOU WOULD NEVER MASTER THAT CAR." *Tom Walkinshaw on driving the Group A XJ-S*

The opportunity to launch a successful XJ-S race programme did not arrive until 1982, however, when new 'Group A' regulations for the European Touring Car Championship came into force. These suited the XJ-S - which as a nominal four-seater just about qualified as a 'touring car' - and so Walkinshaw approached the Jaguar management in 1981 with a proposal: that he would run the XJ-S privately in 1982 if Jaguar would supply a car, parts and some technical liaison.

John Egan's remarkable programme to hoist morale and improve quality at Jaguar was by then well underway and he quickly recognised that Walkinshaw's proposal had real merit. He knew how success on the track could pay off and had already authorised Group 44 to build a car for the IMSA series in the United States. He agreed to provide covert support for the 1982 season.

Tom Walkinshaw delivered the goods. The two black XJ-Ss, with Tom himself the lead driver, secured four outright ETC victories that first season, at Brno, Nürburgring, Silverstone and Zolder. The Czech event was particularly satisfying. "The thing about Brno is that it was mega-quick," Tom recalls. "It had fast corners and it suited the Jaguar well. The XJ-S could stretch its legs there, and that's what it wanted to do." But perhaps more significant was the win in Germany on BMW's home turf; there, Walkinshaw and 'Chuck' Nicholson finished well ahead of BMW's ace pair, Hans Stuck and Dieter Quester, in their 528i. This was also the final 6-hour international event to be held on the original Nürburgring circuit.

The TWR-Jaguar team's third place in the ETC championship was highly promising and for 1983 Walkinshaw received official support from Jaguar. The newly-liveried cars - now

Below: The effort by Ralph Broad to make the XJ12C a race winner in 1976/77 was a brave one, but the cars were plagued with unreliability.

predominantly white - were even more competitive thanks to the lessons learned during 1982 with the bonus of extra power (up to some 400 bhp) extracted from the 5.3-litre V12 by TWR's engine man Allan Scott.

It was a season of contrasts: two Jaguars entered the first race, at Monza, but lost due to an engine failure and a loose bonnet fastening, allowing one of an entry of ten new BMW 635CSi 3.5-litre coupés to win. Then both XJ-Ss retired during the Nürburgring round. But at Donington Park, Martin Brundle put in a spectacular wet-weather drive in his XJ-S to beat Dieter Quester's BMW. By the season's end, Jaguar had won five rounds to BMW's six, netting the Coventry marque second place in the championship.

Above: **Long hours are all part of a racing team's life. Here the TWR mechanics prepare the XJ-Ss before the start of a 1984 ETC round.**

Above: **The magnificent sight of the XJ-S lifting a wheel as it charges through the chicane on its way to a glorious victory in the Spa 24 hour race in 1984.**

Would 1984 be third time lucky? Certainly there was now a three-car Jaguar team and it was Walkinshaw's own XJ-S, co-driven by new recruit Hans Heyer, which won the first race at Monza. This was despite, as ever, the thirstier Jaguars having to make an extra pit stop for fuel compared to the lighter BMWs.

Another wet race at Vallelunga produced only a third place after Win Percy - another 1984 recruit - suffered a thrown drive belt, a misfortune which befell Hans Heyer at the Nürburgring. Such belt failures had not previously afflicted the normally very reliable V12, but the engine was now producing much more power - up to 550 bhp - and was revving higher. Tom Walkinshaw explains: "There was much, much more heat in the engines, too, and that was having an effect on components. These days we know all about engines and we know exactly what they are doing, but then we were much less knowledgeable. We were learning things as we went along.

"Things that you would never dream could come off, did come off! Rubber and plastic bits were melting because there was so much heat, and we had to get rid of it as best we could".

Gradually, the team worked through these problems and as the season progressed reliability was restored. Then came the 24-Hour race at Spa, the premier race of the ETC and undoubtedly the most challenging. BMW had dominated at the Ardennes circuit over the previous few years and they looked strong in 1984.

"WE WENT TO SPA WITH A CAR PEOPLE SAID COULDN'T WIN, AND WE PROVED THEM WRONG." *Win Percy*

Sure enough, BMWs and even, briefly, the TWR-prepared Rovers led during the earlier, wet, stages with the two XJ-Ss adopting a wait-and-see strategy behind. One of the Jaguars was driven by Tom Walkinshaw, Hans Heyer and Win Percy, the other by Enzo Calderari, the Belgian Teddy Pilette and David Sears (son of Jack Sears, who had driven for and against Jaguar in the 1960s). After some two hours Calderari spun and damaged the XJ-S sufficiently for it to be retired in the pit lane; the surviving Jaguar endured a night of mist, rain and pace-car laps to emerge the leader as the new day dawned.

Above: **Elation! Win Percy, Tom Walkinshaw and Hans Heyer celebrate their superb Spa 24 hour race win, 28th/29th July 1984.**

Above: One that got away... the XJ-S did not win the ETC round at the Nürburgring (the ETC race on the new, shorter, circuit). BMW was victorious on its home territory.

The remaining hours passed and the XJ-S, now a comfortable three laps ahead of the nearest BMW, circulated faultlessly all the way to the chequered flag. It was a momentous victory, Jaguar's first 24-hour race win for many years and the climax of the 1984 season. The message went out across the world to everywhere motor sport was appreciated: the Jaguar had regained its claws.

For at least one of the drivers it was the climax of his career too. Win Percy: "People ask me what was the most memorable race of my life. I can't single out a race but I can an emotion and that was being on the podium, with a Union Jack, in Jaguar overalls, at Spa which I love. That is probably as close as anything I wish to achieve in motor sport."

Silverstone provided an anti-climax. The race was hit by torrential rain and TWR, in a rare misjudgment, did not bring their cars in quickly enough for rain tyres. Spectacular spins resulted and BMW won. This kept the championship open until Zolder. There, Walkinshaw made no mistake; his third place producing enough points to secure the drivers' championship as his nearest rival, Helmut Kelleners, failed to score.

So Tom Walkinshaw became the first, and to date only, Jaguar driver since Peter Nocker in 1963 to win the European Touring Car Drivers' Championship. Jaguar itself out-pointed BMW in the over 2.5-litre class, having won seven times compared with BMW's four (and Volvo's one). That it should happen in the year when Jaguar was floated on the London and New York stock exchanges as an independent company once again made it all the more satisfying.

But the TWR XJ-S still had more to give. In November the team travelled to Macau where the Schnitzer BMWs were again beaten. The Jaguars were not to be seen in action again that year, but they had one more official duty to perform, in Australia.

That country has long been enthusiastic about touring car racing and, of course, Bob Jane reigned supreme in the mid-1960s with his Mk 2. By the 1980s, the most famous race in Australia was the James Hardie 1000 km at the unique Mount Panorama circuit at Bathurst, New South Wales, and to tempt over the Europeans, it now had a Group A class.

Below: The TWR-Jaguar team completed the 1984 season having scored eight outright victories, two 'seconds' and four 'thirds'. BMW managed only three wins.

In 1984 Tom Walkinshaw, over with the TWR-prepared 3.5-litre Rovers, had driven with Bathurst veteran John Goss in the latter's own XJ-S. Goss had won the 1000 km race back in

1974 with a Falcon (he also won the Australian GP that year) and had entered an XJ-S for three years from 1980. But even with Bob Tullius co-driving in 1982 and encouragement from Jaguar, victory had never come his way again. Unfortunately that pattern continued in 1984; after practising sixth fastest, Tom Walkinshaw was left on the line when the clutch broke at the start - as Mike Cotton put it, "the Jaguar did cover a short distance, only because it was hit up the back by another competitor in the startline mêlée!"

This incident left Walkinshaw determined to win the Australian classic. Three cars were prepared for the 1985 race: Walkinshaw paired himself with Win Percy, Jeff Allam left his Rover to partner local driver Ron Dickson, and BMW ace Armin Hahne teamed up with the ever-hopeful John Goss.

'Major Tom' produced a devastingly quick lap to secure pole position during the 'Hardie's Heroes' top ten qualifying session, and shared the front row of the grid with Jeff Allam, with Goss in the third XJ-S on row three. Surrounding them were BMWs, Mustangs, a Volvo and locally-made Holdens. Walkinshaw and Allam made a good start but the latter soon dropped back, his engine apparently having inhaled a piece of broken glass, though after half an hour Goss was running second to Walkinshaw, the Jaguars followed closely by the legendary Australian saloon driver Peter Brock in his V8 Holden.

Below: **The TWR XJ-S's international career stretched across Europe and extended to Australasia and Asia.**

More drama occurred when the leading XJ-S came in with damage to its oil cooler. This left Goss and Hahne - bracing themselves as best they could in the cockpit after the seat mounting broke - to take an emotional victory after 163 laps. John Goss once more became the darling of the crowd and Tom (who worked his way back up to come third behind a Schnitzer BMW) had achieved his ambition of producing a Bathurst winner. It was a glorious moment in the XJ-S's racing career.

Left: **Spa, 1984 and the Walkinshaw/Heyer/Percy car motors toward victory; the XJ-S's challenge had failed here in 1982 and 1983, but not in the car's final year in the ETC.**

In Europe, the XJ-S was retired but two cars were prepared for the Group A race held at Fuji in November 1986; although competitive, both retired, though one notable feature of the race was when Denny Hulme took a spell at the wheel of an XJ-S. The former World Champion and Mk 2 3.8 driver proved very quick, too.

The swan-song of the XJ-S was heard in New Zealand when two cars contested the Wellington 4-Hour race in January 1987; Armin Hahne crashed and the other Jaguar retired with differential failure. Just one car was entered in what was to be the TWR Group A XJ-S's last event, at Pukekohe on 1st February 1987. Win Percy and Armin Hahne came second to the Hulme/Perkins Holden Commodore, a far from disgraceful result for a car whose development had effectively ended two years before.

The Group A racing initiative by Jaguar and TWR had achieved everything that could have been hoped for, including the 1984 European Touring Car Championship, 20 outright victories, the great 24-Hours win at Spa, and victory at Bathurst. These all added to Jaguar's resurgence under John Egan's optimistic chairmanship of Jaguar during the 1980s, reinvigorating Jaguar's sporting image amongst a new generation of owners and enthusiasts and directly increasing sales of the XJ-S itself - helped by new model variants and Egan's quality drive, XJ-S sales lifted from a mere 1,292 in 1981 to 7,510 in 1985. The car also honed the TWR team's skills and provided the spring-board for an even greater sporting venture: Group C and a triumphant return to Le Mans.

Driving the XJ-S

As a road car, the XJ-S continued a two-plus-two tradition that William Lyons had started with the very first S.S.1 of 1931. In some ways it is contradictory that this large, comfortable and refined coupé eventually became one of Europe's most successful competition cars. Nothing could have been further from the minds of Heynes, Knight and Sayer when they designed it!

The Group A XJ-S proved itself to be the fastest of any car competing in the European Touring Car Championship but it needed skill and courage to drive. Tom Walkinshaw, who created it, explained its mannerisms to sports journalist Mike Cotton in these words:

"It was a car that you always had to drive on power. You had to get on the power and keep on it. The worst thing you could do was to lift off, because it would probably go round on you. You had to be confident

that you could drive it on power, really get the back suspension to sit down, and once you had it the car would give you more and more.

"A lot of drivers could not drive the Jaguar because they had to adapt their driving style for it. You had to understand the car, what was happening to all the weight, where it was going, and once you did it was very, very quick."

Win Percy, who with Tom was the most successful of the XJ-S drivers in the 1980s, concurs:

"Basically the cars were extremely heavy in feel - there was no power steering. I like a more docile car, Tom likes a car that is alive; I like a car that you can let flow.

You needed strong arms and legs - the pedals were also extremely heavy. But you could be very precise with it. You did have to respect the transmission and certainly the brakes; the less time on them the better..."

Win Percy remembers one further factor: the heat generated by that big V12 engine: "They really were like ovens inside. We sat very low in the cars, right alongside the tunnel, and your left foot would be beside the gearbox. It was so hot that my left driving shoe would burn and crack, and I had to throw them away after each race".

The ETC-winning XJ-S demanded respect from its drivers but rewarded them well.

XJ-S Jaguar

Technical specifications

SPECIFICATIONS

STANDARD XJ-S GT COUPE (pre-'HE')

Engine capacity	5,343cc
Power	285 bhp @ 5,500 rpm
Length	15ft 11.5ins
Width	5ft 10.5ins
Weight	3,707 lbs (33.1cwt)
Wheelbase	8ft 6ins
Max. speed	153 mph
0-60 mph	6.7 secs
Mpg	12.5-15
(manual transmission)	

GROUP 44 SCCA 1976 XJ-S COUPE

Engine capacity	5,343cc
Power	475 bhp @ 7,600 rpm
Dimensions as for standard car except:-	
Width	6ft 3.5ins
Weight	3,130 lbs (27.9cwt)
Wheels	Minilite 15ins x 10ins rim
Tyres	Goodyear Blue Streak 25.0x10.0-15 front
	27.0x11.0-15 rear
Max. speed	180 mph-plus
0-60 mph	5.0 secs, 0-100 mph: 10.3 secs
0-120 mph	15.2 secs
Mpg	4.0 (racing)

TWR-JAGUAR 1984 GROUP 4 XJ-S COUPE

Engine capacity	5,343cc
Power	485bhp @ 7,500rpm
Length	15ft 11.5ins
Width	5ft 10.5ins
Weight	3,086 lbs (27.6cwt)
Wheelbase	8ft 6ins
Wheels	Speedline 17ns x 13ins rim.
Tyres	Dunlop 17ins
Max. speed	180 mph plus
0-60 mph	4.3 secs, 0-100 mph 9.8 secs
Mpg	4-5 (racing)

Competition results

COMPETITION RESULTS

XJ-S IN TRANS-AM SERIES

(North America)
Built by Group 44 Inc, raced 1976, 1977, 1978 and 1981 in Trans-Am (Category One); driver's championship in 1977 (Bob Tullius) and driver's and manufacturer's championships in 1978

1976

(Category I results)
Watkins Glen, New York state, July: withdrew after practicing
Mosport, Ontario, August, 4th Category I, R. Tullius, 10th overall
Lime Rock, Connecticut, August, R. Tullius, 1st,
Indianapolis Raceway: oil pump drive failed in practice
Road Atlanta, fastest lap but DNF, R. Tullius
Daytona, IMSA Camel GT race, DNF, R. Tullius

1977

Seattle, Washington, May, R. Tullius, 1st
Westwood, British Columbia, June, R. Tullius, 1st
Portland, Oregon, June, R. Tullius, 19th after third gear failed
Nelson Ledges, June, Ohio, R. Tullius, 8th after ignition failure
Watkins Glen, New York state, July, R. Tullius/B. Furstenau, 4th
Hallett, Oklahoma, July, R. Tullius, 1st
Brainerd, Minnesota, August, R. Tullius, 2nd
Mosport, Ontario, August, R. Tullius/B. Ferstenau, 1st
Road America, Wisconsin, September, R. Tullius, 1st
St Jovite, Montreal, September, R. Tullius, 3rd

1978

Sears Point, California, May, R. Tullius, 9th
Westwood, British Columbia, June, R. Tullius, 2nd
Portland, Oregon, June, R. Tullius, 3rd
St Jovite, Montreal, June, R. Tullius, 1st
Watkins Glen, New York State, July, R. Tullius, 1st
Mosport, August, R. Tullius, 1st
Brainerd, Minnesota, August, R. Tullius, 1st
Road America, Wisconsin, September, R. Tullius, 1st
Laguna Seca, California, October, R. Tullius, 1st, B. Ferstanau, 3rd
Mexico City, November, R. Tullius, 1st

1981

Charlotte, N. Carolina, May, R. Tullius, 2nd,
Portland, Oregon, R. Tullius, 1st
Lime Rock, Connecticut, DNF, R. Tullius
Road America, Wisconsin, unplaced after electrical fault, R. Tullius
Brainerd, Minnesota, R. Tullius, 1st
Trois Rivieres, Quebec, DNF, R. Tullius
Mosport, Ontario, R. Tullius, 1st
Laguna Seca, California, R. Tullius, 5th
Sears Point, California, DNF, gearbox failure, R. Tullius

NB: The tube-frame XJ-S also took part in the 1982 Daytona 24 hours for V12 engine development purposes

EUROPEAN TOURING CAR CHAMPIONSHIP

XJ-S Group A built by Tom Walkinshaw Racing, raced 1982-1987. Won European Touring Car Championship Group A and driver's championship (T. Walkinshaw) 1984

1982

Monza, Italy, March, retired, Walkinshaw/'Nicholson'
Vallunga, Italy, March, Walkinshaw/'Nicholson', 3rd
Zolder, Belgium, April (non-ETC event), T. Walkinshaw, 1st
Donington, UK, April, retired while leading (radiator)
Mugello, Italy, May, retired (valve spring failure), T. Walkinshaw
Brno, Czechoslovakia, June, Walkinshaw/'Nicholson', 1st
Zeltweg, Austria, June, T. Walkinshaw, 2nd
Nurburgring, Germany, July, Walkinshaw/'Nicholson', 1st
Spa-Fracorchamps, Belgium, 24 hours, retired
Silverstone, UK, September, Walkinshaw/'Nicholson', 1st Hallam/Lovett, 2nd
Zolder, September, Walkinshaw/'Nicholson', 1st, Allam/Dieudonne, 2nd

1983

Monza, March, Walkinshaw/'Nicholson', 2nd
Vallunga, April, 'Nicholson'/Dieudonne/Walkinshaw, 3rd
Donington, May, Fitzpatrick/Calderari/Brundle, 4th, Walkinshaw/'Nicholson', 5th
Perdusa, May, Walkinshaw/'Nicholson', 1st
Mugello, May, Walkinshaw/Fitzpatrick, 3rd
Zeltweg, June, Walkinshaw/Brundle, 1st, Dieudonne/Calderari, 2nd
Nürburgring, July, DNF (both cars)
Salzburgring, July, Walkinshaw/'Nicholson', 1st
Sap-Francorchamps, July, DNF (one car)
Silverstone, September, Walkinshaw/Diedonne, 9th
Zolder, September, Walkinshaw/Brundle/Percy, 8th

1984

Monza, April, Walkinshaw/Heyer, 1st
Vallelunga, April, Walkinshaw/Heyer, 3rd
Donington, April, Percy/'Nicholson', 1st
Pergusa, May, Calderari/Brundle, 1st, Walkinshaw/Heyer, 2nd, Percy/'Nicholson', 3rd
Brno, June, Walkinshaw/Heyer, 1st, Percy/'Nicholson', 2nd, Calderari/Sears, 3rd
Mugello, June, Walkinshaw/Heyer, 1st, Percy/'Nicholson', 2nd
Salzburgring, July, Percy/'Nicholson, 1st, Calderari/Sears, 2nd
Nürburgring, July, unplaced
Silverstone, September, Calderari/Sears, 2nd
Zolder, September, Walkinshaw/Heyer, 3rd
Mugello, October, Brundle/Calderari/Sears, 5th
Grand Prix of Macau, November (non-ETC race), T. Walkinshaw, 1st, H. Heyer, 2nd

1985

James Hardie 1000, Mt Panorama, Australia, John Goss/Armin Hahne, 1st, Gary Willmington/Peter Janson, 14th

1987

Wellington, New Zealand, January, Percy/Hahne, 2nd

World Champions

Jaguar's 'modern' racing era began in 1982 and the next eight years brought a steady stream of substantial victories including three World Championships and two glorious Le Mans wins.

"ONE OF OUR MAIN MARKETING TASKS IS TO FIND SOME SPEEDY WAY OF GETTING AN IMPROVED QUALITY MESSAGE TO THE CONSUMER. LONG DISTANCE RACING PROVIDES THAT OPPORTUNITY…"

Mike Dale of Jaguar in North America

American Bob Tullius was responsible for producing the first mid-engined racing Jaguar, Group 44's XJR-5, taking Jaguar officially back into motor sport and to Le Mans for the first time since the works D-types raced in 1956. Later, another equally determined individual, Tom Walkinshaw, took up the torch and achieved unprecedented successes in both Europe and North America against frequently larger and better-funded teams.

John Egan, after his arrival as chairman of Jaguar in April 1980, had begun the long task of raising quality and morale. A year later the results were already beginning to appear: the Series 3 XJ6 saloon and the XJ-S coupé, always desirable, were now becoming reliable too. Egan, together with Mike Dale and Graham Whitehead at Jaguar's US sales headquarters in New Jersey, wanted to get that message over to the buying public in North America, still Jaguar's biggest export market. Motor racing appeared to be a cost-effective way of doing this - there was an ideal series for a GT prototype Jaguar, and there was the trusty Bob Tullius, who had already

Below: A vital factor in the success of Group 44 was the team's efficiency in the pits (the pit crew were led by Lanky Foushee). Here the XJR-5 takes on fuel and new tyres in its first race, at Road America.

secured championships for Jaguar with the E-type and XJ-S ready and waiting.

Yes, it would cost money, but sponsors would contribute. In any case the rationale was still there, as Mike Dale explained: "It takes no effort to spend a million dollars in prime time TV in one evening, and while this could be extremely effective for Chevrolet, it is not anywhere near as efficient for a highly specialised low-volume product such as Jaguar." Jaguar also needed to race in long-distance events "to show the durability of its products. That is why we have chosen a GTP car that can use Jaguar's basic engine line so that we can relate our, anticipated, success to the products we sell".

Above: Group 44 opened Jaguar's mid-engined account with the XJR-5, the Lee Dykstra-designed car being built at the team's Winchester, Virginia headquarters in 1982. Its race debut was at Road America, Wisconsin on 22nd August 1982. Tullius came third overall and won the GTP class.

So in January 1982 Jaguar announced the car which would become known as the XJR-5. It was constructed at Group 44's new facility in Winchester, Virginia, the chassis being designed by Lee Dykstra, notable as the only American who had shown himself able to design cars on a par with the best from Europe; he came recommended by Al Hobart, a good friend of Bob Tullius.

The 6-litre Jaguar V12-powered XJR-5, with its honeycomb aluminium monocoque and Kevlar bodywork, first raced on 22nd August 1982 at Road America. This 500-mile event was part of the Camel GT series being run by IMSA - International Motor Sports Association, founded as a rival race organisation to the Sports Car Club of America - and the XJR-5 completed it flawlessly, Tullius and Bill Adam finishing third and first in their class.

The XJR-5's first win was in April 1983 at Road Atlanta (Tullius and Adam again); three more wins followed, and at the close of the season, Bob Tullius, with 121 points, was runner-up to Al Hobart (March-Porsche) with 201 points in the IMSA Championship. It had been a good start, although the season's disappointments were non-finishes in the Daytona 24-Hours in January, and the Sebring 12-Hours in March - a race that had been won by the D-type back in 1955.

For 1984, the two XJR-5s were effectively new cars with many improvements; in addition, one of the cars had Lucas electronic fuel injection. Veteran Brian Redman - who had cut his teeth with the Red Rose lightweight E-type in the 1960s - joined the Group 44 team and this time the XJR-5 did finish at Daytona. Tullius, David Hobbs (who had test-driven the XJ13) and Doc Bundy took third place while Redman in the second car made fastest lap while catching up after drive belt problems.

The Budweiser Miami Grand Prix a few weeks later produced one of the best, and best-remembered, Group 44 results. On the tight street circuit Brian Redman and Doc Bundy won the three-hour race, with Bob Tullius and Pat Bedard second. The event was televised worldwide and the Jaguars were popular winners. It certainly converted Bob Tullius's desire to take the XJR-5 to Le Mans into a certainty.

Group 44 did not record another win in 1984 but continued to impress with the competitiveness and smart turn-out of their cars. But the 1985 season was even tougher, despite another 50 bhp. Just one victory was recorded, the XJR-5's last, at Road Atlanta in April. Brian Redman and Hurley Haywood were the winners, with Bob Tullius and Chip Robinson second.

"WE HAD TO HAVE THE NICEST LOOKING CARS, THE CLEANEST CARS AND PERFORM RIGHT AT THE TOP" *Lanky Foushee, Group 44.*

It was Chip Robinson, the newcomer from a successful Super Vee season, who placed Group 44's achievements in perspective, pointing out to the *Tampa Tribune* that, uniquely, the team were designing the cars, building their engines, and racing them. Every other team raced cars or used engines built elsewhere. Only Group 44 did everything, and it is a huge credit to the team that the two XJR-5s were statistically more reliable than the six (later nine) Porsche 962s racing in IMSA. At the end of 1985, however, the XJR-7 appeared. Another Lee Dykstra design, it was a development of the XJR-5 with lower drag and higher downforce for better cornering - still V12-powered, although the capacity for 1986 was increased to 6.5 litres, giving 690 bhp.

Above: **Night-time stop for Adams/Ballot-Lena/Robinson XJR-5. It was to retire from the Daytona 24 Hours with low oil pressure.**

Throughout its life the XJR-7 met with fierce competition, from the Porsche 962 in particular. Brian Redman maintained, with complete justification, that the XJR-7 was the "best stopping and best handling" car in GTP racing, but it was also heavy. However, a fine win came at the end of the 1986 season, in the Daytona 3-Hours in October (Tullius/Robinson), while in 1987 the car won at Riverside and West Palm Beach.

By this time TWR in Britain had already built their own sports prototype and the writing was on the wall for Group 44. A new car - the XJR-8 - had been built but, as designer and crew chief

Left: The V12-engined XJR-7 arrived in December 1985 and ran in 1986 as a GTP car only; it brought Group 44 a single win during that very tough season, the three hour event at Daytona in October (Tullius/Robinson). In 1987 it won at Riverside and West Palm Beach - the latter was Group 44's final race win, the car shown here carrying most of the team on the victory lap! Drivers were Hurley Haywood and John Morton.

Lawton 'Lanky' Foushee explains, "We never got to race it. It was in the pipe when the programme ended because we had to be working so far in front of ourselves that we had to have something for the '88 and '89 seasons if they happened.

"The racing was handed over to Walkinshaw - we would loved to have continued but we knew it was going to end. We knew from the beginning that they eventually wanted to have it all English.

"And I think Jim Randle (Jaguar's engineering director) actually had visions of building the cars in the factory as they did in the 50s. So we had high hopes that we could do such a good job that they would keep us on longer. But that wasn't the way it ended up.

"I think we did our job but you know, time moves on, things change. We had no regrets."

Group 44 at Le Mans

Amongst the American team's many achievements was to return the Jaguar name to Le Mans for the first time since the last E-type ran in 1964. It had been a personal dream of Mike Dale's to see this happen, and Bob Tullius made it a reality in 1984.

The presence of the two gleaming white XJR-5s were warmly welcomed in France where they added a fresh sparkle. Though slower in practice than the leading teams, once the race began there was an early moment of glory when Bob Tullius (co-driven by Redman and Bundy) actually led the race - taking advantage of pit stops. Even at half distance the Jaguars were running sixth

and seventh, but then Tony Adamowicz in the second car went off the road after a tyre deflated and retired back in the pits. The Tullius car then ran into gearbox problems, and although after a 45-minute stop for repairs it regained eighth place, the gearbox again began to seize again with a few hours to go and no. 44 was retired.

In 1985, the team at least achieved a finish…While the XJR-5 driven by Redman/Haywood/Adams retired with driveline failure, the Tullius/Robinson/Ballot-Lena car, although suffering engine problems, managed to complete the 24 hours and take 13th place, so recording a Jaguar finish at Le Mans for the first time in 22 years.

Group 44's efforts at Le Mans had certainly paved the way for greater things there and contributed usefully to the resurgence of the Jaguar name in competition.

Above: Group 44 kept Jaguar's name in the North American sporting scene during the mid-1980s and began the highly successful XJR series of sports-racing cars. Today the 'R' designation is carried by Jaguar's Formula One car and by performance variants of the road car range.

Below: Martin Brundle and Mike Thackwell took the XJR-6 to fifth place at Spa in 1985, amidst the Porsches and a couple of quick Lancias.

Tom Walkinshaw and the Sportscar World Championship

While Group 44 were allowed a further year in North American events, Jaguar had responded well to Tom Walkinshaw's suggestion that he should run a team of Jaguars in the Sportscar World Championship, Group C. John Egan, for the same reasons he had approved the Group 44 programme, could see the worth of the proposal. He also wanted to raise Jaguar's profile against

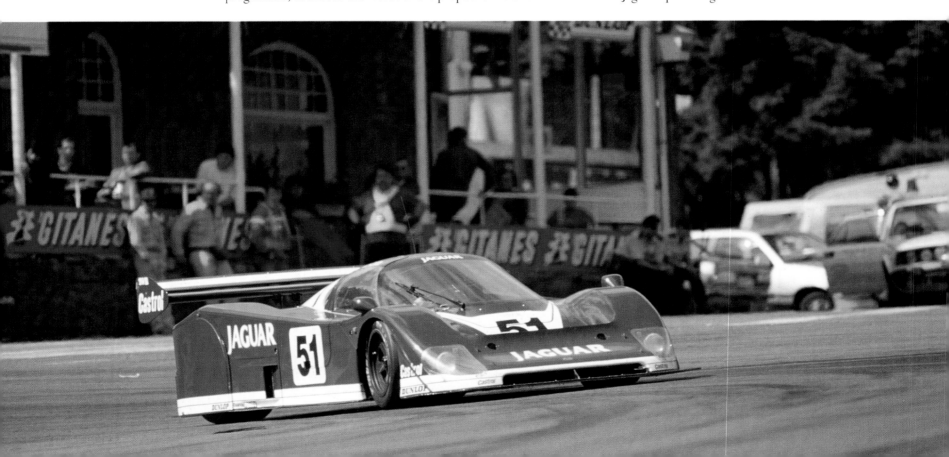

its major rivals - Mercedes-Benz, BMW and Porsche. Agreement came in February 1985 and
TWR very rapidly produced the XJR-6 (which borrowed its name from Group 44's sequence of
identification), the car having been on the stocks ever since the 1984 ETC programme had ended.

The Tony Southgate-designed car used a very light and immensely strong carbon fibre and
Kevlar composite chassis/monocoque. The underside of this featured 'ground effect' twin
venturis, made possible by the Jaguar engine's 'V' shape, which helped suck the car down onto
the road. This was something the Porsche's
flat six engine layout would not allow.

A key change in motor racing,
compared with Jaguar's programme of the
1950s, was the importance of sponsorship:
the sport at international level was now
hugely expensive, and if Jaguar were to
compete successfully against the all-
conquering Porsche, more funds than
Jaguar could afford would be needed.
Accordingly John Egan's sales and

Above: **January 1988 and the XJR-9 hammers round the Daytona banking on the way to victory in the 24 hour race. Drivers were John Nielsen, Martin Brundle and Price Cobb.**

marketing director, Neil Johnson, brought in sponsorship specialist Guy Edwards to locate
suitable partners for the project. He succeeded with Peter Gilpin, chairman of the tobacco giant
Gallaher International: by October 1985 a deal was in place and the Silk Cut Jaguar team was
born. Egan was pragmatic about the health issues which even then surrounded tobacco; he was
prepared to take the money and accept some criticism for it.

The XJR-6 made its entrance at Mosport, Canada, in August 1985, painted British Racing
Green rather than the later mauve and white Silk Cut livery. A third place resulted, enough to
give the Porsche drivers a severe shock.

The team's first full season, 1986, began with an historic win at Silverstone, Warwick and
Eddie Cheever always looking the favourites in the Kouros 1,000 kms. No further wins were
recorded that season but enough points had been amassed by the final round at Fuji so that if
Warwick finished first or second, he would win the Drivers' Championship and Jaguar the new
Teams Championship. Minor problems resulted in a third place, but nevertheless it was a brilliant
start by the Silk Cut Jaguar team.

In 1987 everything came good. The new XJR-8 - in reality an evolutionary XJR-6 - used a 7-
litre, 720 bhp version of the Jaguar V12 engine and proved to be the dominant car of the season.
Eight wins from ten races was easily enough to bring Jaguar its first World Championship ever in
sports car racing, while Raul Boesel became World Champion driver. It went a long way to
making up for a disappointment at Le Mans that year.

The new XJR-9 contested the 1988 season, and started in the best way possible by winning the Daytona 24-Hours in January - John Nielsen, Martin Brundle and Price Cobb the drivers. Then came wins at Jarama, Monza and Silverstone before, finally, a Jaguar was victorious at Le Mans once more. A total of eight wins were recorded in 1988, Martin Brundle and Eddie Cheever between them accounting for five of these. Brundle became World Champion driver and Jaguar kept hold of the Teams' Championship. It all helped, perhaps, to further encourage the decision by Ford to purchase Jaguar, which they did just a year later.

By contrast the 1989 season was considerably less successful; 1988 had shown the increasing strength of the turbocharged cars and TWR produced the V6 turbocharged XJR-10 and 11 in response - but they took considerable 'sorting' and the 750 bhp XJR-11 (the 3.5-litre WSC car) posted its first win only in May 1990, at Silverstone. However, the majority of the results in 1990 (including at Daytona and Le Mans) were obtained by the 'old' V12-engined machines, which amassed enough points for the Silk Cut team to come second to Team Sauber Mercedes in the Teams Championship, Andy Wallace coming fourth in the Driver's Championship.

The mainstream car for 1991 added yet another type designation to the somewhat bewildering tally of XJR Jaguar sports cars: XJR-14. It was the first designed for Jaguar by Ross Brawn and the third all-new XJR. The engine was the Ford-Cosworth HB V8 Grand Prix unit and conformed to the FIA's new 3.5-litre formula for the 1991 Sportscar World Championship.

Very light (it needed to be ballasted to reach the 750 kg minimum weight), the 14 was virtually a two-seater Grand Prix car and intended for short races only; the 24-hour events were left to the V12 cars. The XJR-14, with its characteristic two-tier rear wing, raced in seven Group C events and won three of them (Monza, Silverstone and - especially satisfying - Nürburgring), gaining enough points to make Teo Fabi World Champion driver and Silk Cut Jaguar the World Champion team.

Below: **The V12-engined XJR-9 continued to race in 1989 but suffered from lack of development - most of the effort was now being put into the turbocharged XJR-10 and XJR-11. This is the car at Donington in September 1989.**

Above: The TWR Jaguar transporter was highly artistic: here the XJR-16 is cleaned prior to an outing at Portland, 1991. Tony Dowe, team manager, ran a tight ship and TWR's IMSA team was one of the most efficient in the series despite its relatively small size.

This highly satisfactory result was the last of three World Championships gained by Tom Walkinshaw and the XJR sports cars. The Gallaher sponsorship deal came to an end and the Jaguars gracefully withdrew at the end of 1991. In any case, the increasingly poorly-supported Sportscar World Championship was voted out of existence by the FIA in October 1992, ending world championship status for sports car endurance racing that had existed since 1953. But it had been the arena for a wonderful run of success for Jaguar that was of enormous benefit in re-establishing the sporting credentials of the marque to a new generation of enthusiasts and potential customers.

Jaguar and IMSA

When Group 44's contract ended in 1987, the Jaguar IMSA team was formed, operating from Valparaiso, Indiana: team manager was Tony Dowe and Ian Reed the engineer. Guy Edwards secured Castrol as the major sponsor - the contract was signed on 19th October 1987 and he, and Jaguar, were perhaps fortunate because, that very day, Wall Street plunged to be followed by the London Stock Exchange. 'Black Monday' had hit. One day's delay and the deal might never have been struck.

The new XJR-9 was given its debut by the IMSA team, with its V12 in 6-litre form to comply with Grand Touring Prototype regulations. In January 1988, the TWR Castrol car - driven by John Nielsen, Martin Brundle and Price Cobb - promptly won the opening race of the season, the Daytona 24-Hour, ending the Porsche domination of the event which had existed since 1976!

Tony Dowe was all the more pleased with this result since the win had been produced only 16 weeks after the team moved into an empty factory in Valparaiso. "We worked 20 hours a day to get there," he told journalist Ken Wells. "We had to find staff, kit out the factory, prepare the cars and everything else..."

One other win came in 1988, at the final meeting in October at Del Mar. But just as Bob Tullius had found, driving against turbocharged cars was extremely difficult: the ability to wind up or turn down boost to either gain speed or reduce fuel consumption gave the turbo cars a huge advantage over normally aspirated ones, and it was to counter this that the XJR-10 (and its sister XJR-11) was developed by Tony Southgate. For IMSA, the capacity was three litres and the car first raced in May 1989 at Lime Rock, Connecticut, where it finished second to Geoff Brabham's Nissan. Wins followed at Portland in July (Cobb/Lammers) and at Del Mar again in October (Lammers).

Above: **The XJR-11 was based on the XJR-10 turbocharged V6 design which had already been racing in IMSA events. This is the 3.5 litre car at Monza, 1990.**

In February 1990 the TWR Castrol team, now on Goodyear tyres, scored a great first and second in the Daytona 24-Hours, using the V12-engined XJR-9. Lammers, Wallace and Jones drove the winning car, followed by Brundle, Cobb and Nielsen. It was a moment to savour. The XJR-10 provided victories at Lime Rock and Portland in 1990, but the Castrol Jaguar team were unable to amass enough points to win their championship.

The following year, 1991, the team had the XJR-16 development of the '10', produced with an eye to coping better with the bumpy track conditions often found on American circuits. Competition, meanwhile, was hotting up, the team now having to contend with very fast cars from Toyota, Chevrolet and Nissan. The particular needle match was with Nissan, and a fair bit of gamesmanship went on between the two teams - "mind games" is what Tony Dowe called it. "We will use any and every means to unsettle them," he said, expecting them to do exactly the same.

It was also a fact that Nissan had over 200 people working in their team. At Valparaiso there were just 32 staff, "including receptionists etc." Yet by 1991 the team was really working well and in that year won six times - two with the XJR-14 and four with the XJR-16 - compared with just seven victories over the previous three years. However, Nissan still won the Manufacturers' championship, with 220 points against TWR's 188.

That was pretty much the end for the hard-working Castrol Jaguar team in North America, though the XJR-14 won at Road Atlanta and Mid-Ohio early in 1992, driven on both occasions by Davy Jones. But hopes of winning the IMSA Camel GT Championship faded thereafter, with the

XJR-14 increasingly outpaced by the Dan Gurney-prepared AAR Toyota Eagles. Nevertheless the TWR Castrol had maintained the Jaguar name in North American motor sport at a high level, and gained considerable respect.

TWR-Jaguar at Le Mans

Jaguar's motor racing policy of the late 1980s and early 1990s greatly differed from the company's approach in the 1950s. Then, Le Mans and only Le Mans had been the goal; other races were entered on the basis of, "well, it won't interfere with Le Mans and we have to keep the drivers busy..." In the 'modern' initiative, though, the objective was, for the first time, to gain a championship. Which, as we have seen, was done - three times over.

Le Mans still soared above all other races in stature, however, and remained the single most important objective for Tom Walkinshaw and John Egan. For a start, nothing else received anywhere near the same media coverage - TV satellite broadcasting had now arrived and half the 1988 race was carried live throughout Europe, while TV networks in five continents and 15 countries also broadcast live coverage; another 43 countries took edited highlights and CBS had

six crews covering the action and life around the circuit. Even the Japanese Asahi TV network had a 30-man team in place and broadcast eight hours live.

The Silk Cut Jaguar team's assault on the 24-Hour race began in low-key fashion. At the first attempt, in 1986, none of the three 6-litre V12 XJR-6s entered lasted the distance: the Redman/Haywood/Heyer car retired after six hours, the Brancolli/Percy/Haywood entry in the

Above: **The Lammers/ Watson/Percy XJR-8LM which crashed out of the 1987 Le Mans at 3am.**

10th hour, while the Warwick/Cheever/Schlesser car lasted until the 17th hour. But Tom Walkinshaw had never promised immediate victory...

The 1987 Le Mans did not produce the goods either, despite the Jaguars dominating the World Sportscar Championship. Despite most of the Porsches being eliminated by engine failures (they had been forced to run on commercially available fuel for the first time), only the Cheever/Lammers/Boesel XJR-8LM finished, and that down in fifth place. The Brundle/Nielsen car retired in the 16th hour but that was after the most memorable Jaguar episode of the 1987 Le Mans - the crash which took out Win Percy! He tells the story well:

"I was heading down Mulsanne and the car started to buck. I was doing 240 mph but I kept my foot buried, and just at the 300 metre mark there was an explosive noise and the car took off.

"It went up in the air like a leaf in the wind, up, up and up! I thought, 'this is going to hurt' so I hunched up and even closed my eyes. Then I opened them and I was literally above the trees. It crashed after 600 metres, barrel-rolled and crashed onto the Armco very fast - after Jo (Gartner)'s accident it was three rather than two layers and I think that's what saved my life. That and the strength of the car, to be honest.

"I remember it slid on its side for quite a long way, I could feel the heat of my helmet against the track - then it slowed and slowed and stopped. I just undid my belts and got out! I remember standing by the wreck on Mulsanne and I couldn't believe it. But I still took care to take the mike lead out - otherwise I'd get a rollicking from Tom because they cost £1 each!"

Everything gelled for the Jaguar team in 1988. Five Silk Cut Jaguar XJR-9LMs were entered, the drivers told by Roger Silman (the modern equivalent of Lofty England) to set their own pace. They could also set up the cars to their own taste - either for greater downforce for better cornering, or with less downforce and greater speed along the Mulsanne straight. Jan Lammers

Right: The XJR-16 was evolved from the XJR-10 by Ross Brawn and although it was campaigned for less than a season, in 1991 Davy Jones won four races out of ten with it.

chose the least drag, and was the quickest along Mulsanne at 244 mph. Some heat was removed from the situation when the two Sauber Mercedes withdrew before the start with tyre problems, but the threat of the Porsche 962Cs remained.

When the race began on 11th June, Porsche's Hans-Joachim Stuck led the 49 starters for the first six laps, and at a couple of other times early on in the race but after the first hour was never in contention, losing nearly two laps when co-driver (with Derek Bell) Klaus Ludwig almost ran out of fuel. Problems also afflicted the other potential Porsche threats and after 11 hours, the Jaguars had little opposition.

Except, that is, for fate itself. The Brundle/Nielsen car overheated and had to be retired, and a broken gearbox input shaft sidelined the John Watson/Henri Pescarolo/Raul Boesel entry. The American-piloted car of Danny Sullivan, Davy Jones and Price Cobb held third for a while but lost some three hours on a transmission rebuild in the pits.

So it was all down to Jan Lammers, Johnny Dumfries and Andy Wallace. John Egan described the last few hours as "torture"; it was a little like 1951 all over again. Would the only Jaguar left in genuine contention last out? With five hours to go it began to rain - "the least slip by Jan

Above: **Routine refuelling pit stop for the car which was to win the 1988 Le Mans 24 hour race. A quick clean of the screen, too.**

Lammers could have turned Jaguar's day into a total disaster," recorded Mike Cotton, watching the race unfold from the pits. "Pulse rates quickened each time the Dutchman was due, and each time hundreds of voices across the road signalled his approach before he could be seen."

The emotion as the travel-stained XJR-9LM crossed the line after the 24th hour affected everyone and more than a few tears were surreptitiously shed by those who had waited many, many years to see a Jaguar win once more at Le Mans. The crowds surged around the winning car and under the balcony where the drivers joined Tom Walkinshaw, Roger Silman and John Egan to receive their trophies. It was a wonderful moment.

Above: **John Nielsen and Martin Brundle in animated conversation before the 1987 Le Mans. Any discussions about tactics were doomed to failure, however - the car retired during the 16th hour.**

For Tom, it was simply the successful application of the right strategy. "We knew it was going to be a hard race," he said, "but we didn't think it would be any harder than it was. We expected to cover 295 laps and we did 294. If it hadn't rained on Sunday morning we'd have done 297, far more than anyone had ever done before, and we weren't wrong."

The only sad fact about the whole occasion was the BBC's woeful decision, later regretted, not to cover the event. Many British enthusiasts therefore lost out on being part of an historic British sporting victory.

At Le Mans in 1989 the team could not repeat its 1988 success. All the cars were affected by vibrations from the tyres which began turning on the rims. Gearbox and then engine problems put out the XJR-9LM of Davy Jones, Derek Daly and Jeff Kline, after Jones had set a cracking pace to lead from Jochen Mass' Mercedes, while the Alain Ferte/Eliseo Salazar Jaguar, in fifth place, lost third gear which necessitated a gearbox change (it was to finish eighth, but at least Alain Ferte put up fastest lap while catching up). Then at 5.30 on the Sunday morning, the Nielsen/Wallace/Cobb car dropped out with a failed head gasket. Jan Lammers, Patrick Tambay and Gilbert Scott finally managed to get home in fourth place; Sauber Mercedes were first and second, the Stuck/Wolleck Porsche third.

It had to be better in 1990. And it was.

The 1990 Le Mans 24 Hours saw a wide-ranging entry in which, along with the traditional marques (Porsche was going for its 13th win, Jaguar for its seventh, Mercedes its third), Mazda, Nissan and Toyota were offering strong challenges from Japan. An unknown factor had also been thrown in: two chicanes were now in place on the Mulsanne straight, to reduce maximum speeds.

The Jaguar challenge was in the form of the new XJR-12LM, the final expression of the XJR V12 series which had been developed in America by TWR Inc. for Daytona and Sebring. The type's Daytona win in January 1990 certainly raised hopes for Le Mans, and four of the 7-litre, 750 bhp cars were entered.

While the race was not without drama, it soon became clear that the most consistent performer was the Nielsen/Cobb XJR-12LM, which circulated steadily near the front for ten hours, playing a waiting game. Then, as the "very subdued" Porsches hit trouble, the Jaguar slipped into the lead at 3 am on the Sunday. As his car had broken, Brundle was put behind the wheel at 7.20 am and after that the only concern was the gearbox which lost fourth gear less than six hours from the end.

"That made it hard," recounted Nielsen afterwards. "Le Mans is mainly fourth and fifth gear corners so it was extremely difficult to get our lap times … It was still possible to do the times, but it was pretty damned hard."

In fact the Dane, "built like a rugby player", spent 12 hours 51 minutes behind the wheel, compared with Price Cobb's six hours 56 minutes and Martin Brundle's four hours 13 minutes.

Below: **Jaguar's seventh Le Mans win was greeted with rapture by British race fans.**

Thus Jaguar's seventh Le Mans win was secured, the victorious Jaguar having covered 359 laps at 126.80 mph average. The Lammers/Wallace/Conrad XJR-12LM was second (355 laps), with the Needell/Sears/Reid Porsche 962C third (351 laps). Again, emotions ran high as the Jaguars finished.

Top left: **Two out of four XJR-12LM Jaguars entered in the 1990 Le Mans survived - and achieved a wonderful first and second. Here they cross the line after the end of the 24 hours.**

Bottom left: **Price Cobb, Martin Brundle, John Nielsen, Tom Walkinshaw and Sir John Egan just after the 1990 Le Mans win. It was a joyous occasion for them and the tens of thousands of Jaguar supporters at Le Mans.**

As for 1991 - well, as the old adage says, no one remembers who came second. So it is that while Tom Walkinshaw rates the 1991 Le Mans as one of the greatest finishes Jaguar ever achieved at the circuit, few people recall what happened that year because a Jaguar did not win. The race caused some controversy too: besides four XJR-12LMs, Tom Walkinshaw had entered a single XJR-14 and, in fact Andy Wallace was quickest in qualifying in his 3.5-litre class. But the car was withdrawn, much to the dismay of the Automobile Club de l'Ouest who had chosen the car to illustrate its race posters! But the XJR-14 had not been built for endurance racing and, in any case, the engine had been damaged.

"I'VE GOT A LOT OF TIME FOR THE XJR-15, IT'S A WONDERFUL BEAST." *Win Percy*

The great surprise of 1991 was the rotary-engined Mazda. It was not thought to stand any chance of lasting the distance, although it was favoured by a low (830 kg) minimum weight - the Jaguars and Mercedes had to weigh at least 1,000 kg. But, to cut a long story short, the Mazda, driven by

Johnny Herbert, Bertrand Gachot and Volker Weidler not only survived but became the first Japanese car ever to win Le Mans. The Jaguar team was somewhat shocked, but admired the effort just the same.

Had it not been for the Mazda's speed, fuel economy and endurance, Jaguars would have finished first, second and third. As it was, they finished one notch down from that: the Jones/M. Ferte/Boesel car was second, the Fabi/Wollek/Acheson Jaguar third, with Nielsen, Warwick and Wallace bringing up in fourth. One of the Jaguars failed to finish: the TWR Suntec, Japanese-entered XJR-12LM, looking very different in British Racing Green and white, suffered a couple of crashes and finally a broken drive shaft.

One consolation was that the best of the three Mercedes C11s managed only fifth (one of its drivers was a talented young hopeful called Michael Schumacher), and the results boosted the Jaguar team's chances in the Teams Championship.

The 1991 race brought down the curtain on Jaguar's return to Le Mans. While the XJR-12 continued to compete until the Daytona 24-Hours in January 1993, after that we would have to wait until the year 2000 before we saw a full Jaguar team race officially again. Then, it would be Formula One rather than sports car racing which would beckon.

Below: **Le Mans 1991 and the XJR-12LMs put in one of the best-ever Jaguar performances at Le Mans, finishing second, third and fourth.**

Driving the XJR sports prototype

Chassis no. 001 was the car that took the Jaguar name back into world-class motor sport in 1982 - the founding father, if you like, of all Jaguar's 'modern' racing successes and therefore a very appropriate car to feature here.

This XJR-5 (seen below) was completed in July 1982 by Group 44 in North America to the design of Lee Dykstra. It was taken to Lockheed Marrietta that month for wind-tunnel testing and was first raced in a 500 mile race at Road America, Elkhart Lake, in August where it came third (and first GTP) driven by Bill Adam and Group 44 chief Bob Tullius.

After suffering a tyre blow-out at nearly 200mph in the 1983 Daytona 24 hour race, it won its first event on April 10 1983 at Road Atlanta (Tullius and Adam again). That year it was taken to the UK and

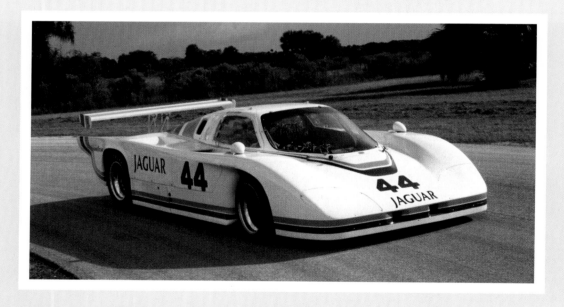

tested at Silverstone by Derek Bell, so becoming the first mid-engined Jaguar, apart from XJ13, to run in the UK. Then after running in the Mosport 6-hour race in Canada it was retired to duties as Group 44's spare car, eventually coming into the custody of that great Jaguar enthusiast in Florida, Walter Hill. It was in 1990 that Walter demonstrated this historic V12-engined projectile on his private circuit, and this is what I wrote at the time:

"A few warm-up laps and it was time for me to get strapped in beside the driver. Modern mid-engined cars aren't easy to get into - there's a massively wide 'sill' to climb over and only certain parts of the bodywork can be trod on or grasped - and once you are 'in' you are certainly 'in', sunk down into the hard bucket seat and feeling a little trapped behind the vast windscreen as the semi-gullwing door comes down to cut you off from the real world.

"Once on the move you are indeed in a different world. First there's the noise, a raucous, nerve-jangling cacophony of transmission whine, mechanical engine noise, the crash of the near-solid suspension over every tiny ridge and, over and above all else, the rising scream of the V12's exhaust.

"Then there are the g-forces, perhaps unimaginable to anyone who hasn't experienced the effect of 650bhp in a car that weighs no more than a small saloon. You experience them three ways, too - on acceleration, where suddenly all is a blur except for the rapidly approaching horizon, on braking when but for the belts you'd be through the screen, and on cornering when you find it almost impossible to keep your head from lolling to one side as the car goes one way and it wants to go another.

"Walter took the car up to 7,000rpm in the first three gears and gave me a couple of quick laps before I indicated that my stomach would not stretch to any more. Bathed in sweat and more than a little dazed I struggled out of my seat - gratefully, I almost said, but it was an experience I'd not have missed for the world."

XJR Jaguar

Technical specifications

RESUME OF TYPES 1982-1993

XJR-5
Built by Group 44 Inc., USA. 6.0 litre, 600-650 bhp.

XJR-7
Built by Group 44 Inc. 6.0/6.5 litre (1986), 650/690 bhp.

XJR-6
Built by Tom Walkinshaw Racing. 6.2/6.5 litre, 650/690 bhp.

XJR-8 & 8LM
Built by TWR. 7.0 litre, 720 bhp.

XJR-9 & 9LM
Built by TWR. 7.0 litre/750 bhp (6.0 litre, 650 bhp IMSA spec.).

XJR-10
Built by TWR. Turbocharged 3.0 litre 650 bhp V6 based on Metro 6RA engine.

XJR-11
Built by TWR. Turbocharged 3.5 litre 750 bhp V6.

XJR-12 & 12LM
Built by TWR. 7.0 litre/750 bhp, (7.4 litre/750 bhp Le Mans 1991, 6.0 litre/650 bhp IMSA).

XJR-16
Built by TWR to a Ross Brawn design to suit bumpy IMSA courses, with turbocharged 3.0 litre V6 engine.

XJR-17
Built by TWR for possible use in IMSA Camel Light category and FIA cup category with (respectively) non-turbocharged 3.0 or 3.5 litre V6 engines, chassis based on XJR-16.

XJR-14
Built by TWR for Sportscar World Championship, Group C and IMSA. First design by Ross Brawn for TWR and third all-new XJR for TWR. Ford Cosworth HB 650-700 bhp V8.

XJR-15
Built by JaguarSport for the Intercontinental Challenge. Based on the XJR-9LM but with Peter Stevens-designed body, wider chassis and engine based on JaguarSport XJR-S 6.0 litre V12 giving approx. 450 bhp.

XJ220C
Built by JaguarSport for GT racing; announced 2nd January 1993. The XJ220C was essentially a lightweight racing version of the production XJ220. Engine was a JaguarSport turbocharged 500 bhp 3.5 V6.

Competition results

XJR-5
Raced 1982-1985. Won 1983 IMSA championship. Le Mans: retired 1984, 13th 1985 (1st GTP).

XJR-7
Raced 1985-1988.

XJR-6
Raced 1985-1986. Won Silverstone 1,000 km 1986. Le Mans: retired 1986 after lying 2nd for 16 hours.

XJR-8 & 8LM
Raced 1987. Won eight races and Team and Driver World Championships (Silk Cut Jaguar/Raul Boesel). Le Mans: 5th 1987.

XJR-9 & 9LM
Raced 1988-1989. Won nine races and Team and Driver World Championships (Silk Cut Jaguar/Martin Brundle). Le Mans: 1st, 4th and 16th 1988, 4th and 8th 1989. Won Daytona 24 Hours 1988.

XJR-10
Raced 1989-1991. Won six IMSA races including Miami GP April 1991.

XJR-11
Raced 1989-1990. Group C version of XJR-10. Won one race, Silverstone 480 kms 1990.

XJR-12 & 12LM
Raced 1990-1993. Won three races including Daytona in 1990 and 1992. Le Mans: 1st 1990, 2nd, 3rd, 4th 1991.

XJR-16
Raced April to August 1991 only. Won 4 IMSA races, driven by Davy Jones.

XJR-17
Tested January 1992 but never raced by TWR. Subsequently appeared in private hands at UK club meetings.

XJR-14
Raced 1991-1992. Won three Group C races, and two IMSA races.

XJR-15
Raced 1991.

XJ220C
First raced May 1993 and won GT race at Silverstone (driver Win Percy), a warm-up in preparation for Le Mans, June 1993 - one car out of the three XJ220Cs entered finished, in 15th place and first in the GT category (though this was disputed by the ACO, the organising club). Won GT class, IMSA at Elkhart Lake, July 1993. Two Le Mans cars subsequently purchased by Tony Brooks and entered privately at Le Mans 1996, one finishing,

XJR
Results: see Jaguars at Le Mans page 158-159.

XJ220
In the USA in 1993, twelve standard XJ220s took part in the Jaguar/Havoline sponsored Fastmasters series for invited veteran race drivers. Entries included Parnelli Jones, George Follmer, Brian Redman, David Hobbs, Bobby Unser, Bob Bondurant, Derek Bell, Guy Edwards and Paul Newman. The oldest Fastmaster was Roger Ward, 72. The two highest qualifiers in the five preliminary rounds went forward to the finals - won by Bobby Unser (aged 59) on 21st August 1993. He collected the $100,000 purse.

LISTER STORM
Following a tie-up with Lister-Jaguar constructor of the 1950s Brian Lister, Laurence Pearce of WP Automotive in Leatherhead, Surrey, UK produced in the 1980s and 1990s a series of highly modified XJ-S road cars using the Lister name. In 1994 Pearce built an entirely new front-engined, 6,996cc V12 Jaguar powered car, the Lister Storm, which raced in GT events plus the 1995 Daytona 24 hours and Le Mans (it failed to finish either race). In 1996 a Lister Storm driven by Needell/Lees/Reid finished 19th overall at Le Mans and 11th in the GT1 category. However, the two Storms entered in the 1997 Le Mans race failed to finish.

With sponsorship from the Newcastle United football team, and after several promising seasons, in the 2000 season the Lister Storm proved to be the quickest car in the FIA GT championship, beating Chrysler Viper, Ferrari 550 Maranello and Porsche 911 GT2 opposition. Successes included winning the British Empire Trophy race - witnessed by Brian Lister who had also been present when Archie Scott Brown won the same trophy driving a Lister-Jaguar in 1957...

Formula One

On Tuesday, 25th January 2000, to a spectacular accompaniment of lights and music, the Jaguar R1 Grand Prix car emerged through clouds of dry ice. Jaguar, for the first time in its history, had entered Formula One motor racing.

"ALMOST 50 YEARS AGO JAGUAR SET OUT ON A JOURNEY WHICH LED TO ITS FAMOUS VICTORIES AT LE MANS… TODAY WE ARE STARTING A NEW ERA IN JAGUAR'S DEVELOPMENT - WE ARE RE-OPENING THE BOOK AT A NEW CHAPTER. I INTEND IT TO BE JUST AS SUCCESSFUL." *Dr Wolfgang Reitzle*

The announcement of Jaguar's Formula One campaign - in a cavernous pavilion erected alongside the new press centre at Lord's Cricket Ground in London - was reckoned to be the biggest, most expensive and most flamboyant ever for a new Formula One team.

It was certainly a momentous step for the company: Grand Prix racing is simply an order of magnitude above any other form of motor sport. Yet there had long been links between the Coventry firm and Formula One - through successive investigations into a Jaguar Grand Prix car and, especially, through Jaguar drivers.

The World Championship of Drivers was established in 1950, and the tally of Formula One World Champions who drove Jaguars or Jaguar-engined cars is impressive - Mike Hawthorn

Below: **Stirling Moss, one of the world's greatest Formula One drivers, secured the first major success of his career with the Jaguar XK 120. Here he is being congratulated after that historic win in the 1950 Tourist Trophy race at Dundrod.**

(World Champion in 1958), Jack Brabham (1959, 1960, 1966), Phil Hill (1961), Graham Hill (1962), Jim Clark (1963, 1965), Denny Hulme (1967) and Jackie Stewart (1969, 1971, 1973). Sir Stirling Moss, of course, heads the list of Grand Prix drivers who drove Jaguars but never won the World Championship - people like Martin Brundle, John Watson and Eddie Cheever.

In the 1950s F.R.W. 'Lofty' England, with his background in motor racing, knew how to choose the best drivers for his works team. Jaguar's chief engineer (and later engineering director) Bill Heynes was, if anything, more of a motor racing enthusiast than Lofty, and might well have led Jaguar into Formula One at various times in the 1950s and 1960s had circumstances been right.

Above: **Lofty England (far right), who selected and guided the Jaguar team's drivers in 1950s. To his right Peter Whitehead and Peter Walker, winners of the all-important 1951 Le Mans.**

In fact, when the BRM racing effort seemed to be doing more harm than good to Britain's Formula One aspirations, a number of people wished that Jaguar, which had just won the 1951 Le Mans, would produce a Grand Prix car. "Ascari reckoned Jaguar were the only company that could build a British GP car," says Tom Jones, a member of the C-type design team, recalling the period when all the best F1 cars came from the continent. Around that time the company did embark on a low-key investigation into producing a single seater using C-type components, but this came to nothing. Jaguar had their work cut out producing the D-type.

A further look at Formula One a few years later, when Jaguar had just withdrawn from racing sports cars, was instigated by no less than Sir William Lyons himself. Recalled Lofty England: "In 1956, when Mike (Hawthorn) was driving for BRM and not having much luck, Sir W. decided we should build a single-seater car for him. We borrowed a 250F Maserati to have a look at and the competition shop made a start with a mock-up chassis. However, Mike rejoined Ferrari so the project was dropped."

Jaguar's chief engineer, Bill Heynes, continued to follow the technicalities of Formula One closely - around 1960 Derrick White produced a chassis design for him, influenced by contemporary Lotus and Cooper practice while Malcolm Sayer created a single-seater scale model. For a power unit, Heynes proposed an advanced V8. The car was never built. "I think everybody would have loved to have done it, but it all came back to resources and money," remembers Trevor Crisp, now managing director of Cosworth Racing but then on Bill Heynes' engineering staff.

It was the acquisition by Jaguar of Coventry Climax Engines in 1963 which finally laid to rest any prospect of an in-house Jaguar Formula One car. Instead, Jaguar could enjoy a connection with Grand Prix racing by proxy, through the superb Walter Hassan-designed Coventry Climax 1.5-litre V8 engine which won 18 Grands Prix and took Jim Clark to his first World Championship.

When Jaguar did finally return officially to racing, it was in its traditional field - sports cars. The TWR-built Group C cars won Le Mans twice and together with victories throughout Europe and North America, the racing of the 1980s and early 1990s kept Jaguar's sporting image alive. There were rumours that these successes might have been followed up by a Tom Walkinshaw-initiated Jaguar Formula One venture but with Jaguar now owned by Ford, there was no John Egan for Tom to have a one-to-one with (Walkinshaw instead established a long-term relationship with the Arrows F1 team).

It was over five years later, in 1996, when Jaguar was coming good in the marketplace that Ford took a strategic look at motor sport for all their brands. While the Ford nameplate would be good for rallying, NASCAR and Indy, it was decided, Jaguar seemed to be the natural choice for Formula One.

Another strong influence on the decision was that BMW, Mercedes and Toyota were all now operating within Formula One. Ford President Jacques Nasser's clearly stated ambition was that

Below: **Stepping stone: Jaguar's highly successful Group C programme of the 1980s and 90s took the marque towards Formula One. The final big triumph of the Group C Jaguars was first and second at Le Mans in 1990 - here the Lammers/ Wallace/Konrad XJR-12LM is feted as it secures second place.**

Jaguar should compete in every sense with these luxury brands. With a full, four-car model line scheduled for the first time in decades, plus new quality and efficiency standards, Jaguar would soon be producing cars at much nearer the huge volumes of BMW and Mercedes, instead of having just one tenth of the annual output of either.

To sell these new volumes and fully realise the marque's potential, a new, wider and younger customer base had to be reached. With its massive worldwide following, Formula One represented the best way of achieving this. It would be costly, but sponsors could be found and in any case, Jaguar's vastly increased turnover and aspirations now justified such investment.

There was at least one other factor which justified the costs of a Formula One programme - the cross-fertilisation of ideas and technology between race and production engineering through the interchange of personnel. "The sums are huge, yes, but it's all relative" says Nick Hayes, director of Formula One engineering at Cosworth, Jaguar Racing's engine supplier. "In terms of pay back I think it's a pretty good investment. We can take advantage of technology which exists in Ford and which as a racing company we could never afford, and in return, Ford and Jaguar will have people who will have worked on race programmes." The exposure to the pressures of race engineering and the need for quick and ingenious solutions to problems certainly hones the skills of engineers and, on their return to production work, this can result in reduced lead times and more lateral thinking.

The next decision was - what would be the best way to get Jaguar into Grand Prix racing? The options were very similar to those faced by Ford when, towards the end of the 1980s, it

Above: **Johnny Herbert's brilliant victory for Stewart at the Grand Prix of Europe in 1999 caused Jackie Stewart to describe his team's win as a Constructor as "the most important moment in my racing life". Perhaps it raised unrealistic expectations of the team when it re-formed as Jaguar Racing in 2000 - but Ford were anxious to launch the Jaguar name into F1 that year to coincide with the reinstatement of the US Grand Prix.**

Above: **Barrichello practiced way down in 10th at Monaco in 1997 but finished second to Michael Schumaker; this was only the fifth Grand Prix contested by the new Stewart Grand Prix team. Team-mate Jan Magnusson was 23th.**

decided to enter the premium luxury car business. A new marque could be created (as Toyota did with the Lexus) or an existing one bought. For many of the same reasons that Ford decided to buy Jaguar, Ford elected to purchase an existing Formula One team - especially as it had been working closely with the Stewart Grand Prix team since its inception.

Quite apart from the Jaguars he had raced, and the fact that his family ran a small Jaguar dealership in Dumbartonshire in Scotland, Jackie Stewart had long been associated with Ford both during and after his motor racing career. His son Paul had followed his footsteps into motor racing, competing successfully in Formula Ford 2000, Formula 3 and F3000, and with his father had formed Paul Stewart Racing in 1988. Six years later Paul swopped racing for managing the highly successful team - which by 1999 had secured 130 individual race wins and 13 championships.

In 1996 the team decided to enter Formula One. The re-named Stewart Grand Prix team's first season was 1997 - the establishment was somewhat astonished when Rubens Barrichello took the Ford-Cosworth powered car to second place at Monaco in only its fifth Grand Prix. Then, just after the announcement in September 1999 that the team would become Jaguar Racing the following season, Johnny Herbert won the Nürburgring European GP. The team's early results seemed a good omen. Ford chief technical officer Neil Ressler said at the R1's launch, "These are the people who got us to where we are today, and these are the people who will carry on".

"WE ARE ONE OF THE NEWEST TEAMS IN FORMULA ONE AND WE ALL KNOW WE HAVE A LOT TO LEARN" *Dr Wolfgang Reitzle*

It was as these plans were crystallising that Dr Wolfgang Reitzle joined Ford after resigning from the board of a BMW deeply troubled by its ill-considered acquisition of Rover. In March 1999 Reitzle was appointed vice president of the newly-created Premier Automotive Group, within which would operate all Ford's luxury marques - Lincoln, Aston Martin, Volvo and Jaguar. He was also appointed chairman of Jaguar.

Dr Reitzle immediately endorsed the logic of Jaguar going into Formula One: "The race track is the spiritual home of Jaguar," he said at the R1's launch. "Today we are sending out a clear signal of our plans and future direction, a renewed commitment to that unique blend of emotion and technology which I think makes Jaguar one of the most evocative marques in the automotive world... Maybe only one other company, which traditionally races in red, has the same emotional appeal."

The other major component of Jaguar's Formula One venture was Cosworth Racing. Cosworth had been founded by Keith Duckworth and Mike Costin in 1958 as a general race engineering and chassis-sorting company. But in 1959 the Ford 997cc engine arrived. At their tiny North London premises, Cosworth's development of this tough little unit for Formula Junior established an enduring link with Ford; it also ensured that the company's activities centred around engines.

Below: **Jim Clark, World Champion in 1963 and 1965 with Lotus - a car powered by the Jaguar-owned Coventry Climax engine builder. Clark also drove a Lister-Jaguar earlier in his racing career.**

In many ways Cosworth became the natural successor to the Jaguar-owned Coventry Climax Engines whose remarkable FWMV 1.5-litre V8 Grand Prix power unit had, from 1961, achieved 18 Grand Prix wins, the majority with Jim Clark. But with the coming of the 3-litre formula in 1966, Coventry Climax elected not to remain in Formula One.

So it was the first Cosworth F1 engine - the legendary DFV V8 produced for Ford in 1967 - that powered Jim Clark's Lotus to further wins. Over the next 15 years the DFV won 155 world championship races and 12 world driver championships - a record which has yet to be broken.

A CART/Indycar version of this engine, the DFX,

appeared in the late 1970s. It won 151 races between 1976 and 1989, and every Indy 500 and Champ Car championship for a decade. In 1977 Cosworth Inc. was established in California to provide back-up and technical support to teams using this engine in the United States.

A further link with Jaguar is the often overlooked fact that the Jaguar XJR-14, which won the World Sports Car Championship in 1991, was powered by the Cosworth-Ford HB V8 turbocharged engine.

Meanwhile, in Grand Prix racing, Cosworth's successes were continued by the Zetec-R V8 engine which Michael Schumacher and Benetton-Ford used to win the 1994 World Championship.

Above: **Jackie Stewart and Niel Ressler looking studious in Melbourne; Ford had already invested heavily in Jackie's team from 1996, but wanted full control. They obtained it in 2000, having already decided that Jaguar was the ideal name to be carried by the re-launched team.**

In 1998 Ford purchased Cosworth Racing to secure the link with their race engine source, and during 1999 the new V10 CR-1 engine powered the Stewart-Ford SF-3, with Johnny Herbert winning a F1 race well ahead of the still-new team's expectations. As part of the strategy to draw all these elements together - Jaguar, Ford, Cosworth and Jaguar Racing - Trevor Crisp moved from his job as group chief engineer (power train engineering) at Jaguar to become managing director of Cosworth Racing. In the early 1960s Trevor had been seconded by Jaguar to Coventry Climax Engines for a period, but the FWMV bore little relationship to the enormously powerful Formula One engine that he was now overseeing! The latest Cosworth-Ford CR-2 is thought to produce over 800 bhp.

Bringing Ford into the equation was Neil W. Ressler, vice president of research and vehicle technology at Ford, and the company's chief technical officer. He had been on the board of Stewart Grand Prix since its launch and was also chairman of Cosworth Racing. Not only did Neil Ressler have the authority within Ford to get things done, he was a shrewd manager with a vast technical knowledge, who quickly gained the respect of the team - even if at first, as one of them remarked, "he wasn't used to the dog-eat-dog world of Formula One!"

The day-to-day management of the team originally lay in the hands of Jackie and Paul Stewart, but on the very day of the R1's launch at Lord's in January 2000, Jackie Stewart announced he was stepping down as chairman and chief executive of Jaguar Racing. This came as a complete surprise to nearly everyone, but it was in keeping with Jackie's character: in 1973 he had not announced his retirement from Formula One driving, even to his wife and family, until completing what he had decided would be his last race.

"The last four years", Jackie explained at Lord's, "I've worked harder than I've ever done in any period my life. It's been long hours but very satisfying." However, he cited having turned 60 and his desire to spend more time with his wife, Helen, as the major reasons for relinquishing the reins. He promised continued involvement from the sidelines, though, and Paul Stewart continued as chief operating officer.

Jaguar Racing's headquarters, inherited from Stewart Grand Prix, were in Milton Keynes, just over an hour from London up the M1 motorway. The modern buildings housed some 280 staff and most of the facilities needed to design and build Grand Prix cars: the design office (with no drawing boards: everything was on CAD - computer aided design - from the outset), fabrication shop, composites shop, machine shop, inspection shop and assembly area.

Below: **Jaguar's first ever Formula One World Championship points came on 4th June 2000 at a Monaco Grand Prix made even more extraordinary than usual, as various incidents produced two abortive starts. Coulthard won, but a high drop-out rate plus a flawless drive by Eddy Irvine saw the Jaguar R1 finish fourth.**

The team was proud that 70 per cent of the car was made in house - even the immensely complex steering wheels containing the clutch and gearbox controls and costing upwards of £20,000 each. Tyres (and the engine from Cosworth, of course) were about the only major items out-sourced. But the team's rapidly expanding programme meant that they were already outgrowing the premises as the 2000 season was underway.

Working at Milton Keynes was technical director Gary Anderson, managing Jaguar Racing's design team which included chief designer John Russell (exWilliams GP and BMW Motorsport) and Darren Davis (head of aerodynamics and formerly at March and Jordan).

While the design of today's Formula One car is very much a team effort, Anderson was largely responsible for the Jaguar R1 and his design philosophies tied in neatly with the Jaguar ethos. "I like the car to look nice aesthetically," he told *Jaguar Racing* magazine. "It doesn't really give you any more performance, but if everybody does their job a little better because they're proud of it, then that's better than it being an ugly beast you want to put the car cover on all the time."

When it came to the practical management of the team, Dave Stubbs, race team manager, was responsible for the selection of race team personnel while Andy Miller, as race and operations director, liaised with team engineers and drivers on race strategy and car set-up, and with suppliers and outside technical support for the team.

Of course, Cosworth Racing had a particularly close relationship with the Jaguar team as the supplier of engines. The company operated not too far away at Northampton on a site originally acquired in 1964 - and which was also becoming somewhat overcrowded. As at Milton Keynes,

Right: Johnny Herbert and Eddie Irvine, both in their mid-thirties, provided Jaguar with an enormously experienced, all-British driver line-up. At the beginning of the 2000 season, Irvine had achieved 24 podium finishes out of 97 Grand Prix starts, while Johnny had started in 146 Grands Prix and stood on the podium seven times. Both drivers had won three Grands Prix each.

everything was carried out in conditions of high security: there are some features of the Cosworth CR2 engine which are still confidential.

The logistics of supplying engines to a Formula One team are daunting. Ten engines are needed for each Grand Prix, and at any one time six or eight more are on test. On top of that is the relentless development work in search of more power and less weight. Quips Nick Hayes, director of F1 engineering at Cosworth, of his relationship with Jaguar Racing's engineers: "I always know how much power we've got - which is not enough - and the engine's always too

heavy, and too long, and it uses too much fuel!" A conference with the Jaguar Racing team would be held at least once a week. Says Gary Anderson: "Both of us need different things and you've just got to meet in the middle."

The final, essential, ingredients in the team were the drivers. Jaguar Racing's Essex-born Johnny Herbert had come to Formula One via the classic route of karts, Formula Ford, Formula 3 and F3000: in his first Grand Prix, the 1989 Brazilian GP, he finished fourth (driving for Benetton). Later he drove for Lotus, Benetton again and then, from 1992 to 1994, Lotus once more, finishing eighth in the World Championship in 1993. When Lotus withdrew from racing at the end of the 1994 season he returned to Benetton once more and won twice, in Italy and the British Grand Prix at Silverstone. Herbert spent the 1996 and 1997 seasons with Sauber before coming to Stewart, where he brought the team that fine European Grand Prix victory.

Eddy Irvine, from Newtonards, Northern Ireland, had started competing with his father's Formula Ford car in 1983 at the age of 17. His later Formula Ford successes included two championship wins in 1987, before moving in 1988 into Formula 3, finishing fifth in the British F3 championship that year. In 1989 he drove in F3000 for Jordan, a period which included three seasons in Japan (and second place in the national championship that final year): his Grand Prix debut was at the 1993 Japanese GP at Suzuka where he finished sixth.

Above: Eddie Irvine provides a fine view of the Jaguar R1's tyres - in a typical season, a two-car team will use over 550 tyres at a cost of around £750 each, though they are supplied by Bridgestone (joined in 2001 by Michelin). After stalling at the start, Eddie came 13th in this, the Canadian Grand Prix of June 2000; Johnny Herbert retired with gear selection problems.

In 1996 Eddie moved to Ferrari where he was number two to the extraordinary Michael Schumacher. His best season there was in 1999 when he won in Australia, finished second to Schumacher at Monaco, and took second place at Silverstone when Michael had his terrifying crash. Two more wins and other points-scoring 'places' as lead Ferrari driver while Schumacher recovered took Eddie to second place in the Driver's Championship, only two points behind Mika Hakkinen. In September 1999 Jaguar announced Eddie was to become its new team's number one driver.

Jaguar Racing's test driver, the Brazilian Luciano Burti, followed in Ayrton Senna's footsteps racing karts before travelling to Britain to race in Formula Junior Vauxhall. He then moved to Paul Stewart Racing, and entered Formula 3 in 1998. Two highly successful seasons followed but from 2000 he started testing the new Jaguar R1 full time - and was the first driver to take it onto the race track.

"WE'VE GOT TO BE THE BEST OF THE REST, AND THEN MOVE FORWARD AND ATTACK THE OTHERS." *Johnny Herbert*

Jaguar Racing's first season could fairly be described as having a sharp learning-curve; it began at the very first race, the Australian Grand Prix at Albert Park, Melbourne, on 12th March. This was in itself an historic occasion, as the first time a Jaguar had officially taken part in a Grand Prix. Jaguar's huge publicity machine had been hard at work and, remarked one race-goer, it looked as though Jaguar had bought Melbourne. Green was everywhere from the airport on: there was a big laser show, painted trams, and huge posters. The message that 'The Cat is Back' was certainly delivered.

Local enthusiasm was correspondingly high: the Jaguar Racing merchandise stall was almost stripped bare by avid fans on the Saturday, buying 15 times the quantity shifted by

Left: Eddie Irvine in Jaguar's Formula One debut race on March 12 2000 in the Australian Grand Prix at Albert Park, Melbourne (where Jaguars raced in the 1950s). It was not an encouraging start for Jaguar Racing as neither R1 finished. "We know that when it runs the car is fast. It's very frustrating," said Johnny Herbert. Things would get better, though...

Stewart Grand Prix at Melbourne in 1999 - proof, if any were needed, of the value of a high-profile brand name. It went some way to producing the "sea of green" so desired by Wolfgang

Reitzle; though the dominant colour at the circuit was still red...

Qualifying saw Eddie Irvine get the Jaguar onto seventh place on the grid, although Johnny Herbert struggled with the Cosworth engine's known oil-scavenging problem and scraped his R1 into 20th place. The Jaguars survived the start as all 22 cars surged away from the lights, but Herbert was out with a failed clutch on the very first lap, while Irvine spun on lap six after swerving to avoid Pedro de la Rosa's Arrows which was having an accident. The anti-stall device didn't work and Eddie was stranded. Schumacher took the spoils in front of the 125,000 crowd. Nobody had said Formula One racing would be easy - even after Eddie Irvine had gained Jaguar's first championship points with fourth place at the Monaco Grand Prix in June.

"There have been races this year when we deserved to get points - today we got them, but it was a big struggle," said Irvine. "It's what the team needs... Jaguar has been investing properly, it

Above: **Much hard work resulted in a faster, more reliable car for Jaguar Racing's second event, the Brazilian GP at Interlagos. Irvine (shown here) held fifth for a while, then "I was pushing harder than I should and just lost the back end," he said. Herbert achieved ninth before retiring.**

has the right people and is on the way up," observed Jackie Stewart.

By this time the news had come that Paul Stewart had been diagnosed with cancer of the colon in April; fortunately this was treatable but it meant that a key member of the team would be out of action for some time. This, combined with Jackie Stewart's reduced involvement, did not help at a critical time in Jaguar Racing's development. Accordingly, in May 2000, Neil Ressler took over the day-to-day running of the whole team; his place as Ford's chief technical officer was taken over by colleagues, leaving him free of production car issues and so allowing him to concentrate entirely on the team's activities and progress.

Ressler's career had not followed the pattern of many other Formula One team bosses - like Sir Frank Williams, Eddie Jordan or Ron Dennis - but a corporate background hid a true

Below: Johnny Herbert's R1 suffered from heavy steering at Monaco, and Johnny had to wave Eddie by. That June 2000 race was won by David Coulthard after Michael Schumaker's Ferrari dropped out with rear suspension damage. The Jaguar R1's paint scheme, with specially-formulated green paint costing £600 ($900) a litre, was designed by Ian Callum and Fergus Pollock of Jaguar's styling department.

enthusiasm for and involvement in motor sport. As a young man Ressler built his own hot rods and did a "fair amount" of drag racing. At Ford he was involved with the link with the Benetton

team, and with CART racing. And even before he became the ultimate boss, Ressler had gained the respect of the Jaguar team members.

Symbolically, perhaps, he took over Jackie Stewart's office at Milton Keynes, a sign that he was in total charge. "Whether I'm a dictator or not has to do with management style," he told *Jaguar Racing* magazine in June 2000. "I have no intention of calling Jaguar Cars or the Ford Motor Company to ask them what to do. We're going to do what we think is right and if the results are what we want, we'll be fine, and if they're not, I'll have to go and explain!"

When success will come was not being predicted by anyone at Jaguar; it would be a long hard road, as the team had to improve at a faster rate than its rivals ahead: a tall order in the fiercely competitive world of Formula One.

The deafening wail of today's 800-bhp Jaguar R1 is a very different sound to that made by the chugging, 14-bhp Harley-Davidson that William Lyons rode in 1922; yet by competing in those early seaside sprints, and by his measured enthusiasm for competition, Lyons set in train a series of events which would culminate in the name of Jaguar achieving some of the highest honours in motor sport - from Monte Carlo to Le Mans, from Spa to Daytona. Now, against this rich backdrop of its sporting heritage, Jaguar is set to scale the heights of the very pinnacle of motor sport. Every previous goal has been achieved; surely, one day, the Formula One World Championship will be Jaguar's too.

Above: **Monaco GP, Irvine Eddie on his way to three Championship points at Monaco. This picture shows Eddie tucked well down in his Lear safety seat. Computer moulded to the driver's body, it is made of Kevlar and carbon fibre, padded with foam and covered in fireproof Nomex. After an accident, it can be lifted, complete with driver, clear of the car - potentially a life-saving feature.**

Following spread: **Johnny Herbert was able to put in a good number of laps in the Canadian Grand Prix even if he did not finish this, Jaguar Racing's second-ever Grand Prix.**

Driving the Jaguar R1

Only one other person apart from the Jaguar Racing team's own three drivers had driven the Jaguar R1 when this book went to press in the summer of 2000, and that is former race driver, now TV and magazine journalist, Tiff Needell. He wrote about his experience with Johnny Herbert's car at Barcelona in BBC's Top Gear magazine:

"A Grand Prix car…is something alive in your hands, so built around your body that you and it are at one. You feel everything.

"You twitch and it will twitch. The acceleration punches the air out of your lungs. The wail of revs rising behind you assaults your senses. The (gearchange) lights flash. You flick a finger; the tone drops momentarily. The lights flash again; the tone drops again. This time it rises slightly more slowly, with the aerodynamics beginning to squish it into the ground, the half-ton car has an effective weight of two tons…

"The lights flash again…sixth gear…the bridge at the end of the straight is looming large and my vision

begins to blur. I force myself to blink… I've gone from a hundred miles an hour to two hundred and I just want to keep going!

"I brake gently at first, surprised to find it's my left foot doing the work. I pull the left paddle four times, the management blips the throttle for me, gears engage without protest. There's violence on the outside yet harmony within…

"I haven't time to think about where I'm going before I'm there. The sensation is mesmeric. The power steering adds to the ease of control yet provides superb feedback. There's a constant contrast to how small my inputs are and how great the reactions are.

"I finally get my first dab of opposite lock out of the final tight left-hander and the Jaguar at last becomes fully alive within my hands. I want to do more of this. I haven't forgotten this feeling, but I've locked it away because it's a

dangerous drug to crave for. There's no compromise in a Grand Prix car; it is the ultimate racing machine.

"You're very aware of how narrow the front track is - the wheels seem so close together. I have no idea where the limit is through the faster corners - and have no intention of getting anywhere near it, yet I'm already cornering far faster than I would in the Lister Storm racer...

"The next couple of laps are an awesome reminder of a world in which only the very best can excel. The over-riding memory is of the responsiveness of the engine and its searing acceleration. I never cornered like Irvine or Herbert, never braked as deep as them, but I accelerated just as fast.

"Next time you feel like laughing at a joke about Minardi tail-ender Gaston Mazzacane, don't. OK, he may have qualified last in the Spanish Grand Prix and he may only have finished 15th, but he ran 63 laps of the Catalunya circuit flat out, just three seconds off the pace of Mika Hakkinen. I was feeling the strain after just three, and was nowhere near even his times.

"Like I said at the start, you can't just hop straight in and drive one of these machines. It is a world where only the very talented can survive - and I'm just extremely grateful that Jaguar trusted me to rekindle those feelings of just what a special world it is."

Jaguar R1

Technical specifications

CHASSIS

Composite monocoque, designed and built in-house, incorporating engine as fully-stressed member

SUSPENSION

Front	Upper and lower carbon wishbones and pushrods, torsion bar springing, Jaguar/Penske damper layout
Rear	Upper carbon fibre wishbone and lower hybrid composite steel, torsion bar springing, Jaguar/Penske damper layout
Brakes	AP Racing lithium alloy six-piston caliper, Carbon Industrie carbon fibre discs and pads
Wheels	12in x 13in (front), 13.4ins x 13ins (rear)
Tyres	Bridgestone

ENGINE

Type	Ford-Cosworth V10 CR-2, 2,998cc, 72 deg.' V' 10 cylinder. Power output (estimated) 815 bhp at 18,000 rpm
Construction	Cast aluminium block and heads, forged aluminium pistons, steel crankshaft
No. of valves	40
Weight	210 lbs (95 kg)
Length	22.4 ins
Width	20 ins
Height	(inc. airbox): 19.3 ins

ELECTRONICS

Cosworth Racing ignition system, Visteon VCS single box integrated engine/chassis electronic control system

DRIVERS 2000

Eddie Irvine (35)
Johnny Herbert (36)

Jaguar Racing website and supporters' club: www.jaguar-racing.com

Sponsors and Partners

PRINCIPLE SPONSORS AND PARTNERS

HSBC HOLDINGS PLC

Major partner. Leading banking and financial services organisation. Five year association began with Stuart team and will continue through to the 2001 World Championship season

MCI WORLDCOM CORPORATION

Major partner. Industry-leading communications company operating worldwide. Webistes: www.wcom.co, and www.mciracing.com

BECKS

Major partner "The most international of all German beer brands", exported to 120 nations worldwide. Established 1875

THE HEWLETT-PACKARD COMPANY

Major sponsor and technical partner. Leading global provider of computing and imaging solutions. Provides a range of advanced IT and design facilities to Jaguar Racing

DHL WORLDWIDE EXPRESS

Major partner. Air express company serving 635,000 cities in 227 countries. Website: www.dhl.com

LEAR CORPORATION

Technology partner. One of the world's largest automotive suppliers including car interiors, already serving Jaguar Cars. Produces state-of-the-art carbon fibre/Kevlar seating for Eddie Irvine and Johnny Herbert, and energy absorbing systems between seat and 'tub' on the R1

BRIDGESTONE

Technological partner. In 1997 the Tokyo-headquartered Bridgestone company supplied four Formula One teams and on the withdrawal of Goodyear in 1998, now supply tyres to 11 teams. All F1 activities are handled by a dedicated motorsport unit at High Wycombe, Buckinghamshire, UK

TEXACO

Technological partner. Texaco originally supplied lubricants to James Hunt's 1976 World Championship winning Texaco McLaren-Ford, and today supply initial-fill and after-care lubricants to Jaguar Cars. Associated with Stewart Ford from 1997. Caltex, a joint marketing venture with Chevron in Asian, Australasian and South African markets, will be participating as well, with the Caltex star being carried on the nose of the Jaguar R1 in Australia and Malaysia

VISTEON

Technology partner. Provides leading-edge electronic race systems including the innovative Vehicle Control System (VCS). Engine management, drive-by-wire throttle, clutch and gearshift control systems are also supplied to Jaguar Racing, with Visteon engineers working on-site with team personnel

UNIGRAPRAPHICS SOLUTIONS

Technology partner. Supplier of product modelling, analysis, simulation, manufacturing planning (CAD/CAM) and product data management. Website: www.ugsolutions.com

OFFICIAL SUPPLIERS:

s.Oliver: team clothing for the Jaguar Racing team; also, a 'Green Line' collection using the famous Jaguar Racing Green will be available to customers at s.Oliver retail stores throughout Europe and the middle East

William Grant: Grant's Family Reserve Scotch Whisky is the world's fourth largest Scotch whisky brand

Corporate Jets Plc: Motor sport is the largest user of corporate jets worldwide. Corporate Jets Plc logo on tyre warmers, transporters and pit walls. The company uses Learjet aircraft and flies Jaguar Racing personnel to various venues. Corporate Jets specialises in 'fractional' ownership jet aviation, and also supply aircraft to individuals and groups

Barr Soft Drinks: Scotland's no. 1 selling soft drink is flagship brand Irn-bru, while Tizer and Orangina are also supplied to Jaguar Racing

Sodick Co. Ltd, Japan: the official supplier of CNC wire erosion machine tools. The company is situated in Coventry

ACKNOWLEDGEMENTS

No-one researching Jaguar's competition history could do so adequately without referring to the two major books on this topic written by the late Andrew Whyte, and published by J.H. Haynes. I gratefully acknowledge my debt to Andrew. Other authors or journalists whose valuable work I have drawn on include John Bolster, Peter Cahill, Michael Cotton, John Dugdale, Doug Nye and David Tremayne, all of whom I also thank.

Over the years I have also been privileged to have talked with many of the great figures from Jaguar's past including F.R.W. "Lofty" England, R.E. Bob Berry, Tom Jones, George Buck, William Munger Heynes CBE, R.J. Knight MBE and Norman Dewis. I did question the Founder on some topics, but Sir William's main comment on competition matters was to assert vigorously that he had not, as I had suggested, chosen the fastest SS 100 for the all-Jaguar race he won at Donington in 1938!

On the American perspective, Bob Tullius and Mike Dale have always been most forthcoming, as has Group 44's designer and crew chief Lawton "Lanky" Foushee.

Especially in relation to D-types and their Lister and Cooper cousins, I am very grateful to John Pearson of Forge Garage, Whittlebury. I would also like to thank Michael Elmer for allowing me to make use of his unique period tape recordings of Brian Lister; David Chamberlain for relating his experiences with the Cooper-Jaguar and Kirk Rylands for insights into owning and racing HWM-Jaguars. Further much-appreciated assistance came from Terry McGrath, Leslie Thurston and Ted Walker.

From the modern era, various members of Jaguar Racing and Cosworth Racing have been of great help, especially Trevor Crisp, Managing Director of Cosworth Racing, and Nick Hayes, director, Formula One engineering, while Roger Putnam, Jaguar's director of sales and marketing, provided valuable perspectives.

Last but by no means least are those who look after Jaguar's past. The Jaguar Daimler Heritage Trust gave me every facility I needed and I am very grateful to archivist Julia Simpson, and highly knowledgeable volunteer assistants Derek and Margaret Boyce and Penny Graham, for their willing help (just as this book was going to press, Anders Clausager joined as chief archivist). The JDHT preserves all Jaguar's competition records and has custody of the company's 110-plus historic vehicles which include the very first D- and C-types as well as the unique XJ-13.

Jaguar North America archives are extremely well cared for by archivist Karen Miller who spent a considerable time researching illustrations, helped by former Jaguar North America PR head Mike Cook. I am extremely grateful to both of them.

There have been many others not named here who have assisted in many valuable ways but space does not permit me to mention their names - or my memory fails! Thanks, however, to them all for contributing to this record of Jaguar's sporting heritage.

PICTURE CREDITS:

COURTESY OF JDHT: pages 7, 8, 9, 12 top and middle left, 13 top and bottom, 16 top, 22/23, 26, 29 top, 34 bottom, 35, 40, 41, 44/45, 46, 47 both pics, 48, 49, 50, 52 bottom, 53, 56, 58, 59, 78, 82 bottom, 89, 90, 92, 95, 96 bottom, 110, 112, 113 bottom left and right, 114, 119, 121, 122, 135, 153, 164, 167, 180, 181, 183, 192/193, 198/199, 200, 202 both, 203, 204, 205, 206, 207, 208, 209, 217, 218 both, 219, 220, 223, 224, 225, 226, 227, 228 both, 229, 230, 231, 232/233, 237, 238

COURTESY OF JAGUAR CARS ARCHIVES, NORTH AMERICA: pages 61, 126, 195, 212/213, 214, 210/211, 222

JAGUAR MOTORSPORT COMMUNICATIONS: pages 234/235, 242, 243, 244, 245, 246, 247, 248, 249, 250/251252, 253, 254/255

COURTESY OF PAUL SKILLETER: 10/11, 12 bottom right, 13 both middle, 14, 15, 16 bottom, 17, 18, 20, 21, 24/25, 29 bottom, 30/31, 32, 34 top, 37, 37, 51, 52 top, 63, 64/65, 67, 68 both pics, 69, 70, 71, 72, 73, 74/75, 79 both pics, 80, 81, 82 top, 85 bottom, 86, 88, 91, 94, 97, 98/99, 100, 101, 102/103, 105, 106/107, 108/109, 111, 113 top, 115, 116/117, 118, 120, 123, 124, 125, 127, 132, 133, 134, 136, 137, 138, 140/141, 142/143, 145 bottom, 146, 152, 155, 157, 165, 174, 176, 177 bottom, 182, 184, 186, 187, 189, 190/191, 194, 221, 236

JAMES MANN: pages 1, 62, 76/77, 104, 160/161, 178/179, 185, 201

L.A.T. PHOTOGRAPHIC: pages 4/5, 239, 240, 241

FERRET FHOTOGRAPHICS: pages 19, 66, 139, 144, 145 top, 147 both, 148, 156 both, 163 bottom, 168/169, 170, 173, 188

BARC: pages 54/55, 84, 96 top, 130/131, 150, 151, 154, 171, 172, 175

M. R. HARRIS: page 83,

PHOTOS BY KAREN MILLER: pages 197 both pics, 215, 216,

MICHAEL BOWLER: page 163 top,

COURTESY CORSA RESEARCH: page 128

PHOTO BY JOHN LEA: page 57

COURTESY OF DAVID CHAMBERLAIN: page 149

PHOTO BY MARGARITE JENNINGS: page 162

PHOTO BY RICHARD DEARNELL: page 166

Every effort has been made to source and contact copyright holders.
If any omission do occur, the publisher will be happy to give full credit in subsequent reprints and editions.